Windows NT
Shell Scripting

Tim Hill

MACMILLAN
TECHNICAL
PUBLISHING
U·S·A

Windows NT Shell Scripting

By Tim Hill

Published by:
Macmillan Technical Publishing
201 West 103rd Street
Indianapolis, IN 46290 USA

Printed in the United States of America   4 5 6 7 8 9 0

ISBN: 1-57870-047-7

Library of Congress Cataloging-in-Publication Data: 97-80990

Warning and Disclaimer

Publisher   *Jim LeValley*

Executive Editor   *Linda Ratts Engelman*

Managing Editor   *Caroline Roop*

Acquisitions Editor
Jane Brownlow

Development Editor
Lisa M. Gebken

Project Editor
Brad Herriman

Copy Editor
Susan Hobbs

Technical Editor
Louise Hudgins

Market Reviewers
Ryan Maley
Robert Marsh

Team Coordinator
Amy Lewis

Book Designer
Gary Adair

Cover Designer
Aren Howell

Production Team
Argosy

Indexers
Craig Small
Chris Wilcox

About the Author

Tim Hill is an independent software developer specializing in systems software and operating system architectures. He has designed several real-time operating systems, including RMOS and PKS, which has been used extensively in mission-critical embedded systems such as ATMs and banking automation systems.

Tim consults extensively on all aspects of Windows NT integration and implementation, and is a Microsoft Windows NT MVP. He is also currently chief technical officer at Document Technologies, Inc., a developer of specialized medical and business imaging systems, in Sunnyvale, California.

Trademark Acknowledgments

About our technical reviewers . . .

These reviewers contributed their considerable practical, hands-on expertise to the entire development process for **Windows NT Shell Scripting.** *As the book was being written, these folks reviewed all of the material for technical content, organization, and flow. Their feedback was critical to ensuring that* **Windows NT Shell Scripting** *fits our readers' need for the highest quality technical information.*

Louise Hudgins is a network telecommunications analyst and LAN administrator at Thomas Nelson Community College in Hampton, Virginia. She is a Microsoft Certified Systems Engineer (MCSE) and Microsoft Certified Trainer (MCT) for Windows NT 3.51 and 4.0, and is currently working towards a degree in computer science. Louise believes that the best place to shop around is in the marketplace of ideas.

Bob Marsh has been a Windows NT user and administrator since NT 3.1 beta in 1993. He is a co-founder and vice president of engineering at Document Technologies, Inc. in Sunnyvale, California. He is the holder of three U.S. patents and is co-inventor of one of the first personal computers, the Processor Tech Sol-20, which debuted in 1976. This machine is now on display in the Smithsonian's Museum of American History in Washington D.C. Bob is also one of the co-founders of the Homebrew Computer Club in Menlo Park and has been featured in two books on the history of personal computing: *Fire in the Valley* and *Hackers*. He is an alumnus of the University of California, Berkeley (class of 1970) and is a lifelong resident of Berkeley.

Dedication

To Donna.

Acknowledgments

My appreciation and thanks go to the editorial and production teams at Macmillan Technical Publishing for their help and encouragement throughout this project. In particular, I would like to thank Linda Engelman for letting me write this book, and Jane Brownlow and Lisa Gebken for all their help and (above all) patience as I juggled writing and a full-time career.

I would also like to thank my colleague Bob Marsh for all his efforts in uncovering technical errors in the manuscript. As usual, Bob was unwavering in his attempts to find as many mistakes as possible in my work.

Finally, thanks go to my two children, Alex and Becky, for putting up with dad disappearing to "play on the computer" instead of with them.

Contents at a Glance

Table of Contents

Introduction

Today, GUI (Graphical User Interface) applications and tools dominate the Windows world, including Windows NT. Buttons, mouse devices, and icons make computers more accessible than was ever dreamed when the only interface to a computer was an ASCII terminal.

So why a book about Windows NT shell scripting? Aren't scripts just MS-DOS batch files with a fancy name? And everyone knows Microsoft hasn't changed batch files for years!

Well, batch files *have* changed. With the release of Windows NT 4.0, the command shell has been given enough new features to fill a book . . . this book, in fact. Did you know you could do arithmetic with environment variables? Or walk a complete directory tree with a FOR command? If you're an NT power user, administer NT systems and servers, or use logon scripts, then these and other new script language features enable you to automate many mundane or difficult tasks.

With its widespread acceptance as both a server and client platform, many other script languages have been ported to Windows NT. Many of these languages, such as Perl, Awk and Tcl, come from the Unix world. Others, such as REXX, come from OS/2. Each of these languages has its own strengths and limitations, but none are quite as suited to systems management as the native scripting of Windows NT. Quite apart from anything else, the built-in scripting of Windows NT is always available on every installation. This *universal availability* makes a good knowledge of NT scripting virtually mandatory, particularly if you manage large NT installations.

I designed this book as a complete reference for Windows NT scripting. To do this, I've drawn together material from many different sources: on-line help (GUI and command line), printed documentation, the Microsoft Knowledge Base and web site (http://www.microsoft.com/kb), and (most importantly) my own years of working with Windows NT. Some of the most useful features of the Windows NT scripting language have been poorly or incorrectly documented (if at all). Therefore, one of my goals in this book is to ensure that these errors and omissions are corrected, allowing use of the rich scripting features now available in Windows NT.

A word about programming: This is *not* a book about programming—it's about *scripting*. Although scripting has many of the same trappings as programming (such as loops, control flow, and variables), it is more pragmatic, and focused on quick solutions to small problems. In this spirit, you will find very little in the book about structuring code, or good techniques for comments, or any of the other more formal aspects of writing good programs. Such things are less important for short scripts. I do, however, assume that the reader is familiar—in principle at least—with the basic ideas of programming, such as subroutines and variables.

Windows NT Resource Kit

Early in the process of creating this book, I also decided to describe many of the command-line utilities available in the Windows NT Resource Kit. The resource kit is now almost *de rigueur* for any serious Windows NT user (and not just for the command-line tools). Where a tool is available only in the resource kit, I have tagged the use of that tool in the text with [RK]. Nevertheless, where possible, I use standard commands rather than resource kit tools, so that most of the sample scripts will run on any out-of-the-box NT installation.

One of the issues with the Windows NT Resource Kit is that many of the tools shipped in the kit overlap each other in functionality (for example, there are many tools for managing the registry). Where this overlap occurs, I have focused on the most complete and up-to-date tools, and omitted those tools that have been superseded or have little additional functionality. I have also omitted from the reference section some tools that are highly specialized, such as command line interfaces for the DNS and DHCP services. For reference, these tools are listed in Appendix B.

How This Book Is Organized

This book is divided into three parts. Part I provides a complete description of the Windows NT scripting language, including a detailed description of shell command syntax. Part I is the core of the book, and should be read by anyone who wants to understand the Windows NT script language.

Part II provides a set of real-world scripting solutions. These solutions are presented as complete, ready-to-use, scripts. Each script can be used as-is, or modified to suit local conditions. The sample scripts can be found at **http://www.macmillantech.com**.

Part III provides a complete alphabetical command reference for all Windows NT scripting commands. In this reference, I have focused on commands and options which are lesser known and documented, and more concisely touched on those which are familiar to any user of (say) MS-DOS 4.0 or later. In this way, this book not only shows you how to use Windows NT scripting, but can also be used as a convenient reference when you are developing your own scripts. In fact, my goal with the reference section is that this book should be the *only* reference you will need.

The information in the book is based on Windows NT 4.0 Service Pack 3 or later, and the Windows NT 4.0 Resource Kit supplement 2 or later. Users of earlier versions of Windows NT should find most of the material in this book applicable, but I have not attempted to distinguish features that are only available on the 4.0 platform. Therefore, before you use a specific feature on an older version of Windows NT, you should check that the feature is compatible.

Conventions Used in This Book

Throughout this book, commands, switches and arguments are shown in upper case within the text, and in lower case (except environment variables and script labels) in the example scripts. However, this is merely a convention and, except where noted, commands and switches are not case sensitive, and can be entered as desired. Environment variables and script labels are shown in upper case in scripts to offset them from the lower case commands. The example scripts in this book contain line numbers in front of each line. These numbers are present only for reference purposes, and are not part of the script text—scripts do not contain line numbers.

When describing the syntax of a command (instead of showing an example), items that must be entered exactly are shown in uppercase. Placeholders that must be replaced by appropriate values are shown in lowercase italic. Optional items are shown in brackets. Vertical bar characters separate alternatives, where one item from a list must be selected. For example, the AT command syntax is:

```
AT [\\computer] /DELETE [/YES ¦ /NO]
```

This example shows one possible use of the AT command. It shows the AT command itself, followed by a computer name prefixed with two backslash characters. The computer name is shown in brackets, and is therefore optional. This is followed by the /DELETE switch, and then optionally followed by the /YES or /NO switch. The following examples show valid AT commands:

```
1. at /DELETE
2. at /delete /yes
3. at \\mothra /delete
```

Also note that the numbers in lines of code are for reference purposes only. They are not to be included in any code commands or instructions.

Tip

Tips are given throughout the book, which provide you with useful short-cuts and other hints.

Troubleshooting Tip

In addition, troubleshooting tips point out common problems and pit-falls, and how to avoid them.

Part I

The Script Language

Chapter 1

The Basics of Scripts

- **What is a script?**
  Here, we introduce scripts and provide some history about the origins of the Windows NT script language. A very simple script is shown, to illustrate the mechanics of script development.

- **The Console Window**
  Since scripts are console applications, a good knowledge of the Windows NT console window is important. This section provides a full description of the console window, and shows how it can be customized.

- **Introducing Scripts**
  This section provides additional information on how scripts are constructed and executed.

- **Script Arguments**
  Like other command-line commands, scripts can accept arguments. Here, we introduce the basic syntax for accessing command-line arguments from within a script.

- **Special Script Lines**
  To make a script user-friendly, it's advisable to start each script with a standard preamble. This section shows a standard preamble that can be used with any script.

What Is a Script?

This is a book about Windows NT scripting. In Windows NT, a *script* is a record, in a text file, of a sequence of shell commands. (A *shell command* is approximately the same as a command typed into a command prompt window.) Once created, a script can be executed as if it were an executable program; for example, by double-clicking a script file from Windows Explorer, or by typing the name of the script in a command prompt window.

When a script is executed, the commands it contains are themselves executed, one-by-one, in the same order that they are listed in the script file. Thus, a script, in its simplest form, is just a way of saving typing. Instead of repeatedly entering the same sequence of commands, you can create a script file and just execute the script.

In the earliest PC operating systems (such as CP/M and MS-DOS) this was just about all scripts could do—store a set of pre-written commands and execute them upon demand. Because they stored blocks of commands for execution, scripts like these were called *batch commands*, and the files that contained the commands were called *batch files*.

Today, Windows NT scripting is far more sophisticated, and has evolved from this simple beginning into a full programming language. But its roots in MS-DOS batch commands can still be seen; script files are still frequently called batch files, and they still have a file type of .BAT (for *batch*). Windows NT scripts are also *forward compatible* with MS-DOS—you can execute almost any MS-DOS batch file on Windows NT. (The reverse is not true, however. Neither Windows 95 nor MS-DOS can execute Windows NT scripts.)

Tip

Throughout this book, the term script refers to a Windows NT script. Where necessary, the term script file refers to the file in which a script is stored.

In comparison with the Windows NT graphical user interface (GUI), scripting is often seen as outdated and more or less irrelevant. However, while the GUI is recognized for its ease of use, Windows NT scripting is far more powerful. A single script can perform operations that would require many different GUI tools. Scripts excel at repeated operations; no one relishes the idea of creating 1,000 new user accounts in NT using User Manager. A script can automate this entire process by creating the account, creating a home directory for each account, setting up a server share, and even sending out a "welcome" message to each new user via email.

This example highlights the primary use of Windows NT scripting: *automation*. Some other examples of this include extracting and collating system information (such as event log data), automating backup operations, managing user accounts, and, most importantly, Windows NT logon scripts.

Since it is now virtually mandatory to start any book on programming or scripting with a "Hello, world!" program, here is a single line Windows NT "Hello, world!" script:

```
echo Hello, world!
```

The ECHO command simply echoes its arguments by displaying them in the command prompt window. In Windows NT scripting, each command is placed on its own line, and any arguments for that command follow the command name on the same line. Generally, individual arguments are separated by spaces, but the ECHO command treats everything that follows on the line (spaces included) as text to be echoed.

The easiest way to create this simple script is to use Windows Notepad editor. Start Notepad and type the ECHO line as previously shown. Press Enter at the end of the line (all script lines should end with a new line, even the last). Save the file in a convenient directory, giving it the name HELLO.BAT.

Now start a Windows NT command prompt. Switch to the directory in which you saved the file HELLO.BAT, type **HELLO**, and press Enter. The ECHO command is displayed following a command prompt, and then the output of the ECHO command appears on the next line:

```
1. C:\scripts>hello
2. C:\scripts>echo Hello, world!
3. Hello, world!
```

Troubleshooting Tip

If the HELLO script does not work as expected, check that you are in the correct directory. The command shell will give the following error if it cannot locate a command.

```
The name specified is not recognized as an internal or external command,
operable program or batch file
```

The Console Window

Scripts are character-based, rather than GUI, programs—they interact with users through a character interface window called a console window. Figure 1.1 shows a basic console window. A *console window* is a software emulation of a traditional computer terminal. The default console window in Windows NT displays 25 lines by 80 characters of text. As new lines appear at the bottom of the window, prior lines scroll up and are eventually lost off the top of the window. Console window output can be paused for viewing by pressing Ctrl+S, and restarted by pressing Ctrl+S again. While output is paused, any program attempting to perform console output is suspended until output is restarted.

Console windows are used as the output windows for all Windows NT console applications. In fact, Windows NT defines a *console application* as one that generates output for a console window. The most common Windows NT

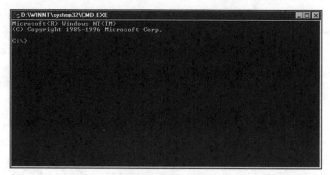

Figure 1.1. *A Windows NT console window*

console application is the Windows NT command shell, CMD.EXE. Technically, not every console window is associated with a copy of CMD.EXE; other console applications do exist. However, almost all console windows are associated with the command shell.

Certain characteristics of the console window can be configured to suit individual requirements. These characteristics include fonts, text color, background color, and character size of the window. They can be set in three different ways:

- Using the Console settings in the Control Panel. Open the Windows NT Control Panel and double-click the Console icon. Changes made in the Control Panel alter the default values used by Windows NT if no shortcut settings are applicable.

- Using the Properties page for a console application shortcut. Right-click on the shortcut and select the Properties command.

- Using the System menu of an open console window. Click the icon in the upper left of the window and select the Properties command. Changes made in the System menu alter the settings for the current console window. In addition, if the console window was opened via a shortcut, Windows NT prompts to allow these changes to be updated in the shortcut as well.

Each method of altering the console window characteristics displays a property page. Four tabs on this page alter the console window: Options, Font, Layout, and Colors.

The Options Tab

The Options tab (Figure 1.2) controls various console options. The Cursor Size buttons alter the size of the text cursor in the console window. The Display Options buttons switch the console window to and from full screen mode. You can also press Alt+Enter to switch to or from full screen mode. The Command History options control the buffers used for the command history feature. Command history is described in Chapter 2, "The Windows NT Command Shell."

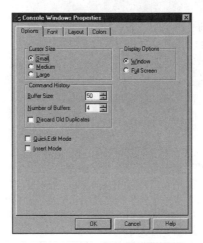

Figure 1.2. *The console window Options tab*

Quick Edit mode uses the mouse for cut and paste operations. When Quick Edit is unchecked, the System menu Mark command enters cut and paste mode. In this mode, the mouse is used to select a block of text to copy to the clipboard. The System menu Copy command then places this text in the clipboard. When Quick Edit is checked, the Mark command is not required. Text can be directly selected with the mouse by dragging. Quick Edit mode is not compatible with applications that use the mouse.

Insert mode sets the default line edit mode to insert, rather than overwrite. This mode can also be changed using the DOSKEY command. When editing a command, the mode can also be toggled using the Insert key.

The Font Tab

The Font tab (Figure 1.3) controls the font used to display characters in the console window. Both the typeface and the font size can be altered. The Preview window shows how the console window will appear on the desktop for the selected font size.

The Layout Tab

The Layout tab (Figure 1.4) controls the layout of the console window. The Screen Buffer Size options set the width and height of the screen buffer, in character units. The *screen buffer* is the logical size of the console window. The

Figure 1.3. *The console window Font tab*

Window Size options set the width and height of the console window in character units. The *window size* is the physical size of the console window. Typically, both Screen Buffer Size and Window Size are set to the same values. Scroll bars will appear if the Window Size is smaller than the Screen Buffer Size.

Using a screen buffer which is larger than a window buffer allows command output to be reviewed even if it has scrolled off the top of the console window. In many cases, using a longer screen buffer avoids the need to use the MORE command to paginate command output.

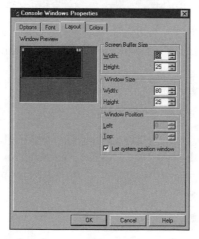

Figure 1.4. *The console window Layout tab*

The Window Position options set the position of the console window. Typically, the Let System Position Window option is checked, giving Windows NT control of the initial window position. Uncheck this option and enter the window position (in pixels) to set a fixed initial window position.

The Colors Tab

The Colors tab (Figure 1.5) controls the colors used in the console window. Four different color values can be set: screen text, screen background, popup text and popup background. Popup colors are used with the Command History popup window described in Chapter 2. The colors can be selected from a palette of standard colors, or individual colors can be mixed using the RGB color model.

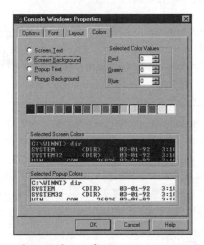

Figure 1.5. *The console window Colors tab*

Screen text and background colors can also be set using the COLOR command (see Chapter 2) or the /T switch of the CMD command.

If you are working with a high-resolution display it is useful to set up a "Big Command Prompt" shortcut and place it on your desktop. This is most easily done as follows:

1. Right-click on the Start button and select the Open option. In the Start Menu window, double-click on the Programs item.

2. Hold down the Ctrl key and drag the Command Prompt item from the Programs window onto the desktop. Close the Programs and Start Menu windows.

3. Right-click the new Command Prompt icon on the desktop and select the Properties command.

4. Change the Layout and Font options to suit your taste. Try setting both Screen Buffer and Window Size to 43 lines, then adjust the font size to provide a suitable fit.

5. Run the new Command Prompt by double clicking the icon.

Introducing Scripts

As previously described, a Windows NT script is a text file containing one or more shell commands to execute. Shell commands are interpreted by the Windows NT command shell, CMD.EXE, which is the subject of Chapter 2. The shell can execute commands typed at the keyboard or read from a script file. With one or two exceptions, any command that can be entered at the keyboard can also be used in a script, and vice versa. Some commands only make sense when used interactively, while others (such as the GOTO command) have no meaning outside a script file.

Script files have a file type of .BAT or .CMD. The .BAT type was inherited from MS-DOS, while the .CMD type came from OS/2. However, the command shell treats both file types identically. The .BAT file type is used in this book, but .CMD can be used if preferred. Once a script file is created, you can execute it simply by typing its name (with or without the file type) as a shell command. For example, to execute the script HELLO.BAT, type **HELLO** or **HELLO.BAT** at the command prompt and press Enter:

```
1. C:\>hello
2. C:\>echo Hello, world!
3. Hello, world!
4. C:\>hello.bat
5. C:\>echo Hello, world!
6. Hello, world!
```

If the script name includes a directory path (and optional drive letter), the shell looks for the script in the specified directory. If the script does *not* include a directory path, the shell looks for the script file in the current directory. If the script is not found in the current directory, the shell then searches the list of directories specified by the current search path. The search path is specified using the PATH command (described in Chapter 2) or by altering the PATH environment variable via the System icon in Control Panel. Figure 1.6 shows the PATH variable in the Control Panel.

Figure 1.6. *Altering the* PATH *environment variable in the Control Panel*

> *Tip*
>
> *One useful convention is to create a directory for all scripts (for example, C:\SCRIPTS) and then add this directory to the system path. All scripts placed in this directory are then available for execution from any command shell.*

Once the shell locates the script file, it begins reading, interpreting, and executing the commands in the file. Each command typically occupies one line, and the commands are read and executed in the order they are listed in the file. By default, the command shell echoes each command before executing it. Script execution ends when the end of the script file is reached—there is no explicit END or STOP command.

> *Tip*
>
> *Press Ctrl+C or Ctrl+Break to interrupt script execution. The shell will ask for confirmation before terminating the script. Press Y to terminate the script, or N to continue script execution.*

Script Arguments

Arguments can be passed to a script from the command line. Script arguments are entered on the command line, separated from the script file name and each other by spaces. The following shell command executes the script SCRIPT1.BAT (or .CMD) and passes it three arguments: C:, E:\ and /P.

```
C:\>script1 c: e:\ /p
```

Within the script file, script arguments are referred to as %1 for the first argument, %2 for the second argument, and up to %9 for the ninth argument. These argument references are called *parameters*, or more correctly, *formal parameters*. The replacement of parameters with actual arguments is called *parameter substitution*. Arguments and parameters are described in detail in Chapter 3, "Script Parameters and Variables."

Parameter substitution can be understood most easily with an example. Use Notepad to create a one line script called ARGECHO.BAT, containing:

```
echo You entered: [%1] [%2] [%3] [%4]
```

Now execute the script, and enter any desired arguments. For example:

```
1. C:\>argecho one alex becky
2. C:\>echo You entered: [one] [alex] [becky] []
3. You entered: [one] [alex] [becky] []
```

The ECHO command is first echoed, and then executed. Notice that the parameters have already been replaced by the actual arguments before the command is echoed. Also notice that the %4 parameter is replaced by nothing, since in this example, only three arguments were entered.

Experiment with different arguments by modifying the ARGECHO.BAT to include additional spaces or tabs between arguments. Try placing an argument in double quotes. Finally, modify ARGECHO to echo %0 in addition to the other parameters. These and other properties of script parameters are discussed fully in Chapter 3.

Special Script Lines

Virtually all the sample scripts in this book follow a similar outline. This outline is as follows:

```
1. @echo off
2. @if not "%ECHO%"=="" echo %ECHO%
3. @if not "%OS%"=="Windows_NT" goto EXIT
4. .
5. . (rest of script)
6. .
7. :EXIT
```

These "magic" script lines perform some basic housekeeping. The individual commands used are described in detail in Chapters 2, 3, and 4. In outline, however, these commands operate as follows:

- Prefixing a command with an @ character stops the command shell from echoing the line when it is executed, resulting in a less cluttered display.

- The ECHO OFF command (line 1) turns off command echo for the script. This stops *all* commands from being echoed by the shell, thus reducing clutter when the script runs, as only the output of commands is displayed.

- The first IF command (line 2) is used as a debug aid. It can be interpreted as follows: If a variable named ECHO exists, execute an ECHO command using the contents of the variable ECHO as the only argument. If no ECHO variable exists, this line does nothing. If, however, the variable does exist, the ECHO command is executed. If the variable ECHO contains the text ON, then the ECHO command that is executed will be:

```
echo ON
```

This command enables command echo, reversing the operation of line one. The combined result of the first two lines is therefore to disable command echo *unless* a variable called ECHO exists and has a value of ON. In this case command echo is enabled, allowing script echo to be turned on for all scripts simply by executing the command:

```
set ECHO=on
```

This SET command defines a variable called ECHO with a value of ON. The ability to quickly switch command echo on or off for all scripts is very useful when debugging a script.

- The second IF command (line 3) checks that the script is executing on Windows NT. If the script is running on Windows NT, the IF command will do nothing, and execution will continue at the next line. If, however, the script is executing on MS-DOS or Windows 95, the GOTO EXIT command will execute. This causes the shell to jump ahead to the last line of the script and immediately stop script execution.

- Line 7, containing :EXIT, is the target label for the GOTO statement in line 3. It should be the last line in the script.

Tip

The use of a variable named ECHO within an ECHO command might appear confusing. This is one place where the use of uppercase for variables and lowercase for command names helps improve readability by clearly distinguishing between the ECHO variable and the ECHO command.

In Windows NT, there are actually more elegant methods to achieve the effect of this script outline, but these methods are not backward compatible. The outline shown has the virtue of being compatible with MS-DOS version 3.x onwards and all versions of OS/2.

Chapter *2*

The Windows NT Command Shell

- **Command Shell Basics**
  The command shell is introduced, along with the basic command syntax.
  The difference between CMD.EXE and COMMAND.COM is explained.

- **Starting a Command Shell**
  Learn how to start, stop and nest command shells. Command line switches accepted by the command shell are also detailed.

- **Command Line Editing**
  Find out about the various command text-editing features, including less well-known features such as command completion and the command history.

- **DOSKEY and Command Macros**
  The features available through the DOSKEY command are described here, including command macros.

- **Launching Applications from the Shell**
  This section provides complete details of how the shell launches applications, including how they are located and how file associations are used. The role of the PATH and PATHEXT variables is explored, as well as the use of the START command.

- **Controlling Script Output**
  Various commands allow control over script output, such as ECHO and TITLE.

- **Command Redirection**
  Find out how to capture command output, redirect command input, and send the output of one command to the input of another.

- **Running Multiple Commands**
  Complex command lines execute multiple commands; learn about multi-line commands and the use of parentheses to group commands together.

- **Using Command Filters**
  The filter commands, such as MORE and SORT, are described here.

- **The Windows NT Command Scheduler**
  This section describes the Windows NT command scheduler, the Schedule Service and the AT command.

Command Shell Basics

The previous chapter introduced the Windows NT console window. By far the most common use for a console window is to execute the Windows NT *command shell*. The command shell defines the Windows NT scripting language and is responsible for processing scripts, as well as commands typed at the keyboard.

The command shell is a *console application*. As explained in chapter 1, console applications are Windows NT applications that interact via a console window, rather than via GUI elements such as windows and dialog boxes. When you start a command shell, Windows NT creates a console window for that shell. All commands that are run from within a shell (including other command shells) share the same console window for output. The only exception to this is the START command, which can be used to create additional console windows.

To start a default command shell in a console window, click the Start button, select the Programs item, and then select the Command Prompt command. The section "Starting a Command Shell" details additional ways to start a command shell.

Command Shell Modes

By default, command shells run in *Interactive mode*. In this mode, the shell displays a prompt and then waits for keyboard input. When a command line is entered, it is immediately interpreted and then executed. After execution completes, the shell displays another prompt, and the whole sequence begins again. This continues until the EXIT command ends the command shell session. Figure 2.1 shows this basic command execution sequence.

If a command entered is the name of a script file, the command shell switches to *Script mode*, and begins reading, interpreting, and executing commands from the specified script file. Figure 2.2 shows the command execution sequence while the shell is in script mode. Execution of the script ends when the shell reaches the end of the script file. At this point, the shell returns to interactive mode, displays another command prompt, and waits for keyboard input.

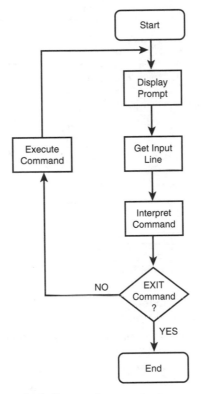

Figure 2.1. *Interactive mode shell execution sequence*

The Command Shell Prompt

The command shell displays the shell *prompt* when it is ready to accept a command in interactive mode. The default shell prompt is the current drive and path name, followed by a > character. When the command shell is in script mode, prompts are only displayed if command echo is enabled. The ECHO command, described in the section "Controlling Script Output," controls command echo.

The PROMPT command changes the command shell prompt. Follow the PROMPT command with the text of the new shell prompt. For example:

```
1. C:\>prompt ???
2. ???
```

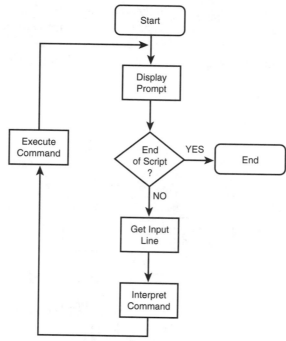

Figure 2.2. *Script mode shell execution sequence*

This example changes the command prompt to three question marks. Notice that the shell uses this prompt on line 2 in the example. To revert to the default prompt, enter a PROMPT command without any prompt text. For example:

```
1. ???prompt
2. C:\>
```

The prompt is restored to the default.

The command prompt text can contain special characters used as placeholders for additional information. For example, $T in the command text is replaced with the current time when the prompt is displayed, and $G is replaced with the > character. The following example shows this:

```
1. C:\>prompt $T$G
2. 14:23:50.35>
```

Using $G to represent the > character might seem unnecessary, as this character can simply be typed. However, this does not work, because the command shell reserves certain characters for special purposes. These reserved shell characters all have $c equivalents, so that they can be used in command prompts. For example, $A is used for an ampersand, $L for a < character, and so on. Table 2.1 shows the complete set of special characters recognized in a command shell prompt.

Table 2.1. Special Characters in a Shell Prompt

Character	Description
$A	Ampersand character.
$B	Pipe (I) character.
$C	Left parenthesis.
$D	Current date.
$E	Escape code (ASCII 27).
$F	Right parenthesis.
$G	Greater than character.
$H	Backspace character.
$L	Less than character.
$N	Current drive letter.
$P	Current drive letter and directory path.
$Q	Equal sign.
$S	Space.
$T	Current time.
$V	Windows NT version number.
$_	New line.
$$	Dollar sign.
$+	A series of "+" signs, corresponding to the number of pushed directories on the PUSHD stack. See the PUSHD command in Part III.
$M	The remote name (UNC name) for the current drive.

The $+ special character works in conjunction with the PUSHD and POPD commands (see Part III). These commands manage a push-down stack of directories and drives, and the $+ special character displays a sequence of + characters in the command prompt, one for each level in the push-down stack.

If the current drive is a network drive, the $M special character displays the remote UNC name of this drive in the form *server**share*. If the current drive is a local drive, then $M does not display anything.

The current prompt text is stored in the PROMPT environment variable. Changing the prompt changes the value of this variable and vice versa. Thus, these two commands have the same effect:

```
1. C:\>prompt [$p]
2. C:\>set PROMPT=[$p]
```

Simple Command Syntax

As described in chapter 1, simple shell commands consist of a command name followed by any required arguments. The command name and arguments (if any) are separated by a space. A command is always entered in response to a shell prompt. Figure 2.3 shows a simple shell command.

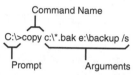

Figure 2.3. *Simple command syntax*

In Figure 2.3, the command name describes the action to be performed, while the arguments provide additional information needed to carry out this action. The syntax of the command arguments is specific to each command. However, there are a number of well-established conventions for command argument syntax. These are only conventions, however, and each individual command is free to interpret the supplied arguments however it chooses:

- First, multiple arguments are normally separated from one another by spaces. In Figure 2.3, the command has three arguments, `c:\*.bak`, `e:\backup`, and `/s`. Occasionally, other characters are used as argument separators. For example, the `COPY` command can use + characters to separate multiple filenames.

- Second, any argument that contains spaces or begins or ends with spaces must be enclosed in double quotes. This is particularly important when using long file and directory names, which frequently contain one or more spaces. If a double-quoted argument itself contains a double quote character, the double quote must be doubled. For example, enter `"Quoted" Argument` as `"""Quoted"" Argument"`.

- Third, command switches always begin with a slash / character. A *switch* is an argument that modifies the operation of the command in some way. Occasionally, switches begin with a + or - character. Some switches are *global*, and affect the command regardless of their position in the argument list. Other switches are *local*, and affect specific arguments (such as the one immediately preceding the switch).

- Fourth, all reserved shell characters not in double quotes must be escaped. These characters have special meaning to the Windows NT command shell. The reserved shell characters are:

  & | ( ) < > ^

To pass reserved shell characters as part of an argument for a command, either the entire argument must be enclosed in double quotes, or the reserved character must be *escaped*. Prefix a reserved character with a carat (^) character to escape it. For example, the following command example will not work as expected, because < and > are reserved shell characters:

```
1. C:\>echo <dir>
2. The syntax of the command is incorrect.
```

Instead, escape the two reserved characters, as follows:

```
1. C:\>echo ^<dir^>
2. <dir>
```

Typically, the reserved shell characters are not used in commands, so collisions that require the use of escapes are rare. They do occur, however. For example, the popular PKZIP program supports a -& switch to enable disk spanning. To use this switch correctly under Windows NT, -^& must be typed.

Tip

The carat character is itself a reserved shell character. Thus, to type a carat character as part of a command argument, type two carats instead. Escaping is necessary only when the normal shell interpretation of reserved characters must be bypassed.

- Finally, the maximum allowed length of a shell command appears to be undocumented by Microsoft. Simple testing shows that the Windows NT command shell allows *very* long commands—in excess of 4,000 characters. Practically speaking, there is no significant upper limit to the length of a command.

CMD.EXE and COMMAND.COM

Be aware that a command shell is *not* an MS-DOS command prompt, even though it shares the same icon. The Windows NT command shell is a full 32-bit Windows NT console application that resides in the CMD.EXE executable file. The MS-DOS command prompt is a 16-bit DOS application that resides in the COMMAND.COM executable file. Because COMMAND.COM is a 16-bit DOS executable, Windows NT executes this shell within a Windows NT virtual DOS machine (VDM). COMMAND.COM is supplied primarily for compatibility with MS-DOS.

Surprisingly, however, both the Windows NT and the MS-DOS shells have almost identical features. Here is a sample IF command entered into a Windows NT command shell, followed by the command output:

```
1. C:\>if /i a==A echo MATCH
2. MATCH
```

The IF command compares the letter "a" to the letter "A" and echoes MATCH if they compare. The /I switch compares the two letters without regard to letter case. Therefore, not surprisingly, the command echoes MATCH.

Here is the same IF command entered into an MS-DOS 16-bit COMMAND.COM shell (running on Windows NT on the same computer):

```
1. C:\>if /i a==A echo MATCH
2. MATCH
```

The output of both commands is identical. This is surprising, as the /I switch is a new feature of the Windows NT command shell (CMD.EXE) which is not understood by COMMAND.COM when running under actual MS-DOS.

This behavior reveals a quite subtle feature of Windows NT that is very important. The 16-bit MS-DOS shell (COMMAND.COM) that ships with Windows NT is specially designed for Windows NT. When a command is entered for execution by this shell, it does *not* actually execute it. Instead, it packages the command text and sends it to a 32-bit CMD.EXE command shell for execution. Because *all* commands are actually executed by CMD.EXE (the Windows NT command shell), the 16-bit shell inherits all the features and facilities of the full Windows NT shell.

You can see COMMAND.COM automatically execute a 32-bit CMD.EXE shell by using the Windows NT Task Manager application. Follow this procedure:

1. Right-click in an empty area in the taskbar. From the popup window select the Task Manager command to start Task Manager.

2. Click the Processes tab to display the list of running Windows NT processes.

3. Click the Start button in the taskbar and select the Run command.

4. In the Open box, type **COMMAND**. Then click OK to start a 16-bit command prompt.

5. Now examine the list of processes in the Task Manager window. You should see at least one NTVDM process. This is the Windows NT VDM, which NT starts to allow COMMAND.COM to execute.

6. In the COMMAND.COM window, enter any command which generates lengthy output (DIR /S is a good choice). When the output begins scrolling, press Ctrl+S to pause the command.

7. Switch to Task Manager and examine the list of processes again. Notice that a new CMD.EXE (command shell) is running. Figure 2.4 shows a typical Task Manager window.

8. Switch to the COMMAND.COM window and press Ctrl+S again. Wait for the command to complete.

9. Switch to Task Manager again. Notice that the CMD.EXE shell has disappeared from the Processes list.

10. To close the COMMAND.COM window enter an **EXIT** command.

This simple experiment shows that every command entered for execution, regardless of the shell used, is ultimately executed by CMD.EXE, the Windows NT command shell.

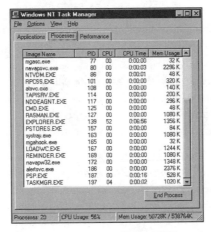

Figure 2.4. *Task Manager showing automatic CMD.EXE execution*

Starting a Command Shell

You can start a Windows NT command shell in a number of different ways:

- Select the Programs item in the Start menu, and then select the Command Prompt command.

- Select the Run command in the Start menu, enter **CMD** in the Open box and click OK.

- Enter a CMD command in an existing command shell.

- Enter a START command in an existing command shell, and specify CMD as the command to execute.

- Double-click a .BAT or .CMD script file in an Explorer window.

All these methods except the last start a command shell in Interactive mode. The last method starts the command shell in Script mode.

Like most other commands, the command shell CMD.EXE accepts several switches that control various shell options. Table 2.2 shows these switches, which are described in detail in the "Command Reference" in Part III.

Table 2.2. CMD.EXE Switches

Switch	Description
/X	Enables command extensions (default).
/Y	Disables command extensions.
/A	Command output to files or pipes will be ANSI (default).
/U	Command output to files or pipes will be Unicode.
/T	Sets foreground and background window colors.
/C	Executes command specified and then terminate shell.
/K	Executes command specified and then prompts for additional commands.

To specify shell switches, place them after the CMD command on the command line. It is not possible to directly enter shell switches if the shell is started from the Start menu Command Prompt command, or by double-clicking a .BAT or .CMD script file (the first and last methods in the preceding list).

Without any switches, a command shell starts in Interactive mode with command extensions enabled. *Command extensions* are certain features added to the command shell since Windows NT was first released. In general, these extensions are backward compatible, but they can occasionally cause older Windows NT and MS-DOS scripts to fail. In this case, the /Y switch disables the extensions and, in effect, runs an MS-DOS compatible command shell.

The /C and /K switches directly execute a command. The command to execute is specified following the switch. For example:

```
1. C:\>cmd /c echo Run this...
2. Run this...
```

All command line arguments following the /C or /K switch describe the command to execute. The /C switch executes the specified command, and the command shell then terminates. The /K switch executes the specified command, and the shell then enters Interactive mode. The /K switch is particularly useful to set up a command shell to a predetermined state before the first command prompt is displayed.

The /C and /K switches both accept any valid shell command, including the name of a script file to execute. In this case, the shell enters script mode and executes the specified script. This is the method the Windows NT Explorer uses to start a script file when it is opened. For example, if you double-click on the file SCRIPT.BAT, Explorer actually executes this command:

```
cmd /c script.bat
```

Terminating a Command Shell

In Interactive mode, the EXIT command terminates a command shell. If a console window was created for the command shell, the console window closes. If the command shell was invoked from within another program (including another command shell), that program regains control of the console window.

> **Tip**
>
> *Closing the console window also terminates a command shell. This method is valid only for the 32-bit CMD.EXE shell. The 16-bit COMMAND.COM shell should not be terminated in this manner.*

The EXIT command can also be used in script mode. The command should be used with care, however, as the shell terminates immediately, effectively aborting script execution. Scripts should normally end by executing to the end of the script file, or by the GOTO :EOF command (see Chapter 4).

If a script file is running in a shell that was started using the /C switch, the command shell terminates when the script reaches the end of the file.

Nesting Command Shells

A command shell can be started from within another command shell, commonly referred to as *nesting a shell*. This can be done either with the START command or by entering a CMD command directly at the command prompt. Nesting shells is useful if a command or script must be executed using different options to the current shell. For example, command extensions can be disabled in the nested command shell, or the command redirection mode changed. For example:

```
1. c:\>prompt [$p]
2.
3. [c:\]cmd /y
4. Microsoft(R) Windows NT(TM)
5. (C) Copyright 1985-1996 Microsoft Corp.
6.
7. [c:\]prompt
8. c:\>exit
9. [c:\]
```

The first PROMPT command changes the prompt. A new command shell is then invoked with the /Y switch (to disable command extensions). Notice that the new command shell inherits the prompt from the previous shell. The second PROMPT command returns the prompt to the default, as can be seen in the subsequent shell prompt (c:\>). The EXIT command exits the nested command shell, reverting to the previous (original) shell. Notice that the prompt reverts to the modified form, showing that the second command shell has indeed terminated.

The inheritance of the current command prompt by nested command shells is not a special feature of the shell. It occurs because the current command prompt is stored in an environment variable, and all commands executed from a shell inherit the current shell environment. The environment and inheritance is described fully in Chapter 3.

Nested command shells are useful when used with the /c switch. Suppose the script SXT.BAT was designed to run correctly only if command extensions are enabled. The following command executes this script correctly regardless of the state of command extensions for the current shell:

```
C:\>cmd /x /c sxt.bat
```

Another use of nested command shells—capturing all script output—is described in the upcoming section, "Controlling Script Output."

Command Line Editing

When in interactive mode, the command shell provides a rich set of tools to assist in command entry and editing. Most of these tools are applicable to all console applications that use line by line input. The command-line editing tools include:

- Basic character editing, such as Backspace and Delete.

- Template editing, which operates with a copy of the previously entered command.

- Command history editing, which allows quick recall of previously entered commands.

- Command completion, which automatically completes partially entered file and directory names.

- Command macros, which are described in "DOSKEY and Command Macros."

The "Command Line Editing" section in the "Command Reference" describes the full set of command-line editing commands.

Basic Character Editing

Basic character editing includes familiar commands such as Backspace, which erases the character to the left of the cursor, and Delete, which erases the character to the right of the cursor. Use the Left Arrow or Right Arrow keys to move the cursor left or right one character. Use these keys with Ctrl to move the cursor left or right one word. Use Home to move the cursor to the start of the command line, and End to move to the end of the command. Press the Esc key to delete the entire command, and press Enter to execute the command. The cursor does not have to be at the end of the line when Enter is pressed.

By default, the character editor operates in *Overwrite mode*. New characters typed overwrite characters at the current cursor location. Pressing the Insert key switches to *Insert mode*. In Insert mode, characters to the right of the cursor are shifted to the right as new characters are entered at the cursor location. Repeatedly pressing Insert toggles back and forth between the two modes. The cursor changes shape to indicate the mode—Insert mode is indicated by a larger, block shaped cursor. The mode resets when the Enter key is pressed.

The default Insert/Overwrite mode can be changed from Overwrite to Insert either by the DOSKEY command or via the Console Window property sheet's Options tab, as described in Chapter 1.

Template Editing

The second editing method, *template editing*, works in conjunction with a hidden command buffer, the *template*, which contains a copy of the most recently entered command. Template editing is present for compatibility with MS-DOS, and the newer command history editing commands generally make template editing obsolete.

The template F4 command is useful to quickly delete blocks of characters in a command line. Position the cursor at the first character to delete and press F4. A popup prompt appears. Enter a single character, and all characters in the command line from the cursor up to (but not including) the first instance of the specified character are deleted.

Command History Editing

Command history editing provides quick access to a list of recently executed commands, also known as the *history buffer*. Commands in this buffer can be re-executed, or recalled to the command line and edited as desired.

Each time a shell command executes, the command text is added to the command history buffer, and is then available for later recall. The maximum number of stored commands is set by the DOSKEY command or via the Console Window property sheet's Options tab, as described in Chapter 1.

The F7 key displays the command history buffer. Press F7, and a popup window appears containing the contents of the history buffer, with the oldest commands listed first.

Figure 2.5 shows a console window with a command history popup displayed. Each command is numbered, starting with 1 for the oldest command. The Up

Arrow and Down Arrow keys move up and down through the list of commands, while the Page Up or Page Down keys move to the start or end of the command list. The Esc key closes the history buffer popup window without executing a command.

Figure 2.5. *The command history buffer popup window*

To recall a command from the history buffer and execute it:

1. Press F7 to display the command history popup window.

2. Use the up arrow and down arrow keys in the popup window to highlight the command to execute.

3. Press Enter to execute the command.

When editing a command, use the up and down arrow keys to directly recall commands from the history buffer for editing. This differs from using these keys within the command history popup window. Press the keys repeatedly to cycle through all commands in the command buffer. The Up Arrow key moves back through the command history (starting with the most recently entered command) while the Down Arrow moves forward through the command history. The Page Up key moves to the oldest command in the history buffer, and the Page Down key moves to the newest command in the buffer. Once a command is recalled to the command line, it can be edited as needed and then executed by pressing the Enter key.

The F8 key searches the history buffer. Begin by typing the first few characters of the command that is required into the command line. Press the F8 key, and the first (most recent) command in the history buffer that begins with the characters entered is recalled to the command line. Repeatedly pressing F8 continues to search for additional matching commands in the history buffer.

The F9 key recalls commands from the history buffer by number. Command numbers are displayed in the command history popup, accessible by pressing F7. Press F9, and a popup window appears asking for the command number.

Enter the command number, and the specified command is recalled to the command line ready for editing or execution. The F9 key can also be used while the command history buffer popup window is displayed.

Windows NT supports command history editing for any program which reads keyboard input on a line-by-line basis. Each program maintains its own command history, so multiple command shells each have an independent command history buffer.

Command Completion Editing

Command completion automatically completes the typing of long file or directory names. Before this feature can be used, it must be enabled by changing a setting in the Windows NT registry. The value to alter is:

```
HKEY_CURRENT_USER\Software\Microsoft\Command Processor\CompletionChar
```

The default value for this is 0x0, which disables command completion. To enable command completion, set this value to the ASCII code for the key to use as the command completion key. The Tab key, value 0x9, is a good choice since it is not normally used in commands. The value is located in the per-user portion of the registry, and is therefore enabled on a per-user basis.

Once enabled, command completion operates as follows:

1. When entering a file or directory name, type the first few characters of the name and press the chosen command completion key (e.g. the Tab key).

2. The shell searches the current directory for a file or directory name which begins with the specified characters, and replaces the typed characters with the complete file or directory name.

3. Pressing the command completion key again cycles through all additional matching file names.

For example, suppose the current directory (C:\BOOK) contains three files, CHAP01.DOC, CHAP02.DOC and CHAPTER.DOC. Type the following, but do not press Enter:

```
C:\book>type chap
```

Press the command completion key. The command line immediately changes to:

```
C:\book>type "c:\book\chap01.doc"
```

The partial file name is replaced with the first file name found in the directory. The full path name is substituted, and the whole argument is placed in double quotes. This ensures that a valid argument is created even if the file name contains spaces. Press the command completion key again, and the command line changes to:

```
C:\book>type "c:\book\chap02.doc"
```

The command completion character can also be used when *no* characters of a file or directory name are entered. Type the command up to the file or directory name, making sure that the last character entered is a space. Then press the command completion key. In this case, *all* file and directory names in the current directory are presented in sequence.

Command completion is a very useful editing tool, particularly when long file and directory names are in use.

DOSKEY and Command Macros

The DOSKEY command provides command line control of various advanced shell command editing features. In MS-DOS, the DOSKEY command was a Terminate-and-Stay Resident (TSR) that needed to be loaded before its features were available for use. In Windows NT, these features are built into the shell and are always available; DOSKEY merely provides an interface to control them.

The DOSKEY command actually provides three distinct functions:

- Insert mode control
- command history buffer management
- command macro management

Insert mode control sets the initial Insert/Overwrite edit toggle. For example, this command sets the initial toggle to Insert mode:

```
C:\>doskey /insert
```

This command sets the initial toggle to overwrite mode:

```
C:\>doskey /overstrike
```

The initial state of this toggle is set for a console window using the console window property sheet Options tab, as described in Chapter 1.

The following DOSKEY command clears the command history buffer (described in the previous section "Command History Editing") of all commands:

```
C:\>doskey /reinstall
```

This command optionally sets a new size for the command history buffer. For example:

```
C:\>doskey /reinstall /listsize=100
```

This example clears the command history buffer and sets the number of commands in the buffer to 100. The command history buffer size can also be set for a console window using the Console Window property sheet Options tab, as described in Chapter 1.

The final set of DOSKEY commands provides control of command shell macros. *Command macros* are shorthand commands for longer, more complex shell commands. Macros can reduce typing or, in scripts, provide simple one-line functions. For example, to define a new macro named LS, which executes a DIR command, enter:

```
C:\>doskey ls=dir
```

The command shell will now accept LS as an alias for the DIR command. For example:

```
1. C:\>ls
2.   Volume in drive C is BOOTFAT
3.   Volume Serial Number is 3F3F-1704
4.
5.   Directory of C:\
6.
7. 05/31/94  01:22p              54,645 COMMAND.DOS
8. ...etc.
```

Command macros, like all shell commands, are not case sensitive. The simple definition of LS is not a direct replacement for the DIR command, however, because it does not accept arguments. For example:

```
C:\>ls *.dos
```

will not work as expected. The *.DOS argument is ignored, and the entire directory is displayed. To pass arguments to a macro, define the macro as follows:

```
C:\>doskey ls=dir $*
```

The special $* argument acts as a placeholder for all arguments entered on the command line. The LS macro is now an exact replacement for the DIR command. The DOSKEY section in the "Command Reference" in Part III lists additional special arguments that can be used within macro definitions.

Obviously, directly replacing one command by an alias is of limited use. However, macros can replace more complex commands. For example:

```
C:\>doskey ls=dir /od $*
```

This definition of the LS macro always provides directory listings sorted in date order. The /OD switch tells the DIR command to sort files according to date and time.

The following macro definition creates a command that displays the user name of the currently logged-on user:

```
1. C:\>doskey myname=for /f "delims=\ tokens=2" %i in ('whoami') do @echo %i
2. C:\>myname
3. TimHill
```

The MYNAME macro uses an advanced FOR command (described in Chapter 4, "Control Flow, Procedures, and Script Nesting") and the WHOAMI command to extract the user name. Typing **MYNAME** is far simpler than entering the complex FOR command. Macros are also very useful when combined with the various compound command symbols described in the section "Running Multiple Commands." For example:

```
C:\>doskey dircount=dir $* $B find "<DIR>" /c
```

This example creates a DIRCOUNT macro that counts the number of directories in a specified directory. The $B argument acts as a placeholder for the pipe symbol (¦). Alternatively, the pipe symbol can be entered directly by escaping it using a ^ character. Pipes are described in the section "Command Redirection."

Macros can be used with any Windows NT application which accepts line-by-line command input. However, each macro is explicitly defined for a specific application. By default, macros are defined for use by the command shell, CMD.EXE. The /EXENAME switch defines a macro for another application. For example, to define an EXIT macro for use with FTP, enter:

```
C:\>doskey /exename=ftp.exe exit=bye
```

The /MACROS switch lists defined macros for the command shell, for example:

```
1. C:\>doskey /macros
2. ls=dir $*
```

The /EXENAME switch lists macros for a specific application, for example:

```
1. C:\>doskey /macros /exename=ftp.exe
2. exit=bye
```

The /MACROS:ALL switch lists macros for all applications. The macros for each application are listed under the application name, which is placed in brackets.

The /MACROFILE switches reads a set of macro definitions from a file, for example:

```
C:\>doskey /macrofile=macros.mac
```

The format of macros in the macro file exactly matches the output of the DOSKEY command with the /MACROS:ALL switch. Therefore, it is possible to define a set of macros interactively and then use DOSKEY to create a macro file. Later, the macros can be recalled. For example:

```
1. C:\>doskey ls=dir /od $*
2. C:\>doskey /exename=ftp.exe exit=bye
3. ...etc.
4. C:\>doskey /macros:all >macros.mac
```

This example uses command output redirection (described in the section "Command Redirection") to capture the macro definitions to the file MACROS.MAC. Later, the /MACROFILE switch can reload the macros. One convenient way to do this is to use the CMD.EXE /K switch. For example:

```
C:\>cmd /k doskey /macrofile=macros.mac
```

This starts a new shell and pre-loads all the macros in MACROS.MAC. If this command is placed in a shortcut, a new command shell can be started and a set of macros loaded automatically without any typing.

Launching Applications from the Shell

As described at the beginning of this chapter, a basic shell command is composed of a command name followed by zero or more arguments. The command name specifies the action to be performed, and the arguments provide additional data used by the command to perform this action. In order to carry out the action specified by the command, the command shell must decode the command. This section describes the steps taken by the shell to decode each command.

Internal and External Commands

Commands can be broken into two main categories: *internal* and *external*. An internal command is one that is built-in to the shell itself. An external command is one that is contained within an executable file on the disk. For example, the COPY command is internal, while the XCOPY command is external (it is contained within the XCOPY.EXE file). Generally, the distinction between internal and external commands is unimportant, except that internal commands have no associated executable file.

The following are all of the Windows NT internal commands:

ASSOC	CALL	CHDIR/CD	CLS
COLOR	COPY	DATE	DIR
DPATH	ECHO	ENDLOCAL	ERASE/DEL
EXIT	FOR	FTYPE	GOTO
IF	MKDIR/MD	MOVE	PATH
PAUSE	POPD	PROMPT	PUSHD
REM	RENAME/REN	RMDIR/RD	SET
SETLOCAL	SHIFT	START	TIME
TITLE	TYPE	VER	

The PATH Command and PATHEXT Variable

Two environment variables are intimately associated with shell command execution: PATH and PATHEXT.

The PATH environment variable defines the Windows NT search path. The *search path* is a list of directories that are searched when the command shell attempts to locate an executable file. Separate directories in the path list with semi-colons. For example, a typical path might contain:

```
d:\winnt40\system32;d:\winnt40;d:\ntreskit;c:\bin;c:\dos
```

The PATH command manipulates the PATH environment variable, although the variable can also be directly manipulated via the SET command (see Chapter 3 for a description of the SET command). To set a new system path, follow the PATH command with a new path list. For example:

```
C:\>path c:\bin;c:\scripts;d:\winnt
```

This PATH command tells Windows NT to search the C:\BIN, C:\SCRIPTS, and D:\WINNT directories for executable files.

Enter a PATH command without any arguments to display the current search path. For example:

```
1. C:\>path
2. PATH= d:\winnt40\system32;d:\winnt40;d:\ntreskit;c:\bin;c:\dos
```

One common use of the PATH command is adding a new directory to the search path. To do this, specify the existing search path as part of the new path. For example, to add a new directory, C:\NEWDIR, to the start of the path, use this command:

```
C:\>path c:\newdir;%PATH%
```

Use this command to add the same directory to the end of the path:

```
C:\>path %PATH%;c:\newdir
```

The PATH variable is initialized from the following sources of information:

- The System Environment, which is set via the Control Panel System icon.

- The User Environment, which is set via the Control Panel System icon.

- Any PATH statements in AUTOEXEC.BAT (if parsing is enabled).

At logon time, path information from the sources listed above is concatenated together to form the initial path. After logging on, the PATH command is used to alter the path.

The PATHEXT environment variable defines the list of file extensions checked by Windows NT when searching for an executable file. Like the PATH variable, semi-colons separate individual items in the PATHEXT variable. The default value of PATHEXT is .COM;.EXE;.BAT;.CMD. The PATHEXT variable is manipulated via the SET command. For example, to add the .PL extension, use the following command:

```
C:\>set PATHEXT=%PATHEXT%;.pl
```

The following section describes how Windows NT and the command shell use the PATH and PATHEXT variables.

Command Search Sequence

When a command is submitted for execution (either by typing or as part of a script), the shell performs the following actions:

1. All parameter and environment variable references are resolved (see chapter 3).

2. Compound commands are split into individual commands and each is then individually processed according to the following steps (see the section "Running Multiple Commands" for details of compound commands). Continuation lines are also processed at this step.

3. The command is split into the command name and any arguments.

4. If the command name does *not* specify a path, the shell attempts to match the command name against the list of internal shell commands. If a match is found, the internal command executes. Otherwise, the shell continues to step 5.

5. If the command name specifies a path, the shell searches the specified path for an executable file matching the command name. If a match is found, the external command (the executable file) executes. If no match is found, the shell reports an error and command processing completes.

6. If the command name does not specify a path, the shell searches the current directory for an executable file matching the command name. If a match is found, the external command (the executable file) executes. If no match is found, the shell continues to step 7.

7. The shell now searches each directory specified by the PATH environment variable, in the order listed, for an executable file matching the command name. If a match is found, the external command (the executable file) executes. If no match is found, the shell reports an error and command processing completes.

In outline, if the command name does *not* contain a path, the command shell first checks to see if the command is an internal command, then checks the current directory for a matching executable file, and then checks each directory in the search path. If the command name *does* contain a path, the shell only checks the specified directory for a matching executable file.

If the command name includes a file extension, the shell searches each directory for the exact file name specified by the command name. If the command name does *not* include a file extension, the shell adds the extensions listed in the PATHEXT environment variable, one by one, and searches the directory for that file name. Note that the shell tries all possible file extensions in a specific directory before moving on to search the next directory (if there is one).

For example, the following command explicitly specifies the path, command name, and file extension:

```
C:\>c:\bin\edit.exe
```

This command executes the program EDIT.EXE found in the directory C:\BIN. If the program is not found, the shell reports an error.

This example omits the path to EDIT.EXE:

```
C:\>edit.exe
```

To execute this command, the shell searches the current directory and then each directory in the search path until EDIT.EXE is found, or reports an error if the file is not found.

This example omits the path and file extension:

```
C:\>edit
```

To execute this command, the shell searches the current directory and then each directory in the search path. Assuming that the PATHEXT variable contains .COM;.EXE;.BAT;.CMD, each directory is searched for EDIT.COM, EDIT.EXE, EDIT.BAT and EDIT.CMD before the shell moves on to the next search directory.

Once the command shell resolves the command name either to an internal command or an external executable file, it executes the command as follows:

- If the command is internal, the shell executes it directly.

- If the command is a 16-bit or 32-bit Windows GUI executable program, the shell runs the program but does not wait for the command to complete.

- If the command is a 32-bit console application, or a 16-bit MS-DOS application, the shell runs the command in the current console window and waits for the command to complete.

- If the command is a script file (.BAT or .CMD), the shell switches to script mode and begins executing the script.

- If the command is a document or data file name associated with an application, the shell executes the appropriate application. The shell applies the previous rules based upon the type of the application associated with the data or document file. See the following section for more information on file associations.

Notice that the command shell does not wait for GUI applications to complete execution before it continues. This behavior can be modified using the START command, described in the following section.

File Associations

Windows NT provides a database, in the system registry, which allows files to be associated with a particular application. The primary use of this association is called *automatic application launching*. This feature is used extensively in the GUI environment: whenever a data file or document is double-clicked, the associated application automatically launches, and the specified file or document then opens within that application.

> *Tip*
>
> *File associations can also be edited using Windows NT Explorer (using the View, Options command). However, the commands presented here have a finer degree of control than that provided by Explorer. For example, Explorer provides no easy way to delete an individual association.*

File associations are also applicable to the command shell environment. For example, suppose Microsoft Word is installed on a computer. During installation of Word, .DOC files are associated with the Word application. Once this is done, it is possible to launch Word and open a .DOC file from a shell command simply by typing its name. For example:

```
C:\>c:\docs\letter.doc
```

This command launches Word and opens the file C:\DOCS\LETTER.DOC. If the file is in the current directory, the path is not required. For example:

```
C:\docs>letter.doc
```

In fact, the command shell applies the same rules when opening a document or data file as it does when searching for any external command. Thus, in the previous example, the shell looks for LETTER.DOC in the current directory and in all directories specified by the search path. If the C:\DOCS directory is added to the search path, the file LETTER.DOC can be opened in Word from *any* directory, merely by typing its name. For example:

```
1. C:\docs>path c:\docs;%PATH%
2. C:\docs>cd ..
3. C:\>letter.doc
```

As previously noted, the file association database is maintained in the Windows NT Registry. Therefore, changes made to file associations are persistent—they are retained even after the computer is reset. In addition, the database is maintained in the HKEY_LOCAL_COMPUTER portion of the registry. Thus, changes made to the file association database effect all users of a particular computer.

The file association database works with three items of information:

- file extensions

- file types

- launch commands

A *file extension* is the familiar file name suffix after the last period in the file name. For example, MYSCRIPT.BAT has a file extension of .BAT. Most file extensions are one, two, or three characters long. A *file type* is a name for a particular class of file. For example, Windows NT scripts might be assigned a file type of Windows.Script. A *launch command* is a prototype command used to launch the associated application. For example, NOTEPAD.EXE %1 is a typical launch command.

When a document or data filename is specified as a command name, the shell uses the file association database to launch the correct application. It does this as follows:

1. The shell extracts the file extension from the specified document file. It then searches the database for a matching file association. If no match is found, the shell reports an error and command processing completes.

2. The shell then obtains from the database the name of the file type associated with the file extension.

3. The shell then searches the database again for the specified file type. If no match is found, the shell reports an error and command processing completes.

4. The shell obtains from the database the launch command associated with the file type.

5. The shell now parses the launch command, replacing any parameters with arguments specified in the original shell command.

6. Finally, the shell executes the parsed command. Typically, this launches the associated application.

This procedure is best understood through an example. Consider this command:

```
C:\docs>letter.doc
```

The shell first extracts the file extension, .DOC, and searches the database for the file type associated with this file extension. Typically, this yields a file type such as Word.Document.8. The shell now uses this file type to search for the launch command. Assume this is WINWORD.EXE %1. The %1 in this command is a formal parameter, which the shell replaces with the document file name (LETTER.DOC). So the final launch command is WINWORD.EXE LETTER.DOC. When this command executes, Word runs, and the LETTER.DOC file is opened.

File types are thus, an intermediary between a file extension and a launch command. They exist to allow multiple file extensions to be associated with the same launch command. For example, a paint program might need to associate .BMP, .JPG, .TIF and .TGA files with a launch command. Rather than entering the same launch command in the database four times, the program uses a single file type and launch command, and then associates the file extensions with this type. Any subsequent changes made to the launch command are then automatically applied to all associated file extensions.

The ASSOC, FTYPE and ASSOCIATE commands are used to manipulate the file association database. The ASSOC command connects a file extension with a file type, and the FTYPE command connects a file type with a launch command.

Use the FTYPE command to create or edit a file type and associate it with a launch command. For example:

```
C:\>ftype REXX.File=c:\rexx\rexx.exe "%1"
```

This creates the file type REXX.File and associates the prototype command C:\REXX\REXX.EXE "%1" with the type. Notice the use of double quotes around the %1 parameter. This ensures that the command is handled correctly even if the specified document name contains spaces.

> **Tip**
>
> *When defining a prototype command, it is advisable to include the full path name of the executable file, unless the directory containing the executable will always be part of the search path.*

The FTYPE command can also display the current launch command for a file type. For example:

```
1. C:\>ftype REXX.File
2. REXX.File=REXX "%1"
```

Finally, the command and file type can be deleted. For example:

```
1. c:\>ftype REXX.File=
2. c:\>ftype REXX.File
3. File type 'REXX.File' not found or no open command associated with it.
```

Once a file type and launch command are set up, the ASSOC command associates file extensions with that file type. For example:

```
1. C:\>assoc .rex=REXX.File
2. .rex=REXX.File
```

The current association of a file type is displayed using ASSOC. For example:

```
1. C:\>assoc .rex
2. .rex=REXX.File
```

Finally, the file extension association can be deleted. For example:

```
C:\>assoc .rex=
```

Notice that for both FTYPE and ASSOC, specifying the file type or file extension *only* displays the current association. Specifying the file type or file extension with a trailing = character deletes the current association.

The ASSOCIATE [RK] command provides a shorthand method to perform an ASSOC and FTYPE in one step. While not as versatile as the ASSOC/FTYPE combination, it is easier to use. ASSOCIATE directly associates a file extension with an application, providing the necessary file type and launch command automatically. For example:

```
C:\>associate .rex c:\rexx\rexx.exe
```

This command directly associates .REX files with the REXX.EXE application. The association can be deleted using the following command:

```
C:\>associate .rex /d
```

More information on the ASSOC, FTYPE and ASSOCIATE commands can be found in the "Command Reference."

Integrating New Script Languages with the Shell

By using a combination of the PATH and PATHEXT variables, along with the application association database, complete integration of new command types into the command shell is possible.

For example, suppose a REXX interpreter, REXX.EXE, is installed in the C:\REXX directory. REXX scripts can then be executed using commands such as:

```
C:\>c:\rexx\rexx myrexx.rex arg1 arg2 arg3
```

This executes the REXX interpreter, REXX.EXE, which then interprets and runs the script MYREXX.REX. In this example, ARG1 etc. are arguments passed to the script.

By adding an association to the file association database, the invocation of the REXX interpreter can be made implicit. For example:

```
1. C:\>ftype REXX.File=c:\rexx\rexx.exe "%1" %*
2. C:\>assoc .rex=REXX.File
```

These commands create the needed associations, so that a .REX file launches the REXX.EXE interpreter. Notice that by including the full path name in the proto-type command the interpreter executes without adding the C:\REXX directory to the search path. In addition, the %1 parameter is placed in double quotes so that .REX filenames containing spaces are correctly handled. Finally, the special %* parameter represents all additional arguments following the first (in this case ARG1 ARG2 ARG3). Now, the original script command can be simplified to:

```
C:\>myrexx.rex arg1 arg2 arg3
```

By adding the file extension .REX to the list of file extensions specified with PATHEXT, the .REX file extension can also be made implicit. For example:

```
1. C:\>set PATHEXT=%PATHEXT%;.REX
2. C:\>myrexx arg1 arg2 arg3
```

At this point, entering a REXX script command to execute is as convenient as entering any native shell command.

Finally, the MYREXX.REX script can be stored in a central directory, and that directory added to the system search path. For example:

```
1. C:\>mkdir c:\rexxscripts
2. C:\>move myrexx.rex c:\rexxscripts
3. C:\>set PATH=%PATH%;c:\rexxscripts
4. C:\>myrexx arg1 arg2 arg3
```

At this point, the MYREXX.REX script can be executed in *any* directory, just by typing its name.

> **Tip**
>
> *File association database changes are persistent. However, changes to environment variables are not. Therefore, the changes to the* PATH *and* PATHEXT *variables shown in the prior examples are lost when the system is shutdown, or the current shell terminated. To make these changes persistent, edit the* PATH *and* PATHEXT *variables in the Environment tab of the Control Panel System applet.*

The START Command

Previous sections described how the command shell implicitly interprets and executes a basic command. The START command explicitly executes a shell command, and provides additional control over how the command is handled by Windows NT.

The syntax of the START command is:

```
START ["title"] [switches] command-name [args]
```

The first item following the START command is an optional window title, enclosed in double quotes. By default, the START command executes the specified command in a new window. In this case, the title text is used as the window title.

Following the title are zero or more switches that control the operation of the START command. A command-name must then be present, which specifies the command to run. Following the command name are zero or more command arguments, which are passed to the specified command.

> **Tip**
>
> All START *switches and options must appear before the* command-name. *Switches and options placed after the* command-name *are passed, unaltered, to the command being started.*

Without any of the optional switches, the START command executes the specified command. It does this as follows:

- If the command is a 16-bit or 32-bit Windows GUI executable program, the START command runs the program but does not wait for the command to complete.

- If the command is a 32-bit console application, or a 16-bit MS-DOS application, the START command runs the command in a new console window but does not wait for the command to complete.

- If the command is a script file (.BAT or .CMD), or an internal command, the START command executes a new command shell (CMD.EXE) in a new console window. The script or internal command is executed using the /K switch. The START command does not wait for the command or script to complete.

- If the command is a document or data file name associated with an application, the START command executes the appropriate application. The START command applies the previous rules based upon the type of the application associated with the data or document file.

Notice that the operation of the START command differs from the default command shell sequence:

- First, the START command never waits for the command to complete.

- Second, all console commands start in a new console window, rather than the current console window.

- Finally, if the command is a script file or internal shell command, the START command executes the command using a new command shell (CMD.EXE) with the /K switch. This means that, after the script of internal command completes, the new command shell does *not* terminate, but instead enters interactive mode. For example:

```
C:\>start "New Window" dir
```

This command executes a DIR command in a new console window, giving the new window the title New Window. Since DIR is an internal command, the new command shell enters Interactive mode and prompts for additional commands after the DIR command completes.

To over-ride this behavior, explicitly execute a new command shell and use the /C switch. For example:

```
C:\>start "New Window" cmd /c dir
```

In this example, the *command-name* for the START command is actually CMD. The /C switch and DIR command are arguments to the CMD.EXE command shell. The START command therefore executes the command CMD /C DIR in a new console window. When the DIR command completes, the new command shell terminates, and the new console window closes.

The START command is most useful when one or more of the optional switches are used. All START switches follow the window title (if used) and precede the command name.

The /D switch specifies a new current drive and directory for the command. Without /D, the command inherits the drive and directory of the command shell. Follow the /D switch with the new drive and directory. For example:

```
C:\>start /dc:\book dir
```

The /I switch controls environment inheritance. Normally, all commands executed by the command shell inherit a copy of the current environment (this is described in detail in Chapter 3). The /I switch causes the command to inherit the environment as it existed when the command shell was first started. Thus, any changes made to the environment within the current command shell are *not* passed to the executed command.

The /MIN and /MAX switches specify the initial state of the new window created by the START command. These switches apply to all applications and commands, including 16 and 32-bit GUI applications. Without /MIN or /MAX, the START command creates the new window using Windows NT default settings. The /MIN switch creates the new window minimized, that is, as a task dbar button. The /MAX switch creates the new window maximized, that is, occupying the entire screen.

The /LOW, /NORMAL, /HIGH and /REALTIME switches set the priority class for the command or application. By default, the START command executes all commands or applications at normal priority. The /LOW switch executes the application at low priority, while the /HIGH switch executes the application at high priority. The /REALTIME switch executes the application at real-time priority.

> **Troubleshooting Tip**
>
> *Use of the* /REALTIME *switch is* strongly *discouraged, as its use can compromise Windows NT stability.*

Using /LOW to execute an application at low priority is a very useful way of running a low priority background task. For example:

```
C:\>start "Cleanup" /low /min cmd /c cleanup.bat
```

This command executes the CLEANUP.BAT script at low priority. The /MIN switch is used so that the script appears only as a button on the task bar.

As described above, the START command does *not* wait for the new command to complete; a new command prompt appears immediately and new commands can be executed at once. When used in a script, the next line in the script executes immediately. The /WAIT switch makes the START command wait for the command to complete before continuing. This switch applies to all commands and applications, including GUI applications.

Finally, the /B switch executes the command without creating a new console window. This switch is application only to internal commands and external console applications—it is ignored if the command specifies a GUI application. Using /B also implies the /WAIT switch.

Controlling Script Output

The command shell provides the following simple commands to control script output:

- The REM command, which is used for script comments.
- The CLS command, which clears the console window.
- The COLOR command, which controls colors used in the console window.
- The TITLE command, which changes the console window title bar text.
- The @ command, which controls command echo on a line-by-line basis.
- The ECHO command, which controls command echo and also displays text.
- The NOW [RK] command, which displays time-stamped text.

REM

The REM (remark) command is the simplest script command because it does nothing. Any text can follow the REM command. REM commands are used for shell comments, and should be used liberally within a script (for example, to clarify complex script commands and document the script logoc). The REM command also suppresses the meaning of reserved shell characters within the remark text. For example, the following is a valid remark:

```
C:\>rem This is valid in a REM statement: &, &&, ¦¦, ^
```

Normally, the shell assigns special meanings to &, && etc., but in a remark command these characters are treated as regular text.

> **Troubleshooting Tip**
>
> *Because the REM command suppresses the normal interpretation of special shell characters, REM commands cannot appear within a multi-line command. For example, the following is invalid:*
>
> ```
> 1. if "%X%"=="ABC" (
> 2.     rem An illegal comment!
> 3.     goto :EXIT
> 4. )
> ```
>
> *The shell combines multi-line commands (like the one above) into a single line before executing them. Therefore, the shell "sees" the command like this:*
>
> ```
> if "%X%"=="ABC" ( rem An illegal comment! &  goto :EXIT )
> ```
>
> *The REM command will include all the text on the line, up to and including the closing parenthesis. The GOTO command is not seen as a command at all, but instead as additional comment text.*

CLS

The CLS command clears the current console window and positions the cursor to the top left of the window. Subsequent command output begins at the top of the window and works down the screen. The screen is cleared using the current window colors. The CLS command is useful when a script needs to present uncluttered output.

COLOR

The COLOR command sets the text and background colors for the console window. When a console window is started, it uses the colors set using the Console Window property sheet Colors tab, as described in chapter 1. The COLOR command without any arguments returns the console window to these default colors. With a single argument, the COLOR command sets the text and background colors. The argument must be two characters long. The first character specifies the background color and the second character specifies the text color. Table 2.3 shows the color codes used.

Table 2.3. COLOR *Command Color Codes*

Code	Color	Code	Color
0	Black	8	Gray
1	Blue	9	Light Blue
2	Green	A	Light Green
3	Aqua	B	Light Aqua
4	Red	C	Light Red
5	Purple	D	Light Purple
6	Yellow	E	Light Yellow
7	White	F	Bright White

For example, this command sets a pleasing white on blue color combination:

```
C:\>color 17
```

TITLE

The TITLE command changes the title bar of the console window to the specified text. The text in the corresponding button on the task bar is also changed. The TITLE command is useful to show the progress of long or complex scripts. It is superior to ECHO for this purpose as it does not scroll text in the console window, and the text is visible in the task bar even when the console window is minimized. For example:

```
C:\>title Backup Drive C:...
```

@

The @ command controls command echo on a line-by-line basis. By default, the shell displays each command in a script before it is executed. Prefix a command with an @ character to suppress command echo. For example:

```
@title Welcome to the script!
```

The @ command can be placed within a compound command (described in the upcoming section "Running Multiple Commands") to control echo of individual portions of the command, although the utility of this is questionable. For example, this compound command will not echo when executed as part of a script:

```
@(echo starting...)&(title Script phase 1)
```

However, the command

```
(@echo starting...)&(title Script phase 1)
```

echoes as:

```
C:\>( )&(title Script phase 1)
```

The @ command controls command echo on a command-by-command basis. The ECHO command controls command echo for an entire script. This command disables command echo:

```
C:\>echo off
```

This command enables command echo:

```
C:\>echo on
```

To display the current state of command echo, enter:

1. C:\>**echo**
2. **ECHO is on.**

ECHO

The ECHO command is typically used at the start of a script to disable command echo for the duration of the script. For example, many scripts begin with this line:

```
@echo off
```

This disables echo for the entire script. The echo of the ECHO command is itself suppressed by using the @ command. (The example above is the first special script line that was shown in the section "Special Script Lines" in chapter 1.) Once echo is disabled (or enabled) in a script, the echo state is maintained within the script and within script procedures and nested scripts. The only exception to this is nested scripts executed via a CMD or START command. These scripts run in a new command shell, which always starts with echo enabled.

Echo can be disabled interactively at a command prompt by entering an ECHO OFF command. In this case, the command prompt is suppressed until echo is enabled again. Typed commands are still echoed during entry, however.

The current echo state is used when the command shell switches from Interactive mode to script mode to begin executing a script. Thus, if echo is enabled interactively, the script begins with echo enabled, and vice versa. However, the shell remembers the original interactive echo state, and recalls it when the script completes. Therefore, after a script ends, the echo state reverts to the value it had before the script began execution.

The ECHO command is also used to echo arbitrary text to the console window. For example:

```
C:\>echo Hello, world!
```

If command echo is disabled, the command itself is not echoed, but the text specified in the ECHO command *is* echoed. When used this way, the ECHO command is the Windows NT script equivalent of the PRINT statement found in many languages. Typically, ECHO is used with environment variable substitution, which is described in Chapter 3.

> **Tip**
>
> The ECHO *command cannot be used to echo an empty line. For example:*
>
> ```
> 1. C:\>echo
> 2. ECHO is on.
> ```
>
> *As can be seen, the* ECHO *command displays the current state of command echo, not an empty line. The nearest equivalent is to echo something inconsequential, such as a single period. For example:*
>
> ```
> 1. C:\>echo .
> 2. .
> ```

NOW [RK]

The NOW [RK] command also displays arbitrary text. However, NOW prefixes the text with the current time and date. This is useful when the time taken to execute a command must be monitored. For example:

```
1. E:\workdir>now Start
2. Wed Oct 21 12:20:07 1997 -- Start
3. E:\workdir>echo Quick command
4. Quick command
5. E:\workdir>now End
6. Wed Oct 21 12:20:18 1997 -- End
7. E:\workdir>
```

Command Redirection

Most console applications and commands generate output, and many accept input. This input or output is in the form of a *stream* of characters (either ANSI or Unicode). Applications generally work with up to three streams, as follows:

- The *command input stream* is used by the application or command to read input. By default this stream comes from keys typed at the keyboard.

- The *command output stream* is used by the application or command to display output. By default, this stream is displayed in the console window.

- The *command error output stream* is used by the application or command to display errors. By default, this stream is displayed in the console window.

The default stream input and output provides normal interactive command operation: input is obtained from the keyboard, and output is displayed in the console window. Note that the distinction between the command output stream and the command error output stream is somewhat arbitrary. An application or command can direct output to whichever stream it wishes. Typically, however, normal output is sent to the command output stream, and errors are sent to the command error output stream.

The command shell provides facilities to change the default stream input and output. These facilities are accessed by placing special command redirection symbols in a command. Table 2.4 shows the command redirection symbols.

Table 2.4. Command Redirection Symbols

Symbol	Description
`>file`	Redirects command output to the *file* specified. You can also use a standard device name such as LPT1, CON, PRN or CONOUT$ as the file name. Any preexisting contents of the file are lost.
`>>file`	Redirects command output to the *file* specified. If the file already exists, all command output is appended to the end of the file.
`<file`	Redirects command input from the *file* specified. You can also use a standard device name such as CON or CONIN$.
`2>file`	Redirects command error output to the *file* specified. You can also use a standard device name such as LPT1, CON, PRN or CONOUT$ as the file name. Any preexisting contents of the file are lost.
`2>&1`	Redirects command error output to the same location as command output. This makes any command output redirection also apply to command error output.
`cmd1 ¦ cmd2`	Pipes the command output of *cmd1* to the command input of *cmd2*. Multiple pipe characters are allowed, creating a chain of commands, each sending output to the next command in the chain.

Command redirection symbols are not visible to the command. The shell processes them before the command is executed and they are *not* passed as arguments to the command. The <, >, and ¦ symbols are reserved shell characters. If these symbols must be passed as command arguments, instead of being used as redirection symbols, then they must be escaped using the ^ character.

The > redirection symbol redirects command output to the specified file. For example:

```
C:\>dir >c:\dir.txt
```

This example creates a text file C:\DIR.TXT containing the output of the DIR command. The > symbol can be placed anywhere in the command, but is typically placed at the end of the command. A space is permitted between the > symbol and the file name. If the file specified by the redirection symbol already exists, any existing contents are deleted before the command is executed.

Tip

Only one command output redirection symbol is allowed per command. It is not possible, for example, to duplicate command output by redirecting the command output to multiple files.

The >> redirection symbol redirects command output to the specified file, but concatenates the output onto the end of the file. For example:

```
C:\>dir >> c:\dir.txt
```

This example adds the output of the DIR command to the end of the file C:\DIR.TXT. If the file specified does not exist, it is created.

The < redirection symbol redirects command input from the specified file. For example:

```
C:\>sort <c:\dir.txt
```

This command sorts the contents of the file C:\DIR.TXT and then displays the result. A space is permitted between the < symbol and the file name. The < symbol is used less frequently than > and >>, since there are few shell commands which accept console input.

The 2> redirection symbol redirects command error output to the specified file. For example:

```
C:\>dir 2>c:\error.txt
```

This example redirects the error output of the DIR command to the file C:\ERROR.TXT. A space is permitted between the 2> symbol and the file name. Notice that this example does *not* redirect regular command output, so the directory listing is still displayed. Only error output (if any) is captured to the file.

The redirection symbols can be combined in a single command. For example:

```
C:\>sort <c:\dir.txt >c:\sortdir.txt 2>c:\error.txt
```

The `2>&1` redirection symbol redirects command error output to command output. This means that command error output is sent to the same destination as command output. For example:

```
C:\>dir >c:\dir.txt 2>&1
```

This command sends both command output and command error output to the file C:\DIR.TXT.

The ¦ (pipe) redirection symbol sends the command output of *cmd1* to the command input of *cmd2*. For example:

```
C:\>dir ¦ sort
```

This example sends the command output of the DIR command to the command input of the SORT command. The output from the SORT command is then displayed. Alternatively, the SORT output can be sent to another command. For example:

```
C:\>dir ¦ sort ¦ more
```

This example sends the command output of the DIR command to the command input of the SORT command. Then, the command output of the SORT command is sent to the command input of the MORE command. Finally, the command output of the MORE command is displayed.

When the command shell processes a pipe (¦) symbol, it actually runs both commands specified simultaneously. The right hand command is suspended until the left hand command begins generating command output. Then, the left hand command wakes up and processes the output. When this output has been processed, the command is again suspended until more input is available. The synchronization of both commands is handled automatically by the command shell and Windows NT.

The pipe symbol is both a redirection symbol and a compound command symbol. Compound commands are discussed in the next section.

Command redirection effects are inherited by nested commands. If a command starts with its command output redirected, and this command then starts additional commands, these commands inherit the same redirection as the parent command. This is frequently used with nested shells to capture all script output to a file. For example:

```
C:\>cmd /c myscript.bat >result.txt
```

This command executes the script MYSCRIPT.BAT in a new shell. Since the new command shell has its command output redirected to the file RESULT.TXT, all commands run by the shell (i.e. those in the script) also have their output redirected.

By default, all command input and output is processed as ANSI (or ASCII) characters. However, if the shell is started with the /U switch (see the "CMD" section in the "Command Reference"), command input and output is processed as Unicode characters. In this case, if a command generates ANSI output, the shell automatically converts ANSI command output to Unicode.

Running Multiple Commands

In previous sections, the simple "command and arguments" syntax of a shell command was described. The shell also supports *compound commands*, where a command line specifies more than one command to execute. Compound commands are indicated by special compound command symbols. Table 2.5 shows the compound command symbols.

Table 2.5. Compound Command Symbols

Symbol	Description
cmd1 & cmd2	Executes command cmd1, then command cmd2. Additional commands can be added using additional ampersand symbols.
cmd1 && cmd2	Executes command cmd1, then executes command cmd2 only if cmd1 completed successfully.
cmd1 ¦¦ cmd2	Executes command cmd1, then executes command cmd2 only if cmd1 did not complete successfully.
( )	Use parentheses to indicate the nesting of complex multi-command sequences. Also used in IF ... ELSE commands.

The &, ¦, (, and) symbols are reserved shell characters. If these symbols must be passed as command arguments, instead of being used as compound command symbols, then they must be escaped using the ^ character.

The simplest compound command symbol is &. The & symbol separates multiple commands on a single command line. For example:

```
1. C:\>echo Command 1 & echo Command 2
2. Command 1
3. Command 2
```

This example shows two ECHO commands on a single line. When & is used to separate multiple commands, the commands execute one at a time, starting with the first command. Each command runs to completion before the next command executes.

Any number of commands can be placed on a single line using the & symbol.
For example:

```
C:\>dir c:\bin >files.txt & dir c:\dos >>files.txt & type files.txt
```

This example accumulates the results of two DIR commands into the file
FILES.TXT and then displays the contents of this file. This example also shows
that command redirection symbols can be used with each individual command
in a compound command.

The && and ¦¦ compound command symbols provide conditional command
execution. The first (left) command is executed. If the && symbol is used, the
second command executes only if the first command completed successfully. If
the ¦¦ symbol is used, the second command executes only if the first command
did *not* complete successfully. A command completes successfully if it returns
an exit code of 0 or no exit code at all. Exit codes are discussed in chapter 3.
For example:

```
C:\>verify on ¦¦ echo Verify command failed!!
```

Since the VERIFY command executed successfully, the ECHO command was *not*
executed. However, in this example:

```
1. C:\>verify ox ¦¦ echo Verify command failed!!
2. An incorrect parameter was
3. entered for the command.
4. Verify command failed!!
```

The ECHO command *was* executed because the VERIFY command syntax was
incorrect, causing the command to exit with a non-zero error code.

Multiple commands can be chained together using additional && and ¦¦ compound command symbols. For example:

```
C:\>dir && copy a b && echo OK!
```

The COPY command executes only if the DIR command succeeds, and the ECHO
command executes only if the COPY command succeeds.

The parentheses symbols (and) are used to resolve command ambiguities and
indicate the binding of compound command and redirection symbols. They are
also used in the IF command and to specify multi-line commands.

For example, the following command collects two directory listings into the file
FILES.TXT:

```
C:\>dir *.exe >files.txt & dir *.com >>files.txt
```

The following command might appear to do the same, but in fact it does not
work:

```
C:\>dir *.exe & dir *.com >files.txt
```

This second example fails because the command redirection symbols have a higher precedence than the compound command symbols. The shell interprets this command as follows:

```
1. C:\>dir *.exe
2. C:\>dir *.com >files.txt
```

This displays the result of the first DIR command in the console window— which is not the desired effect.

The second example can be corrected by using parentheses to alter the binding of the various symbols, as follows:

```
C:\>(dir *.exe & dir *.com) >files.txt
```

This compound command executes two DIR commands, one after the other. The output of both commands is redirected into the file FILES.TXT. The parentheses change the binding of the command symbols. Notice that this command is far cleaner than the earlier example, and that the file FILES.TXT is only specified once in the command.

Parentheses can be nested to specify arbitrarily complex compound commands. For example:

```
C:\>((echo command1) & (echo command2)) && (echo command 3)
```

An opening parenthesis can be placed anywhere on a command where a *command-name* is expected. When a command is enclosed in parentheses, either a closing parenthesis or a compound command symbol marks the end of the command. For example:

```
1. C:\>echo (command)
2. (command)
3. c:\>(echo command)
4. command
```

Notice that the second ECHO command did not echo the closing parenthesis. In this case, the shell treats this as the end of the command, and this parenthesis is not passed as part the ECHO arguments. In the first case, the command itself does not begin with a parenthesis, and so the end of line marks the end of the command. In this case, the entire (command) text is passed to the ECHO command.

Parentheses can also be used to enter multi-line commands. If a command line ends with one or more sets of unbalanced parentheses, the command line is assumed to continue on the next line. If the command was entered interactively, the shell prompts for more input until all parentheses balance. If the command is part of a script, the shell reads additional script lines until all the parentheses balance. For example:

```
1. C:\>(
2. More?echo command1
```

```
3. More?echo command2
4. More?)
5. command1
6. command2
```

The first line consists only of an open parenthesis. The shell detects this, and prompts for more input. Next, two ECHO commands are entered. Finally, a closing parenthesis balances the opening parenthesis and the command is complete. The shell then executes the compound command, which executes the two individual ECHO commands.

Individual commands do not span lines in multi-line commands. The end of a physical line always terminates a simple command (either as typed or as entered in a script file). Notice in the preceding example how the end of the physical line terminated each ECHO command.

Compound commands and multi-line commands are particularly useful with IF and FOR statements. These commands are described in Chapter 4. For example:

```
1. if exist *.bak (
2.     echo Deleteing *.BAK files...
3.     del *.bak
4. )
```

The IF command executes the following command if one or more .BAK files exist in the current directory. Parentheses are used to execute a compound multi-line command. In this example, the ECHO command displays a warning, and then the DEL command deletes the files. The indentation here is not mandatory, but does help to indicate the flow of control.

Tip

Using a parenthesis, even when not strictly needed, is a useful way to increase script readability, and makes explicit the command execution precedence rules.

Using Command Filters

The previous sections showed how individual commands can be combined using command redirection and compound command symbols. Although command redirection can be used with any command, it is most effective with commands that are specifically designed as command filters. Generally, a *command filter* reads command input, permutes, or processes the input in some manner, and then writes the permuted input to its command output. Command filters are typically connected to other commands and each other via the pipe (¦) redirection symbol.

Command filters are frequently used in scripts to extract specific information needed by a script. Typically, a FIND command can filter the output of a command, extracting only the line (or lines) which contain the required information. The script can then further process this filtered data. Many of the sample scripts in Part II use this technique.

Windows NT provides four command filters:

- The MORE command, which is used to paginate command output.

- The SORT command, which can sort command output alpha-numerically.

- The FIND command, which filters lines that contain a specified text string.

- The CLIP [RK] command, which captures command output to the Windows NT clipboard.

MORE

The MORE command breaks its command input into pages. A *page* is the same number of lines as the console window. For example:

```
C:\>dir | more
```

This command displays the current directory, one page at a time. Press the spacebar to advance to the next page. The MORE command supports several switches to control the output format. These are detailed in the MORE section of the "Command Reference."

SORT

The SORT command sorts its command input alpha-numerically, using the ASCII collating sequence. For example:

```
C:\>sort <data.txt
```

This command sorts the contents of file DATA.TXT and displays the result. By default, the SORT command sorts in ascending order. The /R switch sorts in reverse (descending) order. Lines are sorted based on the data at the start of each line. Use the +*n* switch to sort based on data starting at column *n* on each line. For example:

```
C:\>dir | sort +14
```

This command sorts the output of the DIR command based on data starting at column 14 on each line.

FIND

The FIND command filters command input, passing to its command output only those lines which contain a specified string. For example:

```
C:\>dir ¦ find "<DIR>"
```

This command filters only directory lines from the output of the DIR command. The FIND command supports several switches to control the filtering process— these are detailed in the FIND topic of the "Command Reference." One useful switch is /C, which outputs only a count of the lines which match the string, instead of the lines themselves. For example:

```
C:\>dir ¦ find "<DIR>" /c
```

This command counts the number of directories in the current directory.

> **Tip**
>
> *Windows NT also supports the more powerful* FINDSTR *command, which provides more sophisticated filtering capabilities. However,* FINDSTR *works with files as input.* FINDSTR *is described in the "Command Reference."*

CLIP [RK]

The CLIP [RK] command places its command input into the clipboard. For example:

```
C:\>dir ¦ clip
```

This command dumps the output of the DIR command into the clipboard. Once in the clipboard, the text can be pasted into any Windows application.

The Windows NT Command Scheduler

Windows NT provides a special feature called the *Schedule Service* that can execute any command or application periodically or at a specified time and date. Scheduled commands can execute even if there is no user logged on to the computer. The Schedule Service is therefore ideal for running periodic mainte-nance tasks, such as file backups. For example, the REPL.BAT sample script in Part II uses the Schedule Service to provide periodic file replication services.

The Schedule Service is controlled through several shell commands. These com-mands can control the service either on the local computer or any computer on the network (assuming that the user has sufficient rights to access that comput-er). The ability to control the Schedule Service remotely is particularly useful for system administrators managing many servers.

The two most common mistakes made when using Windows NT involve the setup and use of the Schedule Service:

- First, the Schedule Service, like all services, logs on by default as the LocalSystem account. Typically, this account has insufficient rights to per-form many operations (such as accessing network drives).

- Second, because the Schedule Service operates independently of a user logon, drive mappings and other per-user settings are not necessarily available when a scheduled command executes. For example, the environment available to a command executed by the schedule service is restricted to the system environment set via Control Panel.

Fortunately, both these problems are easily solved. Creating a special account exclusively for the Schedule Service (named, for example, ScheduleService) solves the first problem. This account is then assigned whatever access rights and group memberships are needed to ensure that any scheduled commands are successful. Explicitly mapping all required resources within a scheduled script (such as network drives) solves the second problem. Alternatively, use UNC names directly in commands.

For example, assume a logon script maps drive X: to \\SERVER\COMMON. This command, which operates correctly when used interactively, fails when used with the Schedule Service:

```
copy x:\myfiles\*.bak c:\backups
```

The Schedule Service does not execute the logon script, so drive X: is not available. The first solution to this problem uses the NET command to explicitly map drive X: in the script. For example:

```
1. net use x: \\server\common
2. copy x:\myfiles\*.bak c:\backups
3. net use x: /delete
```

The second solution uses UNC names directly. For example:

```
copy \\server\common\myfiles\*.bak c:\backups
```

Virtually all built-in commands, and most external commands, accept UNC names as well as path names as arguments.

The final stage to prepare the Schedule Service for use is starting the service. Typically, the start-up options for this service are changed to require the service to automatically start whenever Windows NT boots. Both of these operations can be accomplished via the Control Panel Services applet. Figure 2.6 shows the Services applet running. The Schedule Service is named Schedule. Click the Start button to start the service, or the Stop button to stop the service.

Click the Startup button to set service startup options. Figure 2.7 shows the startup options dialog box. Typically, the Startup Type should be Automatic, and the Log On As option should be the account setup specifically for the schedule service.

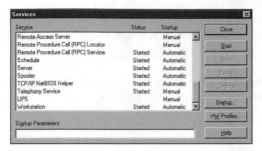

Figure 2.6. *The Control Panel Services applet*

Once the Schedule Service is running, commands can be scheduled using either the AT command or the SOON [RK] command. Refer to the "Command Reference" for a detailed description of these commands. The Windows NT Resource Kit also provides a GUI interface to the Schedule Service, called WINAT.

Figure 2.7. *Schedule Service startup options*

By default, all AT commands manage the schedule service on the local computer. Specify the computer name as the first argument to manage the service on another computer. For example, this command lists all scheduled commands on the current computer:

```
1. C:\>at
2. Status ID   Day                    Time         Command Line
3. ----------------------------------------------------------------------
4. 0    Each F                 8:00 PM      "e:\Tools\NAVNT\NAVWNT" /L
```

This command lists all scheduled commands on the computer CRAFT:

```
C:\>at \\craft
```

Enter an AT command and specify the execution time and the command to execute to schedule a command for execution. For example:

```
C:\>at 23:00:00 /every:monday cmd /c sysbkup.bat
```

This command schedules the command CMD /C SYSBKUP.BAT to execute at 11 p.m. The command is executed every Monday whenever the system clock indicates the time is 11 p.m.

The SOON [RK] command schedules a command to execute a certain number of seconds in the future. For example:

```
C:\>soon 600 "cmd /c sysbkup.bat"
```

This command schedules the command CMD /C SYSBKUP.BAT to execute in 10 minutes (600 seconds) time. SOON can be used to setup a script for periodic execution. Simply place a SOON command as the first line of the script. For example, place this line as the first line in MYSCRIPT.BAT:

```
soon 600 "cmd /c myscript.bat"
```

Then manually schedule MYSCRIPT.BAT to execute *once*. The first time MYSCRIPT.BAT executes, it reschedules a new copy of itself to run in ten minutes. Thus, every 10 minutes, a new copy of MYSCRIPT.BAT is executed.

Chapter 3

Script Parameters and Variables

- **Variable basics**
  Learn how to set and retrieve variable values. Additionally, the variable substitution mechanism and variable scoping rules are described.

- **Advanced SET commands**
  Here, the use of SET to compute arithmetic expressions is detailed.

- **Special variable syntax**
  This section details the string substitution and indexing mechanisms, and develops a simple variable array scheme.

- **Script parameters and arguments**
  The parameter passing mechanisms are described, along with advanced features such as parameter qualifiers.

Variable Basics

As Chapter 1 described, a basic script is simply a text file containing a record of shell commands. Executing a basic script produces an effect identical to typing the commands directly into a command shell. If this were all scripts could do, they would be of limited value. Fortunately, the command shell includes three features that enable scripts to go beyond simple command re-entry. These are:

- Environment variables, which provide data storage for scripts.

- Parameter substitution, which passes script arguments into the body of the script.

- Control flow, such as GOTO and CALL, which enable scripts to branch and loop, and also to execute commands conditionally. Control flow is the subject of Chapter 4.

The use of variables in a script is the key to virtually all advanced scripts. Variables allow a script to maintain *state* information, and act intelligently on that state. For example, a script could use the NET USER command to capture a list of all users into a variable array, and then perform additional processing steps for each user specified in the array.

In Windows NT, each running application (process) contains a set of strings called the *application environment*. Each string is named and can contain any arbitrary text. These named strings are called *environment variables*, or simply *variables*. The name of each string is the *variable name*, and the string itself forms the *variable value*. Windows NT provides Application Program Interfaces (APIs) to allow an application to recover the contents of variables by name and to change variable values or create new variables.

When Windows NT starts a new process, the process *inherits* the environment of the process that created it (its parent process). The new environment is *copied* from the parent process. This means that any changes the process makes to its environment are *local* to the process and do not effect the parent or any other processes running in the system.

These same rules apply to the Windows NT command shell. When a command shell starts, it inherits the environment of its parent process, which is typically the Windows Explorer. Any changes the shell makes to its environment variables are local to that shell. If multiple shells are running at the same time, each shell has its own unique environment. Similarly, when the shell starts an application or external command, that application or command inherits the current shell environment.

The /I switch of the START command modifies the default inheritance behavior. When the START command is used with the /I switch, the command executed inherits the shell environment as it existed when the command shell started execution. Thus, any changes made to the shell's environment (via the SET command) are not passed to the executed command.

Variables are defined and their values set using the SET command, described in the following sections. Variable values are recalled using a process known as *variable substitution*, which is described in subsequent sections.

Environment Variable Sources

Because each process in Windows NT inherits the environment of its parent process, environment variables accumulate from a number of different sources as the system initializes. These sources, in order, are as follows:

- Built-in system variables, or variables derived directly from the hardware during system boot.

- The system environment stored in the HKEY_LOCAL_MACHINE hive of the Registry (and set using the Control Panel).

- Built-in user variables set during the logon procedure.

- The user environment stored in the HKEY_CURRENT_USER hive of the Registry (and set using the Control Panel).

- SET commands parsed in AUTOEXEC.BAT during user logon (if parsing is enabled).

- SET commands in a Windows NT logon script (if one if present).

These individual sources each accumulate additional variables. The cumulative result then forms the initial environment inherited by the command shell. Variables set from a later source in the list over-ride variables of the same name set in an earlier source. Variable substitution, described in the following section, can also be used to add additional values to previously defined variables. For example:

```
set LIB=%LIB%;e:\shared\libs
```

This command appends an additional library directory to the end of the LIB variable.

The first two items in the previous list, built-in system variables and the system environment, are available to all processes in Windows NT regardless of the interactive logon state. All other variables are available only in a logon session. One consequence of this (as discussed in Chapter 2) is that shell scripts executed by the AT command can rely only on built-in system variables and the system environment, because these commands are executed by the Schedule service and do not run in a user logon session.

Built-in system variables are set implicitly by Windows NT. These include values such as the CPU type (PROCESSOR_ARCHITECTURE), the number of CPUs present (NUMBER_OF_PROCESSORS), and other information obtained at boot time. The variable OS is always set to "Windows_NT" by Windows NT. Scripts can use this variable to verify that they are executing on the Windows NT platform, as described in Chapter 1. Additional built-in variables are described in the "Standard Variables" section of Part III, "Scripting Command Reference."

The system environment is stored in a key in the HKEY_LOCAL_MACHINE hive of the registry. Variables stored in this key are loaded as the system boots. This includes values such as the initial search path (PATH), the Windows NT root directory (SystemRoot), and the command shell executable name (COMSPEC).

Windows NT sets built-in user variables during logon. This includes values such as the user name (USERNAME) and profile directory (USERPROFILE).

Additional built-in variables are described in the "Standard Variables" section in Part III.

The user environment is stored in a key in the HKEY_CURRENT_USER hive of the registry. This includes values such as the temporary directory (TEMP) and the user path (PATH). Variables stored in this key are loaded during user logon and are per user.

Finally, additional variables can be defined using SET commands in AUTOEXEC.BAT and a logon script. The logon script is an ideal location to set enterprise environment settings. The "AUTOEXEC" section in Part III describes the parsing of the AUTOEXEC.BAT file in detail.

Accessing Variables Using the Control Panel

The system and user variables stored in the registry are edited through the Control Panel System icon. (Editing system variables requires administrative rights.) To edit a variable, use the Environment tab (shown in Figure 3.1) of the System Properties dialog box. You can display this dialog box quickly by right-clicking on the My Computer icon and choosing the Properties command. Variables displayed in this dialog box are stored in the registry, and therefore persist after a logout or system reboot.

You can perform the following procedures using the System Properties dialog box:

- *Delete a variable.* Click the variable name to select it, then click the Delete button.

- *Edit a variable.* Click the variable name to select it. The name and value appear in the Variable and Value edit boxes. Edit the variable value, and then click the Set button.

- *Add a user variable.* Click an existing user variable name to select it. Type the new variable name in the Variable edit box, and the new value in the Value edit box. To create the variable, click the Set button.

- *Add a system variable.* Click an existing system variable name to select it. Type the new variable name in the Variable edit box, and the new value in the Value edit box. To create the variable, click the Set button.

The System Properties dialog box has one odd characteristic: It adds new variables to the section most recently "visited." For example, if the previous operation edited a system variable, subsequent newly-created variables will appear in the list of system variables. If the previous operation edited a user variable, newly created variables will appear in the list of user variables. The easiest way to ensure that new variables are created in the correct location (system or user) is to first select an existing variable in the appropriate section.

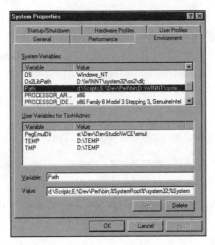

Figure 3.1. *The System Properties Environment tab*

Another point to note is that the variable values displayed in the value lists are shown *after* variable substitution has occurred, but the values displayed in the Value edit box are shown *before* variable substitution has occurred. To see an example of this, examine the value of the TEMP user variable.

The dialog box does not edit the environment itself. Instead, it edits the registry keys that are used to initialize the environment (as previously described). Therefore, changes made to user variables are not applied until the next logon, and changes made to system variables are not applied until the next system restart.

Setting Variables

The SET command is used to create, delete, change, and display the value of environment variables. The command alters variables in the current shell's environment only. To display a list of all environment variables, use SET without any arguments. For example:

```
1. C:\>set
2. BLASTER=A220 I5 D1 H5 P330 E620 T6
3. COMPUTERNAME=GODZILLA
4. ComSpec=D:\WINNT\system32\cmd.exe
5. Etc.
```

To display a partial list of variables, follow the SET command with the first few characters of a variable name. The command displays all variables whose name begins with these characters. For example:

```
1. C:\>set PROCESSOR
2. PROCESSOR_ARCHITECTURE=x86
3. PROCESSOR_IDENTIFIER=x86 Family 6 Model 3 Stepping 3, GenuineIntel
```

```
4. PROCESSOR_LEVEL=6
5. PROCESSOR_REVISION=0303
```

To create a new variable or change the value of an existing variable, follow the SET command with the name of the variable, an equal sign, and the value of the variable. For example:

```
1. C:\>set X=14
2. C:\>set SRCDIR=c:\
3. C:\>set DEFAULT_DESTINATION=c:\Program Files\TestApp\Data
```

The last example shows that *everything* following the = sign forms the variable value, including spaces.

To delete an existing variable, follow the SET command with the name of the variable to delete and an equal sign. For example:

```
1. C:\>set LOCATION
2. LOCATION=d:\bin
3. C:\>set LOCATION=
4. C:\>set LOCATION
5. Environment variable LOCATION not defined
```

Notice the difference between displaying the current value of a variable (the first command in the previous example) and deleting the variable (the second command using set *name=*) .

Virtually any character can be used for a variable name. For example, the following command creates a variable named _%!:

```
C:\>set _%!=An odd variable name
```

Tip

Generally, it is a good idea to confine variable names to letters, digits, and the underscore character. This avoids syntax conflicts with other shell features. Variable names are not *case sensitive, though the shell does preserve the case of a name (for display purposes only) when it is first created. Throughout this book, variable names are defined and shown in uppercase.*

Troubleshooting Tip

The shell accepts the space character as a valid part of a variable name. This can lead to some odd consequences. For example, this command defines a variable called ZZ:

```
C:\>set ZZ=12
```

This command defines a variable called zz *(i.e. ZZ with a trailing space):*

```
1. C:\>set ZZ =13
2. C:\>set ZZ
3. ZZ=12
4. ZZ =13
```

The rule the SET *command follows is that everything from the first non-blank character on the line up to, but not including, the first = character is the name of the variable. One common mistake in scripts is accidentally placing a space before the = sign in a* SET *command. For example:*

```
1. set DEFDIR=c:\src
2. if "%1"=="X" set DEFDIR =c:\src2
```

Presumably, the intention of the second line is to redefine the DEFDIR *variable. However, the extra space instead defines a new variable called* "DEFDIR " *(with a trailing space) and leaves the original* DEFDIR *intact. Bugs such as these can be very tricky to track down. The rule of thumb is never leave a space before the = sign in a* SET *command.*

When creating or changing a variable with the SET command, all of the command text after the first = sign comprises the variables value. This *includes* any leading and trailing spaces and tabs. Reserved shell characters (defined in Chapter 2) such as & can be placed in the command text either by escaping them or by placing the variable value in double quotes. For example:

```
1. C:\>set ZZ=rock ^& roll
2. C:\>set ZZ
3. ZZ=rock & roll
4. C:\>set ZZ="rock & roll"
5. C:\>set ZZ
6. ZZ="rock & roll"
```

Notice that using double quotes to include reserved shell characters also includes the double quotes themselves in the variable value. This happens because all text after the = sign is taken as the variable value, including double quote characters.

The IF DEFINED command is used to test to see if a variable is defined or not. For example:

```
1. C:\>set ZZ=1
2. C:\>if defined ZZ echo ZZ is defined
3. ZZ is defined
4. C:\>set ZZ=
5. C:\>if  not defined ZZ echo ZZ not defined
6. ZZ not defined
```

The IF command is described in detail in Chapter 4.

Variable Size Limits

The command shell does not impose any significant upper limits on the use of variables. Variable values can contain more than 1200 characters, and names can exceed 100 characters in length. In addition, the total amount of space available for storing all variables is limited only by available memory. However, access to variables becomes slow if very large numbers of variables are defined, and so it is generally advantageous to limit the number of variables to, at most, a few hundred.

It is generally considered good practice to delete a variable at the end of its lifetime (for example, at the end of a script). This is most easily achieved using the SETLOCAL and ENDLOCAL commands described in the following sections.

Variable Substitution

Once a variable is defined, it can be used within typed commands and scripts using a process known as *variable substitution*. Variable substitution is the single most powerful tool available for writing scripts, as it is the primary mechanism for a script to modify its behavior based on state information. To use variable substitution, place the name of a defined variable, bracketed by percent signs, anywhere in a command. For example:

```
1. C:\>set ZZ=HELLO
2. C:\>echo Var ZZ contains %ZZ%
3. Var ZZ contains HELLO
```

Notice what happened to the output of the ECHO command in the previous example: The variable name, enclosed in percent signs, is *replaced* by the value of the variable. This substitution process is valid for all variables, including those defined by the system. For example:

```
1. C:\>echo Good morning, %USERNAME%!
2. Good morning, TimH!
```

Frequently, variables contain parameters for commands, as in this example:

```
1. set SRC=c:\bin
2. set DST=d:\backup\bin
3. copy %SRC% %DST%
```

The COPY command that is executed is:

```
copy c:\bin d:\backup\bin
```

Variables used in this and similar ways can be defined in the script, or defined by entering commands into a command shell before the script is run. In addition, one script can define variables containing information needed by another script, and then execute this second script as a procedure (this is described in detail in Chapter 4). When used in this manner, variables can be used to pass arguments to procedures.

Variable substitution is powerful because it occurs *before* the shell interprets a command. Therefore, a command can be built up from command text fragments contained in variables. This allows a script to adapt itself to different circumstances. For example:

```
1. set NETSW=
2. if "%OS%"=="Windows_NT" set NETSW=/persistent:no
3. net use d: \\dataserver\files %NETSW%
```

This script fragment executes a NET USE command to map a network share. The NET USE command is available on Windows NT and Windows 95, but the latter operating system (OS) does not support the /PERSISTENT switch. The IF command in the example tests to see if the operating system is Windows NT. If it is, the NETSW variable is set. If not, the variable remains empty. This means that when the NET USE command executes on Windows 95, the command will be:

```
net use d: \\dataserver\files
```

When the command executes on Windows NT, it will be:

```
net use d: \\dataserver\files /persistent:no
```

When the shell processes a command, variable substitution occurs before all other syntax processing. Thus, a shell variable can contain any syntax or syntax fragment allowed in a command. For example:

```
1. C:\>set AND=^&
2. C:\>echo one %AND% echo two
3. one
4. two
```

In this example, the SET command defines a variable AND containing an ampersand character. Notice the use of the escape to enter the ampersand literally. This is then used in the second command to separate two ECHO commands, just as if an ampersand had been entered literally.

Undefined Variables and Literal Percent Character Handling

If an attempt is made to substitute an *undefined* variable, the result depends upon the current shell mode. In *interactive mode* (commands are read from the keyboard), the variable name and percent symbols are left unchanged. For example:

```
1. C:\>set UNDEF=
2. C:\>echo Undef is %UNDEF%
3. Undef is %UNDEF%
```

The text is echoed literally. In *script mode* (when commands are read from a script file), the variable name and bracketing percent signs are deleted (i.e., replaced by nothing). For example:

```
1. set UNDEF=
2. echo Undef is %UNDEF%
```

When executed, this script displays:

```
Undef is
```

Similarly, the handling of percent signs differs depending upon the shell mode. In interactive mode, any percent sign not explicitly part of a variable substitution is treated literally. For example:

```
1. C:\>echo % by itself is ok, as is %% or 100%
2. % by itself is ok, as is %% or 100%
```

In script mode, however, all literal percent characters *must* be doubled. For example:

```
echo Use %% to enter a literal percent sign in a script
```

When run, this displays:

```
Use % to enter a literal percent sign in a script
```

Recursive Substitution

Variable substitution is not recursive. If a variable's value in turn contains variables to substitute, these will *not* be substituted when the variable is itself substituted. For example:

```
1. C:\>set ZZ=^%YY^%
2. C:\>set YY=Any text
3. C:\>echo %ZZ%
4. %YY%
```

In this example, the variable ZZ contains the literal text "%YY%" as a result of the escaped percent signs. In the last line, the shell substitutes the variable ZZ with the literal text "%YY%", but does not then attempt to substitute the variable YY. In other words, the shell does not rescan substituted text for additional variable substitutions.

There is one exception to this non-recursive rule: the CALL command (which is described in Chapter 4). For example:

```
1. set ZZ=%%YY%%
2. set YY=Any Text
3. call :SUB1 "%ZZ%"
4. goto :EOF
5. :SUB1
6. echo %1
7. goto :EOF
```

When run, this script displays:

```
"Any Text"
```

As in the previous example, zz contains the literal text "%YY%". However, the ECHO command in procedure SUB1 actually echoes the contents of the variable YY. This is because the CALL command performs an additional level of variable substitution. First, the shell expands %ZZ% into %YY% (literally). Then, the additional level of substitution expands %YY% into "Any Text".

The lack of recursion in variable substitution can be a difficulty when more advanced scripts are developed. In particular, accessing variables indirectly (for example, in arrays) or accessing variables whose *name* is passed as an argument to a procedure is difficult. Chapter 4 develops a technique to overcome this using the FOR command, and this technique is presented as the :RESOLVE procedure in the _MTPLIB.BAT library in Chapter 5. Many of the example scripts in Part II of this book use this procedure.

Returning Procedure Values

One very common use for variables is returning a value from a script procedure. The shell does not support any language mechanism for returning values from a script procedure. Instead, an agreed-upon variable is used for this purpose.

Typically, a variable named RET is used to store the return value from a procedure. This is merely a convention, however, and any variable name can be used, as long as both the caller and callee agree on the name. In fact, procedures can "return" multiple values in multiple variables if desired. For example:

```
1. call :SUB1
2. echo Return result is %RET% and %RETV%
3. goto :EOF
4. .
5. .
6. :SUB1
7. set RET=400
8. set RETV=Four Hundred
9. goto :EOF
```

(See Chapter 4 for details of the CALL and GOTO commands.) When executed, this script displays:

```
Return result is 400 and Four Hundred
```

The RET variable is used extensively in the example scripts developed in Part II of this book.

Substitution and Command Syntax

Chapter 2 introduced compound commands and multi-line commands. Variable substitution (along with parameter substitution discussed in the following sections) completes the overall description of how the shell handles commands. When a command is entered, the following steps are performed by the shell:

1. All variable and parameter substitution is resolved. This yields a "plain text" version of the command.

2. The command is scanned for unbalanced parentheses. If unbalanced parentheses exist, additional input lines are read (in script mode) or entered (in interactive mode) until all parentheses balance. Variables are substituted in each additional line as it is read or entered.

3. The final command text is broken into simple commands using the reserved shell characters as separators, as described in Chapter 2. Command redirection symbols in compound commands are resolved at this step.

4. Each simple command is then executed in sequence. Command redirection symbols in simple commands are resolved at this step.

Notice that the entire multi-line command is read and parsed before *any* of the commands are executed. This means that the following will not work:

```
1. C:\>(
2. More? set CP=^)
3. More? %CP%
4. More? )
5. C:\>set CP
6. CP=)
```

The open parenthesis starts a multi-line command. The SET command defines a variable called CP that contains a closing parenthesis character. On the next line, the %CP% is an attempt to end the command by expanding %CP% to a closing parenthesis. However, the prior SET command has not yet been executed, so CP is not yet defined, and %CP% is not expanded. Finally, after the closing parenthesis is entered, the SET command is executed, and CP is then defined.

Troubleshooting Tip

Multi-line commands are a very useful method of improving script readability and structure. However, as previously described, the command shell performs all variable substitution once before an entire multi-line command is executed. This can lead to some unexpected results. For example:

```
1. Set X=Tim
2. (
3.     set X=John
4.     set X=%X% Doe
5. )
```

What is the value of the variable X *after these lines are executed? Surprisingly, perhaps, the answer is* Tim Doe. *The first line simply sets the variable* X *to* Tim. *Then, the multi-line command is executed. The entire command is read by the shell, and processed as one command:*

```
( set X=John & set X=%X% Doe )
```

Before any of the commands are executed, variable substitution occurs. Since variable X *is currently* Tim, *the line is converted by the shell to:*

```
( set X=John & set X=Tim Doe )
```

Now the commands are executed. The first SET *command sets* X *to* John, *but the next* SET *command immediately changes* X *back to* Tim Doe.

To avoid problems such as this, the rule is to never attempt to use the value of a variable in the same multi-line command that sets *the value.*

Variable Scope

The previously described rules governing environment inheritance limit the *scope* of environment variables. Because each application (and hence each command shell) inherits its own environment, SET commands in each shell affect *only* the current shell environment, and not any other (unless that environment is then inherited by another command).

Changes to variables made with the SET command are global *within* a command shell. Any scripts run by the command shell have access to all shell variables defined within the shell. Changes, additions, or deletions to the environment made by a script persist within the command shell after the script finishes. For example, if a script creates a new variable called SRC1, then this variable will exist in the environment when the script ends, and can be accessed interactively or within subsequent scripts.

One way to change this behavior is to execute a script within a nested command shell. For example, to execute the script TEST.BAT within a nested command shell, enter the following:

```
C:\>cmd /c test.bat
```

The new shell inherits the current environment and begins executing the script. However, because the new shell is a distinct process, changes made to the environment within the script are lost when the script (and the nested command shell) terminates. Using a nested shell in this way protects the current environment from changes made within a script. In fact, the current shell is also protected in the same way from other state changes made by the script, such as changing the current drive and directory.

A similar technique uses the START command to run a script. For example:

```
C:\>start test.bat
```

This executes the TEST.BAT script in a nested command shell in a new window. Use the /I switch with the START command to cause the nested command shell to inherit the same environment that the parent shell itself inherited. As with all environment inheritance, the nested shell inherits a copy of all variables.

Using SETLOCAL and ENDLOCAL

The SETLOCAL and ENDLOCAL commands provide additional variable scope control within a script. Both commands are applicable only within a script—they have no effect in interactive mode. When used in a script, SETLOCAL marks the beginning of a new "local" scope for environment variables, and ENDLOCAL marks the end of this local scope. Changes made to the environment *within* a local scope are discarded when the local scope ends. In other words, SETLOCAL takes a snapshot of the current environment, and ENDLOCAL restores the environment to this snapshot state. All variables created within a local scope are deleted, and variables deleted or altered within a local scope are restored to their snapshot values.

By starting a script with a SETLOCAL command and ending it with an ENDLOCAL command, changes to the environment within the script are local to the script. For example:

```
1. setlocal
2. set ZZ=123
3. .
4. .
5. endlocal
```

Within the "brackets" formed by the SETLOCAL and ENDLOCAL commands, SET commands have a local scope. Thus, after the ENDLOCAL command executes in the script fragment above, the ZZ variable is restored to the value it had before the SETLOCAL command was executed. (If the ZZ variable did not exist before the SETLOCAL command was executed, it will be deleted by the ENDLOCAL command.)

SETLOCAL and ENDLOCAL are used in a similar way within script procedures (described in Chapter 4). By bracketing the entire procedure within a SETLOCAL/ENDLOCAL pair, all variable manipulations are made local to the procedure.

The SETLOCAL and ENDLOCAL commands can be nested to create additional local scopes. For example, a procedure with a local scope can call another procedure that contains a local scope. In each case, the ENDLOCAL command restores the most recently saved snapshot. The maximum nesting level for SETLOCAL/ENDLOCAL is 32 levels.

Variable Tunneling

Using local scopes in procedures is strongly encouraged. (Procedures are covered fully in Chapter 4.) However, SETLOCAL and ENDLOCAL within a procedure can cause difficulties. Consider this simple procedure:

```
1. :SUB1
2. .
3. .
4. set RET=500
5. goto :EOF
```

This example defines a procedure called SUB1, which sets the variable RET to 500 and then returns to the caller. As already described, the RET variable is typically used to hold return values from procedures.

Using SETLOCAL and ENDLOCAL to define a local scope enhances this simple procedure. For example:

```
1. :SUB1
2. setlocal
3. .
4. .
5. set RET=500
6. endlocal
7. goto :EOF
```

However, as shown, this procedure will not work properly. The problem is that the SET command that sets the return value, RET, is executed before the ENDLOCAL command. As a result, ENDLOCAL deletes the RET variable, along with all other changes made to the environment, before the procedure returns. This effectively wipes out the return value from the SUB1 procedure.

One solution to this problem is to move the SET command so that it is after the ENDLOCAL command. For example:

```
1. :SUB1
2. setlocal
3. .
4. .
5. endlocal
6. set RET=500
7. goto :EOF
```

For this simple procedure, the alteration works correctly. However, for more complex procedures, the solution fails. Consider this procedure:

```
01. :SUB2
02. setlocal
03. if "%DIR%"=="1" set RET=4
04. .
05. .
06. if "%P45%"=="NEW" set RET=14
07. if "%AUTOSW%"=="3" set RET=56
08. .
09. .
10. endlocal
11. goto :EOF
```

The procedure uses SETLOCAL and ENDLOCAL commands to create a local scope, and sets the return value in RET to a different value depending upon the result of several IF commands. As before, this procedure does not work as written, because the ENDLOCAL deletes the RET variable. In this case, however, the SET commands *cannot* be moved to below the ENDLOCAL command, because they are an integral part of the procedure logic. The SET command somehow has to be both before *and* after the ENDLOCAL command.

Fortunately, there is a simple trick to overcome this problem, which can be thought of as *variable tunneling*. The SUB2 procedure is re-written as follows:

```
01. :SUB2
02. setlocal
03. if "%DIR%"=="1" set RET=4
04. .
05. .
06. if "%P45%"=="NEW" set RET=14
07. .
08. if "%AUTOSW%"=="3" set RET=56
09. .
10. .
11. endlocal & set RET=%RET%
12. goto :EOF
```

This version of SUB2 is identical to the previous version except for the addition of the extra SET command after the ENDLOCAL command. The trick used here involves the order in which the shell evaluates a command. When the shell reaches the line containing the ENDLOCAL and SET commands, the RET variable contains the desired return value. Suppose RET contains the value "56." The shell then executes the command. As entered in the script file, the command consists of:

```
endlocal & set RET=%RET%
```

As previously described, the first operation the shell performs on any command text is variable substitution. In this case, the shell replaces %RET% with the value 56. So, after variable substitution, the command appears as:

```
endlocal & set RET=56
```

The command is a compound command, so the shell executes each simple command in sequence. The first command is ENDLOCAL, so the ENDLOCAL command executes and the local scope, including the RET variable, is deleted. The next command is the SET command, so the shell executes:

```
set RET=56
```

This sets the RET variable to 56. Notice that this is executed after the ENDLOCAL command, and it restores the RET variable to the value it had before the local scope was deleted.

This trick of assigning a variable with its own value on the same line as the ENDLOCAL command allows a variable's value to "tunnel" through a local scope. It can be used for multiple return values. For example:

```
endlocal & set RET=%RET% & set SRCDIR=%SRCDIR%
```

This example tunnels the RET and SRCDIR variables out of the local scope.

Special Variables

The command shell and Windows NT define and use several special variables. In addition, some commands also make use of variables. For example, the DIR command reads additional command switches from the DIRCMD variable.

The COMSPEC variable always contains the full path of the command shell executable. It is considered good practice to use this variable to refer to the command shell, rather than simply using CMD.EXE or CMD. This avoids the possibility of the wrong version of CMD.EXE being executed when multiple OSs are included in the search path. For example, replace this line in a script:

```
cmd /c test.bat
```

with this line:

```
%COMSPEC% /c test.bat
```

The START command automatically performs this substitution if the command name is the literal text "CMD".

The PATH and PATHEXT variables are used when the shell searches for a command to execute. This process is described in detail in Chapter 2. Chapter 2 also describes the PROMPT variable and its use to define the shell command prompt.

The ERRORLEVEL variable is a *substitute-only* variable. This variable does not appear in the list of variables displayed by the SET command, and is not set using the SET command. Instead, the value of the ERRORLEVEL variable is the exit code of the most recently executed command. For example:

```
1. C:\>choice
2. [Y,N]?N
3. C:\>echo %ERRORLEVEL%
4. 2
```

The CMDCMDLINE variable is also a substitute-only variable. The value of this variable is always the exact command line used to invoke the current command shell, including all switches and arguments. For example:

```
1. C:\>echo %CMDCMDLINE%
2. "C:\WINNT\System32\CMD.EXE"
```

Finally, although the RET variable is not technically a special variable, by common convention this variable is used to pass a return value from a procedure back to the calling script. Following this convention can help to make scripts more easily understood.

Advanced SET Commands

The basic SET command is used to set the value of a variable to a literal text value. The advanced SET command evaluates an arithmetic expression and can assign the numeric result of this expression to a variable. To enter an arithmetic SET command use the /A switch. For example:

```
1. C:\>set /a 1+2
2. 3
```

As this example shows, the SET command displays the numeric result of the expression—in this case 1+2. This only occurs in interactive mode. In script mode, expression results are evaluated, but *not* displayed.

Expressions are evaluated using 32-bit signed integer arithmetic. Overflows are not detected, and wrap-around from 2147483647 to –2147483648 and vice versa is allowed.

Basic Expression Syntax

A *basic expression* consists of numbers and arithmetic operators. The arithmetic operators are shown in Table 3.1. The multiplication, division, and modulus operators are evaluated first. For example, the expression 1+2*3 yields 7, not 9. Use parentheses to modify the order of evaluation. For example, (1+2)*3 yields 9.

> **Tip**
>
> *It is always a good idea to explicitly use parentheses to improve the readability of complex expressions. However, some versions of Windows NT 4.0 have a bug that causes the shell to issue an error whenever parentheses are used. The only work-around for this is to construct expressions without parentheses and use intermediate, temporary variables to evaluate complex expressions as a sequence of simpler expressions. The comma character can be used to place these expressions in a single* SET *command.*

Table 3.1. Arithmetic Operators.

Operator	Meaning
+	Addition
-	Subtraction
*	Multiplication
/	Division
%	Modulus (remainder)

Care should be taken when using the modulus operator. The shell uses the % sign for variable substitution. Therefore, to enter a modulus operator in a script, either escape it or use two percent characters. For example:

```
set /a 13 ^% 3
```

Use the = operator to assign the result of an expression to a variable. For example:

```
C:\>set /a x=12+14/5
```

> **Tip**
>
> *The rules governing the use of the = operator in arithmetic expressions are different from those governing normal* SET *commands (those without the* /A *switch). Spaces before or after the = operator are not significant. For example, both these commands define a variable* ZZ *with the value* 14*:*
>
> ```
> 1. C:\>set /a ZZ=14
> 2. C:\>set /a ZZ = 14
> ```
>
> *Generally, spaces are ignored within expressions and can be used freely to improve readability.*

The = operator sets the variable to the expression result. The value is stored as a decimal string of digits, not a binary value (environment variables are always strings). Once set, the variable can be used in variable substitution like any other variable. For example:

```
1. C:\>Set /a X=900*13
2. C:\>echo Result is %X%
3. Result is 11700
```

Variables that contain numeric values can be used within expressions. These variables do *not* need to be placed within percent signs. For example:

```
1. C:\>set /a X=14
2. C:\>set /a X*10
3. 140
4. c:\>set /a %X%*10
5. 140
```

Generally, percent signs are not used, as this improves readability and avoids evaluation order ambiguities (described in the following section). In addition, undefined variables are treated slightly differently, depending upon the presence or absence of percent signs. When used *with* percent signs, normal variable substitution replaces undefined variables with nothing. When used *without* percent signs, the SET command assumes any undefined variables have the value zero. For example:

```
1. C:\>set X=14
2. C:\>set Y=
3. C:\>set /a X + Y
4. 14
5. C:\>set /a %X% + %Y%
6. Missing operand.
```

The variable Y in this example is undefined. The first SET /A command simply treats this as a zero value. The second SET /A command substitutes a null value for %Y%, resulting in a missing operand error.

Tip

There is a minor bug in the evaluation of expressions in the Windows NT 4.0 build 1381 and newer. This expression should display the decimal value of X, which in this case is 14:

```
1. C:\>set X=14
2. C:\>set /a X
3. 0
```

However, the result is always 0, as shown. This is incorrect. The simple work-around is to add zero to the variable, yielding a valid expression. For example:

```
1. C:\>set X=14
2. C:\>set /a X+0
3. 14
```

When the shell obtains a numeric value from a variable, it attempts to locate a valid number at the *start* of the value of the variable. If no number is found, the shell uses the value zero. For example:

```
1. C:\>set X=14 dollars
2. C:\>set Y=19 dollars
3. C:\>set Z=and cents
4. C:\>set /a X+Y+Z
5. 33
```

To be evaluated, numbers must appear at the start of a variable. For example:

```
1. C:\>set X=14 dollars
2. C:\>set Y=and 10 dollars
3. C:\>set /a X+Y
4. 14
```

Because the variable Y does not begin with a number, it yields zero when used in an expression.

Number Formats

All numbers are assumed to be decimal by default. Expression results are always displayed in decimal, and values assigned to variables using the = operator are always decimal.

Hexadecimal (base 16) numbers can be entered in an expression by prefixing the number with 0x. For example, the hexadecimal number 0x100 is equivalent to the decimal number 256. Hexadecimal numbers can contain the digits "0" to "9" and the letters "A" to "F" or "a" to "f."

Octal (base 8) numbers can be entered in an expression by prefixing the number with a leading zero. For example, the octal number 014 is equivalent to the decimal number 12. Octal numbers can contain the digits "0" to "7" only.

> **Tip**
>
> *Be careful not to prefix a decimal number with a leading zero. Doing so causes the number to be treated as an octal number, or causes a syntax error if the number contains the digits "8" or "9" (which are not allowed in octal numbers).*

Binary (base 2) numbers can be entered in an expression by prefixing the number with 0b. For example, the binary number 0b10010 is equivalent to the decimal number 18. Binary numbers can contain the digits "0" and "1" only.

Numbers in any base can be entered literally into an expression in any combination. For example:

```
1. C:\>set /a 0x100+12
2. 268
```

The shell applies the same number format rules to numbers stored in variables. Thus, variables can contain strings representing decimal, hexadecimal, octal or binary numbers. For example:

```
1. C:\>set X=0x100
2. C:\>set Y=12
3. C:\>set /a X+Y
4. 268
```

Although variables can contain numbers in any base, the = operator always stores decimal values. For example:

```
1. C:\>set X=0x100
2. C:\>set /a X=X
3. 256
4. c:\>set X
5. X=256
```

In this example, the variable X is initially set to the string 0x100. The second SET command evaluates this value as an expression and assigns the result back to the variable X. This replaces X with the decimal result of the expression, which is 256.

Logical Bit Operators

In addition to the basic arithmetic operators, the SET command also supports various logical bit operators. These are shown in Table 3.2. The logical bit operators treat the expression value as an unsigned 32-bit binary number. The operators at the start of the table are evaluated first (that is, they have higher precedence). For example,

```
A << C & D
```

is evaluated as

```
(A << C) & D
```

Logical bit operators are evaluated as a group after the arithmetic operators. For example,

```
A << C + D
```

is evaluated as

```
A << (C + D)
```

Table 3.2. Logical Bit Operators.

Operator	Meaning
<<	Left shift
>>	Right shift
&	Logical AND
^	Logical exclusive OR
|	Logical OR

The left shift and right shift operators logically shift the bits in a 32-bit value to the left or the right. Zero bits are shifted in at the left or right as the bits are shifted. For example, `0x100 << 2` shifts the value 0x100 (256 decimal) to the left by 2 bits. This yields the value 1024.

The logical AND, logical OR, and logical exclusive OR perform "bitwise" logical operations by applying the specified logical operator to each bit in the operands in parallel. For example, `0b1001 & 0b0101` yields the value 1, which is 0b0001 in binary.

All of the logical bit operators use characters that are reserved shell characters. Therefore, *all* these operators must be escaped when used in an expression. For example:

```
C:\>set /a X = Y ^<^< 3.
```

Assignment Operators

The basic *assignment operator* assigns the result of an expression to a variable as a decimal number. The assignment operators act as shorthand for a special type of expression. For example, the expression:

```
1. C:\>set X=1
2. C:\>set /a X = X + 1
```

Can be re-written using an assignment operator as:

```
C:\>set /a X += 1
```

Both these SET commands perform the same action: they increment the value in the X variable. The second SET command uses an assignment operator, which provides a more compact expression.

Assignment operators work as follows:

1. The expression to the right of the assignment operator is evaluated to yield a number (in the previous example, 1).

2. The operation specified by the assignment operator (+ in the previous example) is applied between the expression result (1), and the value of the variable specified on the left of the operator (in the previous example, X, which has the value 1).

3. The result of this expression (X+1, which yields 2) is then stored back into the same variable. This assigns the value 2 to the variable X.

The following example multiplies the value in X by 12, placing the result back into X:

```
C:\>set /a X *= 9+3
```

Assignment operators exist for all standard operators; for example, *= for multiplication, &= for logical AND, and so on.

Evaluating Multiple Expressions

The comma character can be used to place multiple expressions in a single SET command. Separate each expression with a comma. For example:

```
1. C:\>set X=1
2. C:\>set Y=1
3. C:\>set /a X+=1, Y+=1, Z=X+Y
4. 4
```

This example increments both X and Y using assignment operators, and assigns the sum of these two variables to Z. When multiple expressions are placed in a single SET command, only the result of the last expression is displayed.

Expressions are evaluated from left to right. In the previous example, both X and Y are incremented before the last expression is evaluated. Thus, Z is assigned the value 4.

Evaluating multiple expressions in a single command is one case where the use of percent signs can make a considerable difference to the result of an expression. The variable Z is assigned the value 4 because the two variables X and Y are incremented to 2 *before* the expression Z=X+Y is evaluated. However, consider this example:

```
1. C:\>set X=1
2. C:\>set Y=1
3. C:\>set /a X+=1, Y+=1, Z=%X% + %Y%
4. 2
```

In this example, the variable Z is *not* assigned the value 4.. Instead, Z is assigned the value 2. This occurs because, as previously described, variable substitution occurs *before* a command is executed. The shell substitutes the values of the variables X and Y before the SET command is executed. This yields a plain-text command that looks like this:

```
C:\>set /a X+=1, Y+=1, Z=1 + 1
```

When the SET command is executed, Z is assigned the value 2.

Special Variable Syntax

Earlier in this chapter, you were introduced to variable substitution, which provides the shell with the capability to add the contents of any variable into the text of a command. The shell supports several enhancements to the basic variable syntax already defined. These are:

- *String substitution*, which allows the substituted text to be edited.

- *String indexing*, which allows portions of the variable text to be extracted.

- *Indexed and named arrays*, which store sets of data in simple tables.

String Substitution

String substitution is an optional feature of variable substitution. String substitution enhances variable substation by replacing, in the variable text, occurrences of a specified string with another string. To specify string substitution, use the following syntax:

```
%var-name:string1=string2%
```

Replace *var-name* with the name of the variable to be substituted. The variable text is then scanned for occurrences of the string *string1*. Each occurrence is then replaced with the string *string2* before the value is substituted in the command text. For example:

```
1. C:\>set X=A normal variable
2. C:\>echo %X%
3. A normal variable
4. C:\>echo %X:a=b%
5. b normbl vbribble
```

In this example, the variable substitution %X:a=b% replaces all occurrences of the letter "a" with the letter "b," as seen in the result of the ECHO command. Notice that both upper and lower case letters are replaced—string substitution is not case sensitive.

String substitution does not alter the value of the variable being substituted, only the command text into which the substitution occurs. Thus, after the %X:a=b% substitution, the variable X is unchanged.

Substitution is not limited to single characters, nor do *string1* and *string2* need to be the same length. For example:

```
1. C:\>set PATH=c:\bin;c:\dos;c:\winnt
2. C:\>set PATH=%PATH:c:=d:%
3. C:\>set PATH
4. PATH=d:\bin;d:\dos;d:\winnt
```

This example replaces all instances of the string c: with d: in the PATH variable, and then uses a SET command to assign the result back to the PATH variable.

The replacement string, *string2*, can be empty. In this case, all occurrences of the search string *string1* are deleted. For example:

```
1. C:\>set X=1,200,456
2. C:\>echo %X:,=%
3. 1200456
```

This substitution strips all comma characters from the variable X in the ECHO command.

String Indexing

String indexing is similar to string substitution. It operates during variable substitution, and causes only a fixed portion of the variable's value to be substituted into the command text. To specify string indexing, use the following syntax:

```
%var-name:~n,len%
```

Replace *var-name* with the name of the variable to be substituted. A portion of the variable, starting at character index *n* and of length *len* characters, is then substituted into the command text. For example:

```
1. C:\>set X=.CMD;.BAT;.EXE
2. C:\>echo %X:~5,4%
3. .BAT
```

The index of the first character in X is zero. Therefore, the index of the . in .BAT in X (the sixth character) is 5. The length of the string .BAT is 4 characters, so the result of the %X:~5,4% substitution is .BAT, which is shown by the ECHO command output.

> **Tip**
>
> *Do not forget to follow the variable name with a colon and tilde character :~ when using string indexing. If you leave out the tilde, the shell interprets the variable substitution as string substitution. This can have unexpected and unpleasant results.*

The *len* argument in a string index can be omitted, in which case all variable text starting at index *n* and continuing to the end of the variable value is substituted. For example:

```
1. C:\>set X=1234567890
2. C:\>echo %X:~4%
3. 567890
```

If either *n* or *len* or the combination of the two specify a string index that is beyond the end of the variable text, then substitution truncates at the end of the text. For example:

```
1. C:\>set X=1234567890
2. C:\>echo %X:~2,20%
3. 34567890
```

In this example only eight characters are substituted, even though *len* calls for 20, because the end of the variable is reached first.

Indexed and Named Arrays

The command shell only supports simple text variables. Arrays are not supported. However, by using a number of tricks, it is possible to simulate arrays in shell scripts quite effectively. An array is simulated by using a set of normal variables in combination with a simple naming convention. The naming convention breaks the variable name into two parts: the array name, followed by the element index enclosed by underscore characters. Each element of the array is then stored in one of these variables. For example:

```
1. C:\>set USERS_12_=MarkP
2. C:\>set USERS_13_=KarenV
```

This creates two new array entries in the array USERS. Array element 12 is set to the value MarkP and element 13 is set to KarenV. This use of variable names is just a convention: To the command shell, the variable USERS_12_ is a normal variable, not part of an array.

Individual elements can also be set indirectly. For example:

```
1. C:\>set X=14
2. C:\>set USERS_%X%_=BobW
```

This command sets element 14 in the array to BobW.

If desired, a DOSKEY macro can be defined to hide the details of the array naming convention (macros are described in Chapter 2). For example:

```
C:\>doskey seta=set $1_$2_=$3
```

This macro can then be used to define new elements. For example:

```
C:\>seta USERS 9 KarlM
```

Although the macro is more elegant than the direct SET command, it has one disadvantage. If the value to be set contains spaces, it must be enclosed in double quotes, and these double quotes become part of the value. For example:

```
1. C:\>seta USERS 17 "Karen Voester"
2. C:\>set USERS_17_
3. USERS_17_="Karen Voester"
```

To display all the elements of an array, use the SET command with the array name and a single underscore character only. For example:

```
1. C:\>set USERS_
2. USERS_9_=KarlM
3. USERS_12_=MarkP
4. USERS_13_=KarenV
5. USERS_14_=BobW
```

Use the SET command to delete an element. For example:

```
1. C:\>set X=12
2. C:\>set USERS_%X%_=
```

Use a FOR command to delete an entire array. The FOR command is described in detail in Chapter 4. For example:

```
C:\>for /f "delims== tokens=1" %i in ('set USERS_') do @set %i=
```

The FOR command uses the output of the SET command to run a series of individual element delete commands. This use of the FOR command is described fully in Chapter 4. Since this is quite a complex command, it is another ideal candidate for a DOSKEY command macro. For example:

```
C:\>doskey dela=for /f "delims== tokens=1" %i in ('set $1_') do @set %i=
```

Now, array USERS can be deleted using the command:

```
C:\>dela USERS
```

Obviously, an individual element can be recalled by specifying the array name and element index. For example:

```
1. C:\>echo %USERS_12_%
2. MarkP
```

Recalling an element when the index is stored in another variable is rather more complex. This command will *not* work:

```
1. C:\>set X=12
2. C:\>echo %USERS_%X%_%
3. %USERS_12_%
```

The ECHO command does not echo the contents of USERS_12_, as was intended, because the shell does not recursively parse substituted text for additional variable substitutions.

There are two solutions to this problem. First, if the contents of the array element is a number, it can be accessed using the SET /A command. For example:

```
1. C:\>set X=12
2. C:\>set USERSIZE_%X%_=100
3. C:\>set /a RET=USERSIZE_%X%_
4. 100
5. C:\>echo %RET%
6. 100
```

The SET /A command works because, when evaluating an arithmetic expression, variable names do not need to be bracketed by percent signs. The %X% variable is substituted before the expression is evaluated, USERSIZE_12_ is then recalled, and its value (100) is stored in the RET variable. As noted, however, this technique works *only* for numeric values. If USERSIZE_12_ contained, say, cows, then RET would be set to zero, as the SET /A assignment only assigns numeric values, not strings.

The second, and more general method to access array elements uses the FOR command. For example:

```
1. C:\>set X=12
2. C:\>for /f "delims== tokens=2" %i in ('set USERS_%X%_') do @set RET=%i
3. C:\>echo %RET%
4. MarkP
```

The FOR command sets the RET variable to the contents of the variable USERS_12_. As with the previous FOR command, this command can be wrapped in a DOSKEY macro. For example:

```
C:\>doskey geta=for /f "delims== tokens=2" %i in ('set $2_$3_') do @set $1=%i
```

This macro can now be used to recall any array element into any variable. For example:

```
1. C:\>set X=12
2. C:\>geta RET USERS %X%
3. C:\>echo %RET%
4. MarkP
```

The first argument of the GETA macro is the name of the destination variable, the second is the name of the array, and the third is the index.

This array scheme, and the macros and commands already demonstrated, is not restricted to numeric index values. Strings can also be used as an index value. For example:

```
1. C:\>seta USERSIZE MarkP 14000
2. C:\>seta USERSIZE KarlM 15000
3. C:\>seta USERSIZE BobW 12
4. C:\>geta RET USERSIZE KarlM
5. C:\>echo %RET%
6. 15000
```

This example creates a three-entry USERSIZE array. The entries are indexed with the strings MarkP, KarlM and BobW.

The array scheme developed here is not limited to one-dimensional arrays. Simply by extending the naming convention, two-dimensonal arrays can also be created, or special index schemes used. Many of the example scripts in Part II of this book make extensive use of arrays.

Script Parameters and Arguments

Chapter 1 briefly introduced script arguments and parameters. Script *arguments* are passed to a script in the same way that arguments are passed to regular commands—on the command line. For example, the command:

```
C:\>myscript c:\bin d:\bin
```

has two arguments, `c:\bin` and `d:\bin`. Arguments are separated from each other by spaces, tabs, commas, equal signs, or semi-colons. To include any of these separator characters in an argument, enclose the argument wholly or partially in double quotes. This is useful when using long file names that might contain spaces. For example:

```
c:\>myscript "c:\Program Files" d:\bin
```

In this example, the first argument is `"c:\Program Files"`. Without the double quotes, the shell would interpret the command as containing three arguments, `c:\Program`, `Files` and `d:\bin`.

Script arguments are accessed within the script using *parameters* (sometimes known as *formal parameters*). A parameter consists of a percent sign followed by a single digit, 0 to 9, for example, `%2`, `%6`, etc. Parameter 1 corresponds to the first argument entered on the command line, parameter 2 corresponds to the second, etc. Parameter 0 contains the name of the script file itself, exactly as entered on the command line. Arguments beyond the ninth argument cannot be accessed directly as parameters; therefore, `%10` is not a valid parameter. Instead, the SHIFT command is used to access additional arguments.

When a SHIFT command is executed within a script, it causes the contents of all parameters to move "down" one index. For example, parameter 0 gets the contents of parameter 1, parameter 1 gets the contents of parameter 2, etc. Parameter 9 then gets the contents of the next argument on the command line (i.e. the tenth argument). The original contents of parameter 0 are lost. Thus, each time a SHIFT command is executed, a new argument from the command line is shifted into parameter 9 and one argument is lost from parameter 0.

The SHIFT command can be used with an optional */n* argument, which starts the shift process at parameter *n*. For example:

```
SHIFT /3
```

This command shifts parameter 4 into parameter 3, parameter 5 into parameter 4, etc., but it will not alter the contents of parameters 1 or 2.

The special parameter `%*` contains *all* arguments entered on the command line except the name of the script file (parameter 0). The parameter contains the exact command line text as entered. This parameter is not affected by the SHIFT command.

Parameter Substitution

When a command is read from a script file, the shell replaces any parameters in the command text with the text of the corresponding argument. This process is known as *parameter substitution* and is similar to the variable substitution described previously in this chapter.

Parameter substitution occurs at the same time as variable substitution. Therefore, the same general rules that govern variable substitution also apply to parameter substitution. For example, parameter substitution occurs before any other parsing of the command. Therefore it is possible to pass fragments of commands into scripts as arguments.

For example, consider a sample script named TEST1.BAT containing these commands:

```
1. echo %*
2. copy %1 %2
```

This script can be used as follows:

```
C:\>test1 c:\winnt\*.bak d:\backup
```

The script begins by echoing all arguments, and then copies all .BAK files from the C:\WINNT directory to the D:\BACKUP directory.

Parameters are frequently used with the IF command to validate that the command syntax was correct. For example, the TEST.BAT script shown previously fails if only one argument is supplied. To correct this, add an IF command:

```
1. echo %*
2. if {%2}=={} (echo syntax error: missing argument)(goto :EOF)
3. copy %1 %2
```

The script now checks that at least two arguments are present before proceeding. Otherwise, it reports an error and aborts. The IF and GOTO commands are covered in detail in Chapter 4.

Special Parameter Syntax

The string substitution and indexing features of variable substitution are *not* available with parameter substitution. Fortunately, there is a trivial workaround for this. Simply assign a parameter to a variable and then use the variable instead of the parameter. For example:

```
1. set PARAM1=%1
2. echo %PARAM1:a=b%
```

If these lines are stored in the script TEST2.BAT, then the following command can be executed:

```
1. C:\>test2 absolutely fabulous
2. bbsolutely fbbulous
```

Parameter substitutions can be *qualified* using special qualifier characters. To qualify a parameter, follow the % character with a tilde, any required qualifier characters, and finally the parameter index digit. For example, %~f1 applies the f qualifier to parameter 1. Qualifiers treat the parameter as a partial or complete file or directory name, and return portions of the file name. Table 3.3 shows the available qualifiers.

Table 3.3. Parameter Qualifiers.

Qualifier	Meaning
f	Expands to a fully qualified path name.
d	Expands to a drive letter and colon character only.
p	Expands to a path name (directory) only, without a drive letter, file name, or file extension.
n	Expands to a file name only, without a directory, drive letter, or file extension.
x	Expands to a file extension only (with a leading period).
s	When used with the n or x qualifiers, expands to a short (MS-DOS) file name or file extension.
$var:	Searches the specified search path and returns the fully qualified path name of the first matching file.

The qualifiers use the current drive and directory to fill in items that are not explicitly specified in the parameter. For example, if the parameter %1 contains d:\bin, then %~d1 returns d: as expected. If parameter %1 contains \bin, then %~d1 returns c:, assuming C: is the current drive. This means that the qualifiers can always be relied upon to return valid information, even if this is not explicitly present in the parameter.

Qualifiers can be combined to yield a composite result. For example, %~nx1 returns the file name and extension from parameter 1.

The $var: qualifier treats *var* as an environment variable that contains a search path (formatted as a list of directories separated by semi-colons). The qualifier then searches the directories for a file name that matches the specified argument, and returns the fully qualified path name of the first file found. For example, if parameter 1 were to contain the text letter.doc:

```
echo %~$PATH:1
```

Then this example searches all directories specified by the PATH variable until it finds one that contains the file LETTER.DOC. It then echoes the full drive, directory and name of that file. To just return the drive and path, combine this qualifier with the d and p qualifiers. For example:

```
echo %~dp$PATH:1
```

Using Double Quotes

When an argument contains spaces, tabs, commas, semi-colons, or equal signs, it must be placed in double quotes. Otherwise, the command shell parses the argument text as several distinct arguments. Arguments that are quoted in this way are passed intact as parameters *including the double quotes*. Generally this behavior yields correct results. For example, consider the sample script named TEST1.BAT again:

```
1. echo %*
2. copy %1 %2
```

Assume the script is executed using the following command:

```
C:\>test1 "c:\Program Files" d:\backup
```

The first argument contains a space in the file name, and so is quoted. The quotes are included as part of the argument, so when the script is executed, the COPY command appears as follows (after parameter substitution):

```
copy "c:\Program Files" d:\backup
```

The double quotes correctly indicate the source directory to the COPY command. Because the double quotes are passed intact as part of the argument, they continue to "protect" the file name from any problems that might occur if they were not present.

Sometimes, however, it may be necessary to strip double quotes from an argument within a script. Unfortunately there is no easy way to do this that works under all circumstances. The simplest method is to copy the parameter into a variable and then use string substitution to delete all double quote characters. For example:

```
1. Set VAR1=%1
2. Echo %VAR1:"=%
```

This deletes the double quotes, but it also deletes any embedded double quote characters, which may not be desirable. Fortunately, embedded double quotes are rare, and using string substitution should work for almost all real-world scripts.

Double quotes provide additional difficulties when dealing with the IF command (which is described in detail in Chapter 4). For example:

```
if "%1"=="c:\temp" goto :TEMP
```

This command will not work if argument 1 already contains double quotes from the command line (for example, `"c:\temp"`). In this case, after parameter substitution, the command will be:

```
if ""c:\temp""=="c:\temp" goto :TEMP
```

This is not legal syntax for an IF command, and the shell will report an error. Leaving out the quotes does not help. For example:

```
if %1==c:\temp goto :TEMP
```

In this case, a quoted argument *will* work, but now the IF command will fail if parameter 1 is empty. In this case, after parameter substitution, the command will be:

```
if ==c:\temp goto :TEMP
```

Again, this is not a legal IF command. Similar problems arise with variables in IF commands. Should *they* be quoted?

To solve this dilemma, observe that a parameter will *never* contain spaces *unless* it is quoted (otherwise the shell would break the parameter into multiple parameters without the spaces). The following guidelines can then be used to avoid syntax errors:

- *Never quote parameters in a script.* As noted above, if a parameter contains spaces, it will already contain a set of quotes, and adding extra quotes will cause an error. If a parameter does not contain spaces, quotes are not needed.

- *Enclose parameters used in IF commands in braces.* Braces satisfy the syntax needs of the IF command but also prevent confusion should a parameter already contain quotes. If the parameter is empty, the braces prevent the IF command from causing a syntax error.

- *Never include quotes within the contents of a variable.* A variable can contain spaces without needing double quotes. Sometimes, it is necessary to quote a variable name within a script. If the variable *content* also contains quotes, two sets of quotes will be included in the script, causing syntax errors.

- *Always delete quotes when copying a parameter to a variable.* Parameters may contain quotes, but variables should not. Therefore, when copying a parameter to a variable, always delete quotes (using string substitution).

- *Quote variables in a script when needed.* Variable substitutions should be quoted if spaces introduced by the substitution would cause a syntax error. Generally, variables are quoted unless they are part of an ECHO or SET command. Variables *should* be quoted when they are used in an IF command.

These rules are best understood by considering the following example script fragment:

```
1. if {%1}=={} goto :END
2. set SRC=%1
3. set SRC=%SRC:"=%
4. if "%SRC%"=="c:\temp" goto :TEMP
5. copy "%SRC%" %2
```

Line 1 shows the use of braces enclosing a parameter in an IF command. This command is syntactically correct regardless of the contents of parameter 1 (even if the parameter contains double quotes or is empty).

Lines 2 and 3 copy parameter 1 to the SRC variable, and then use string substitution to strip out any double quotes. Thus, the SRC variable contains a copy of parameter 1 *without* any quotes.

Line 4, the IF command, compares the SRC variable to the literal c:\temp. Quotes are used here, because we know that SRC *cannot* contain quotes (they have been removed) but it *may* contain spaces.

Line 5 executes a COPY command. The SRC variable is quoted, as it may contain a file name with embedded spaces. However, parameter 2 is *not* quoted. Since it is a parameter, if it contains embedded spaces, then it *must* already be quoted, so extra quotes in the script are not needed.

Chapter 4

Control Flow, Procedures, and Script Nesting

- **Simple control flow**
  This section describes the basic control flow features of scripts, such as GOTO and nesting or chaining scripts.

- **Script procedures**
  More advanced control flow techniques are discussed here, including procedures and parameter passing techniques.

- **Procedure structure**
  This section shows how to use the various core shell features to construct well-behaved procedures and procedure libraries.

- **The IF command**
  This command is the fundamental command used to provide conditional command execution, allowing scripts to alter their actions based upon various testable conditions.

- **Interactive commands**
  Several commands are specifically designed to allow script to interact with the user.

- **The FOR command**
  The FOR command is probably the single most powerful command for script development. This section details how the power of this command can be used in scripts.

Simple Control Flow

To execute a script the shell reads the script file one line at a time. Each command in the script executes in the order in which it is encountered in the file. Script execution terminates when the shell reaches the end of the file. This is the default control flow used in all scripts (and in most other programming languages).

Script control flow can be modified within a script file by using branches. A *branch command* alters the control flow, diverting it to another location within the current script file or another script file. The branch commands supported by the shell are

- Jumping from one script to another by a process known as *chaining*.

- Executing another script by a process known as *nesting*.

- Jumping to another location in the script file using a GOTO command.

- Calling a procedure (subroutine) using a CALL command. The CALL command is described in subsequent sections of this chapter.

Chaining Scripts

The simplest control flow process is chaining. *Chaining* transfers control flow from the current script file to a new script file. The shell discards the current script, stays in script mode, and continues script execution at the first line in the new script file. To chain to a new script file, specify the new script file as a command. For example:

```
1. echo Now chaining to file CLEANUP.BAT
2. cleanup
```

When the CLEANUP line executes, the shell chains to the file CLEANUP.BAT (or CLEANUP.CMD). A directory path can be specified if required, for example:

```
c:\scripts\cleanup
```

If a path is not specified, the shell searches for the script using the normal command search procedure described in Chapter 2. "The Windows NT Command Shell."

Chaining to a new script performs a *jump* operation; execution of the current script terminates. It is not possible to return to the original script and continue execution—when the chained script terminates, script mode terminates and the shell returns to interactive mode.

Any number of chaining operations can be executed. For instance, SCRIPT1 can chain to SCRIPT2, which then chains to SCRIPT3, etc. A script can even chain to itself (either directly or indirectly through a circular chain of scripts), creating a simple loop in which the script(s) repeatedly executes.

Chained scripts acquire the current shell state (such as the current drive and directory), but are given a new set of arguments obtained from the chain command. For example, assume SCRIPT1.BAT contains

```
1. echo Argument 1=%1
2. cleanup c:\backup
```

and CLEANUP.BAT contains

```
echo Argument 1=%1
```

Now execute SCRIPT1:

```
1. C:\>script1 test
2. Argument 1=test
3. Argument 1=c:\backup
```

The first ECHO command shows parameter %1 in the initial script (SCRIPT1.BAT), which is test. The second ECHO command executes in script CLEANUP.BAT, and shows that parameter %1 is now c:\backup, which was the argument passed to CLEANUP within SCRIPT1.

> **Tip**
>
> To *chain to a script with all current arguments intact, use the %* parameter (described in Chapter 3, "Script Parameters and Variables") as the only argument to the* chain *command. For example:*
>
> ```
> cleanup %*
> ```
>
> *This command chains to the CLEANUP.BAT script and passes all of the current arguments to this script.*

Nesting Scripts

Although chaining enables one script to execute another, this feature is of limited value because the shell does not return to the chaining script after the chained script terminates; chaining is a *jump* operation.

Script *nesting* enables one script to execute another as a simple subroutine. The nested script executes to completion, and the nesting script then continues execution. Thus, script nesting enables one script to execute another as a procedure.

Nested scripts execute using nested command shells and use the /C switch to execute the script. For example, assume SCRIPT1.BAT contains:

```
1. echo In SCRIPT1.BAT...
2. cmd /c cleanup
3. echo In SCRIPT1.BAT again...
```

and CLEANUP.BAT contains:

```
echo In CLEANUP.BAT...
```

Now execute SCRIPT1:

```
1. C:\>script1
2. In SCRIPT1.BAT...
3. In CLEANUP.BAT...
4. In SCRIPT1.BAT again...
```

The ECHO command output shows that the CLEANUP.BAT script executes as a procedure of the SCRIPT1.BAT script.

As described in Chapter 3, it is considered good practice to execute nested command shells indirectly using the %COMSPEC% variable. Therefore, SCRIPT1.BAT should be re-written as:

```
1. echo In SCRIPT1.BAT...
2. %COMSPEC% /c cleanup
3. echo In SCRIPT1.BAT again...
```

As with chained scripts, a nested script has its own set of arguments and parameters. Any arguments required by the nested script must be explicitly passed to the script on the command line. For example:

```
%COMSPEC% /c cleanup c:\backup d:\backup
```

This passes c:\backup as parameter %1 and d:\backup as parameter %2. The parameters and arguments of the script calling the nested script are not affected by the nesting process; after the nested script terminates, the arguments (and hence parameters) of the nesting script are unchanged.

Nested scripts execute in nested command shells. Therefore, nested scripts obey the same rules as nested command shells (described in Chapter 2). The nested script inherits the current environment (and hence all variables), and also the current drive and directory. However, if the script makes changes to the environment, current drive, or directory, these changes are discarded when the script terminates. This means that nested scripts cannot pass return results back to the nesting script, except indirectly (for example, via a file) or through an exit code.

Nesting and Recursion

Nested scripts can in turn execute other nested scripts, forming a "stack" of nested scripts. For example, SCRIPT1 executes SCRIPT2, which then executes SCRIPT3. Eventually, SCRIPT3 terminates, allowing SCRIPT2 to continue until it also terminates. Finally, SCRIPT1 continues execution. Each nesting "level" starts another command shell, and so the only limit to the depth of nesting is available memory.

Recursion (either direct or indirect) can also be used with script nesting. *Recursion* is a programming technique where a procedure (or script) calls itself. Typically (as in the following DELM.BAT example) the procedure has a set of data to process, and calls itself recursively to process a subset of that data.

Recursion is an advanced programming technique and should be used with great care, as mis-use can cause significant problems (such as an endless recursion). However, there are several classic computer algorithms, such as tree sorting, which are most easily handled using recursion.

This example script, DELM.BAT, uses recursion to delete up to nine files, each specified on the command line:

```
1. if {%1}=={} goto :EOF
2. del %1
3. %COMSPEC% /c %0 %2 %3 %4 %5 %6 %7 %8 %9
```

For example, this command deletes files x, y, and z:

```
C:\>delm x y z
```

The operation of DELM.BAT, like most recursive examples, is subtle. The IF command in line 1 (described in "The IF Command" section later in this chapter) simply terminates script execution if there are no arguments on the command line. Line 2 deletes the file specified by argument 1. Line 3 provides the recursion: It invokes a new command shell and executes %0, which is DELM.BAT. This new shell is passed all the arguments from the original argument *except* the first.

To understand how this script works, consider the example above, where the script is used to delete the files x, y and z. When the script first executes, %1 is x, and so line 2 deletes this file using the DEL command. Line 3 then nests another copy of DELM.BAT. Once parameters have been substituted, line 3 appears as:

```
cmd /c delm y z
```

Notice that x is no longer present in the arguments, because the %1 parameter is not present in the original command on line 3. The nested script now executes, and line 2 executes again. This time, however, %1 contains y, since this is the first argument, as shown previously, to the nested command shell. So file y is now deleted. Line 3 then executes again, and this time the line is expanded to:

```
cmd /c delm z
```

This causes file z to be deleted, and yet another line 3 to be executed. This time, the line is expanded to:

```
cmd /c delm
```

This nested execution is passed no arguments: All the arguments to the original shell have now been consumed. When this nested script executes, line 1 finally comes into effect. Parameter %1 is empty, and the GOTO statement (covered in the following section) jumps to the end of the file.

The GOTO terminates the innermost command shell. The previous shell then continues execution, and because it is at the end of the script file, it also terminates. This termination process continues for all earlier nested command shells, and this cascade of shell termination completes when the original script file terminates.

> **Tip**
>
> *Do not mistake recursion with chaining a script to itself. When a script chains to itself, execution of the current copy of the script file is abandoned, and the current command shell simply restarts script file execution at the start of the (same) script file. A script file can chain to itself forever with no ill effects (assuming this is the desired behavior).*
>
> *When a script uses recursion, execution of the current copy of the script file is suspended, and another command shell is created to begin execution of the same script file. If the recursion continues indefinitely, many additional command shells are invoked. Eventually, Windows NT exhausts all available resources, and the script fails.*

Labels and the GOTO Command

The chaining and nesting techniques previously described enable control flow *between* scripts. The GOTO command enables control flow *within* a script. The GOTO command works in conjunction with script labels. A *label* identifies a location within a script file. Specify a label by entering the label in the script, prefixed with a colon. For example:

```
:LABEL1
```

Labels must be placed on a separate line from other commands. They *cannot* be placed within a compound command, even if the compound command is broken across multiple lines by parentheses. Spaces are allowed before the colon character and between the colon and the label text. Labels in this book are shown in uppercase, but they are not case sensitive.

Labels can contain letters, digits, and the underscore character. Other characters are allowed, but should be avoided, as they can cause difficulties when labels are used with GOTO and CALL commands. Labels can be very long—in excess of 50 characters.

The GOTO Command

The GOTO command jumps to a specified label. Follow the GOTO command with
the name of the target label. The colon character on the label in the GOTO command is optional, though its use is encouraged for consistency with the CALL
command, as shown in the following:

```
1. :BEGIN_LOOP
2. .
3. .
4. goto :BEGIN_LOOP
```

When a GOTO command executes, script execution continues at the line following the target label. The label can be either before the GOTO command (creating
a loop) or after the GOTO command (jumping ahead in the script).

In MS-DOS and earlier versions of Windows NT, labels and the GOTO command
were used extensively to describe the control flow logic of scripts. However,
the compound command statements make many such uses of the GOTO command obsolete. For example, in MS-DOS this script code was frequently used
to check that a required argument was present:

```
1. if not "%1"=="" goto ARG1OK
2. echo error: missing argument
3. goto exit
4. :ARG1OK
5. .
6. .
7. :EXIT
```

This code can be re-written using a compound command as follows:

```
if {%1}=={} (echo error: missing argument) & (goto :EOF)
```

This single line replaces all the lines shown in the previous example, and is far
easier to understand. If desired, the line can be written as a multi-line
command:

```
1. if {%1}=={} (
2.    echo error: missing argument
3.    goto :EOF
4. )
```

Both the single line and multi-line versions have the same effect. The choice of
which to use should be based on style and clarity of meaning.

The DELM.BAT script shown earlier can be re-written using the GOTO command. Written this way, DELM2.BAT does not use recursion, which makes it

easier to understand, and deletes any number of files specified (DELM.BAT was limited to 9 files). The DELM2.BAT script is

```
1. set /a FILE_COUNT=0
2. :NEXT_FILE
3.     if {%1}=={} (echo %FILE_COUNT% file^(s^) deleted) & (goto :EOF)
4.     del %1
5.     set /a FILE_COUNT+=1
6.     shift /1
7. goto :NEXT_FILE
```

This script loops repeatedly between the :NEXT_FILE label in line 2 and the GOTO :NEXT_FILE command in line 7. The IF command in line 3 terminates the script when there are no more arguments to process (or if none were specified on the command line). Line 4 deletes the first file specified, while the SHIFT command shifts down the arguments. Using SHIFT like this lets the loop process each argument one by one, by shifting each argument into parameter %1. Eventually, all arguments are processed and the IF command terminates the loop.

This version of the DELM script has also been enhanced by adding a file counter and displaying the count of files deleted at the end of the script.

The :EOF Label

The command shell has one pre-defined label that is present in all scripts. The label :EOF means the end of the script file (after all script text). Therefore, the command

```
goto :EOF
```

transfers control to the end of the file. Because script file processing terminates at the end of the file, this command is interpreted as an *end script* command. When a GOTO :EOF command executes in a script procedure, it is interpreted as a *return* command.

Script Procedures

Although much can be accomplished by using the simple control flow constructs previously described, virtually all non-trivial scripts can use *procedures* to improve robustness and reduce maintenance overhead. The virtues of using procedural elements in programs are well known, and include code re-useability, compartmentalization (hiding implementation details within procedures), and structured design (breaking a large problem into a set of smaller ones). All of these virtues can be realized in scripts by using script procedures.

The CALL Command

The CALL command provides explicit support for procedures (or subroutines) within a script. The call command "calls," as a subroutine, another script or part of a script. When the called portion of the script terminates, execution of the current script resumes at the next command after the CALL command.

Although the CALL command is similar to the script-nesting feature already described, it is superior to it for two reasons:

- The CALL command can execute a portion of the current script as a procedure, whereas script nesting only nests entire script files.
- The current shell executes the procedure.

Because the CALL command executes the procedure within the current shell, the procedure shares the environment of the caller, and can therefore modify script variables. In contrast, a nested script *inherits* the shell environment, and cannot modify the caller's variables.

To execute another script file as a procedure (an *inter-file* procedure call), follow the CALL command with the name of the script. For example:

```
call cleanup
```

A directory path can be specified if required. For example:

```
call c:\scripts\cleanup
```

If a path is not specified, the shell searches for the script using the normal command search procedure described in Chapter 2.

To execute a part of the current script file as a procedure (an *intra-file* procedure call), follow the CALL command with a colon and a label. For example:

```
call :SUB1
```

Unlike the GOTO command, the intra-file CALL command requires the colon character before the script label, in order to distinguish an inter-file from an intra-file call.

Regardless of the location of the procedure (a new script file or a label in the current script), the command shell executes the specified procedure until the procedure reaches the end of the script file. Execution then resumes at the command following the CALL command. This can be either the next line or the next command on the same line if the command is a compound command.

Procedure execution ends when the shell reaches the end of the script file containing the procedure. The GOTO :EOF command is typically used to end the procedure and return to the calling script. For example:

```
1. echo Starting...
2. call :SUB1
3. echo Ending...
4. goto :EOF
5. .
```

```
6. .
7. :SUB1
8. echo In procedure SUB1
9. goto :EOF
```

When this script executes, it displays

```
1. Starting...
2. In procedure SUB1
3. Ending...
```

The procedure SUB1 is bracketed by the procedure label at the start and a GOTO
:EOF command at the end. If required, procedures can contain additional GOTO
:EOF commands. The main body of the script also contains a GOTO :EOF command at line 4. Without this command script execution would continue from
line 3 and "fall through" into the SUB1 procedure, accidentally executing the
procedure a second time.

Tip

Place procedures in a script after the main body of the script. Place a GOTO
:EOF *command before the script label (as well as at the end of the procedure), so that if a previous procedure accidentally falls through to the
procedure, it does not execute by mistake. For example:*

```
1. (main body of script)
2. .
3. .
4. rem Procedure SUB1
5. goto :EOF
6. :SUB1
7. (body of procedure SUB1)
8. goto :EOF
```

Procedure Nesting

Procedure calls can be nested; procedures can call other procedures. Any combination of intra-file and inter-file procedure calls is allowed, but all intra-file
procedure calls are relative to the *current* script file. For example, if
SCRIPT1.BAT calls SCRIPT2.BAT using an inter-file CALL command, then any
nested intra-file CALL commands *within* SCRIPT2.BAT will call procedures
within that file (SCRIPT2.BAT).

The nesting of procedures is limited by command shell stack space. Typically,
procedure calls can be nested several hundred deep, far more than is likely ever
to be encountered by typical scripts.

Procedure State and Variable Scope

The CALL command executes procedures using the current command shell. This means that a procedure *can* alter the current state of the shell. For example, a procedure can alter the current drive or directory, or change environment variables. All these changes remain in effect after the procedure completes and control flow returns to the main script body.

A procedure wishing to temporarily alter the current drive and directory can use the PUSHD and POPD commands. The PUSHD command saves the current drive and directory in a push-down stack, and the POPD command recovers the current drive and directory from the most recent entry in that stack; for example:

```
1. :SUB1
2. pushd
3. cd \backup
4. .
5. .
6. popd
7. goto :EOF
```

This procedure alters the current directory. However, by bracketing the procedure within a PUSHD/POPD command pair, changes to the current directory are made local to the procedure. The procedure is "well behaved" and preserves the current directory. This kind of defensive programming avoids unwanted procedure side effects and leads to more robust scripts.

As a convenience, the PUSHD command can switch to a specified drive and directory. For example, the previous example can be written as

```
1. :SUB1
2. pushd \backup
3. .
4. .
5. popd
6. goto :EOF
```

Other uses of the PUSHD and POPD commands are described in Part III, "Scripting Command Reference."

Tip

The PUSHD command can specify a UNC (universal naming convention) name instead of a traditional drive and directory name; for example:

```
pushd \\DataServer\Share1\MyDirectory
```

When used like this, the PUSHD command automatically creates a temporary drive letter mapping for the UNC name. The first free drive letter is

used, starting at Z: and working down the alphabet. Once mapped, the
PUSHD *command then makes this drive and directory the current drive and*
directory.

The POPD *command automatically undoes any UNC drive mappings when*
it executes. Using PUSHD/POPD *to map UNC names is particularly useful in*
scripts that are scheduled via the AT *command. As Chapter 2 explained,*
these scripts cannot rely on user-defined network drive mappings.

Procedures can also alter variables in the current environment. These changes
are global in scope, and so are still in effect after the procedure returns. To
limit the scope of environment variable changes, use the SETLOCAL and ENDLOCAL
commands to bracket the procedure. These commands are described in Chapter 3. For example:

```
1. :SUB1
2. setlocal
3. .
4. .
5. endlocal
6. goto :EOF
```

When either PUSHD/POPD or SETLOCAL/ENDLOCAL (or both) are used, take care to
exit the procedure correctly. For example, the following procedure contains a
significant error:

```
1. :SUB2
2. setlocal
3. .
4. .
5. if {%1}=={} goto :EOF
6. .
7. endlocal
8. goto :EOF
```

The problem in this procedure is the IF command. The procedure executes
within the SETLOCAL/ENDLOCAL command brackets. However, the IF command
executes a GOTO :EOF command *without* executing an ENDLOCAL command first.
This does not generate a syntax error, but leaves the shell stack with an
unmatched SETLOCAL every time SUB2 executes. Eventually, the shell may run
out of stack space.

One way to correct this problem is to add an ENDLOCAL command to the IF
command before the GOTO command. For example:

```
if {%1}=={} (endlocal) & (goto :EOF)
```

This works, but if PUSH/POPD brackets are also used, they must also be added.
Maintenance becomes difficult if the procedure contains many such IF
commands.

A better solution is to always define an exit label within a procedure. This label should appear just before the bracketing commands (like ENDLOCAL). All GOTO :EOF commands within the procedure are then replaced by jumps to this exit label. SUB2 can then be re-written as

```
1. :SUB2
2. setlocal
3. .
4. .
5. if {%1}=={} goto :EXIT_SUB2
6. .
7. :EXIT_SUB2
8. endlocal
9. goto :EOF
```

Passing Arguments to Procedures

As with chained and nested scripts, script procedures are given a new set of arguments obtained from the CALL command. For example, assume SCRIPT1.BAT contains:

```
1. echo Argument 1=%1
2. call :SUB1 SubArg1
3. echo Argument 1=%1
4. goto :EOF
5. .
6. .
7. :SUB1
8. echo SUB1 Argument 1=%1
9. goto :EOF
```

This script executes as follows:

```
1. C:\>script1 MainArg1
2. Argument 1=MainArg1
3. SUB1 Argument 1=SubArg1
4. Argument 1=MainArg1
```

Use the %* parameter to pass all current arguments to a procedure. For example:

```
call :SUB1 %*
```

Within an intra-file procedure, the %0 parameter is the name of the procedure (i.e., the target label of the CALL command). If a procedure needs access to the name of the script, this can be passed explicitly as an argument, or the script name can be assigned to a variable (for example, SCRIPTNAME) before calling the procedure.

Returning Values from Procedures

As Chapter 3 explained, the shell language does not support return values in procedures. Instead the RET environment variable is used to pass a return value back from a procedure to the caller. This is only a convention, however, and procedures are free to use any other return mechanism they choose, as long as both the caller and callee agree upon the details.

Chapter 3 also described how to return a value correctly when using the SETLOCAL and ENDLOCAL commands to enforce local variable scope. The RET variable can "tunnel" across the local scope by assigning the variable to itself on the same line as the ENDLOCAL command. For example:

```
endlocal & set RET=%RET%
```

Procedure Structure

The CALL and GOTO :EOF commands provide the core commands to enable scripts to be structured. They enable the work of a script to be broken into logically distinct blocks of code, each of which performs a particular task. This section provides additional information on various structuring techniques.

Using a MAIN Procedure

When a script file executes, execution begins at the first line in the script file and continues until the end of the file is reached. One method for adding structure to a script is to add a MAIN procedure. Begin the script file with basic preamble code and then immediately call a MAIN procedure. Place all the actual script lines within the MAIN procedure, or procedures called by MAIN.

A skeleton of such a script might be:

```
01. @echo OFF
02. @if not "%ECHO%"=="" echo %ECHO%
03. @if not "%OS%"=="Windows_NT" goto DOSEXIT
04. rem $Workfile: MODEL1.BAT $ $Revision: 4 $ $Date: 7/01/97 3:27p $
05. rem $Archive: /SrcSafe/Proto/MODEL1.BAT $
06.
07. rem Set local scope and call MAIN procedure
08. setlocal & pushd & set RET=
09. set SCRIPTNAME=%0
10. if "%DEBUG%"=="1" (set TRACE=echo) else (set TRACE=rem)
11. call :MAIN %*
12. popd & endlocal & set RET=%RET%
13. goto :EOF
14.
15. rem MAIN procedure
16. :MAIN
17. if defined TRACE %TRACE% [proc %0 %*]
18.
19. goto :EOF
20.
```

```
21. rem Additional procedures go here...
22.
23. rem These must be the FINAL LINES in the script...
24. :DOSEXIT
25. echo This script requires Windows NT
```

The first three lines of this skeleton are the standard lines introduced in Chapter 1. Line 8 deletes the RET variable, so that the default return value from this script is nothing. Obviously, this is only significant if the script executes through an inter-file CALL, but it is good practice to structure *all* scripts so that they include a return value.

Line 8 also creates a local scope and state using the SETLOCAL and PUSHD commands, so that the MAIN procedure (and any other in the script) is free to alter state and variables without creating unexpected side effects.

Line 9 saves the name of the script file in the variable SCRIPTNAME. All the script logic is in the MAIN procedure, but inside this procedure the parameter %0 value is :MAIN, not the name of the script file. Saving the script file name in SCRIPTNAME allows the MAIN procedure (or any other) to reference this information if necessary.

Line 10 sets up script tracing. The shell has no built-in tracing support, but line 10 provides a simple trace facility. If the DEBUG variable is set to 1 before the script executes, tracing is enabled. Otherwise, tracing is disabled. To enable tracing, the TRACE variable is set to echo. To disable tracing, the TRACE variable is set to rem.

To generate trace output, include a line containing %TRACE% and any trace text. For example:

```
%TRACE% This is trace output...
```

If tracing is enabled, %TRACE% is replaced by echo, and so the trace text is displayed. If tracing is disabled, %TRACE% is replaced by rem, and so the trace text is ignored. An example of tracing can be seen at the start of the MAIN procedure. For robustness, this line checks the TRACE variable to verify that it is defined before it executes.

Line 11 calls the MAIN procedure. All command line arguments are passed directly to the MAIN procedure via the %* parameters. The MAIN procedure then executes the script logic.

When the MAIN procedure returns in line 12, the local scope and state are deleted, and the return value in RET (if any) is tunneled back out of the local scope. Finally, line 13 exits the script.

Complete Procedure Skeleton

This chapter introduces several techniques for using procedures properly. A complete, well-behaved procedure skeleton using these techniques appears as follows:

```
01. .
02. .
03. REM XYZ procedure
04. Goto :EOF
05. :XYZ
06. setlocal
07. pushd
08. set RET=
09. (body of procedure here)
10. .
11. :EXIT_XYZ
12. popd
13. endlocal & set RET=%RET%
14. goto :EOF
```

This skeleton places a safety GOTO :EOF command before the procedure start. It uses SETLOCAL and ENDLOCAL commands to give all variables local scope, and uses PUSH and POPD commands to make state changes local. The :EXIT_XYZ label provides a procedure exit label for use within the procedure body. Finally, it returns a value in the RET variable, which is cleared at the start of the procedure. If desired, these commands can be combined into compound commands as follows:

```
01. .
02. .
03. REM XYZ procedure
04. Goto :EOF
05. :XYZ
06. setlocal & pushd & set RET=
07. (body of procedure here)
08. .
09. .
10. :EXIT_XYZ
11. popd & endlocal & set RET=%RET%
12. goto :EOF
```

Script Libraries

The CALL command can either call a procedure within the current script (an intra-file call) or call another script file as a procedure (an inter-file call). Sometimes it is necessary to call an individual script procedure *within* another script file, i.e., perform an intra-file call into another script file. This is called an *indirect* CALL *command.*

The most typical use of indirect CALL commands is accessing script libraries. *Script libraries* contain sets of general-purpose procedures that can be used by other scripts. Although a script library *could* be developed using a series of individual files (one procedure per file), it is more efficient if these scripts can be placed within a single script file.

The shell language does not support indirect CALL commands directly, but these commands can be quite easily simulated, allowing script libraries to be built and deployed. The scheme shown here is thus a convention: Other similar conventions can be developed if required.

A script library using this convention should follow these rules:

- To distinguish a script library from a regular script file, use a leading underscore in the file name, for example _MTPLIB.BAT. This helps to separate script libraries from regular scripts in directory listings.

- If it is executed without any command arguments, the script library should echo a description and version number, and then exit. The library can then be invoked from the command line to check version information, etc.

- Provide an INIT procedure within all script libraries. Any script that wishes to use the library *must* call the INIT procedure before calling any other library procedures. This allows the library to initialize itself before any other procedures are called.

- Provide a dispatch function at the start of the script library to handle indirect CALL commands. This is described below.

- To call a procedure in the library, use an inter-file CALL command and specify the name of the procedure as the first argument. Procedure arguments then follow the procedure name.

Following the last rule described above, the procedure KILLALL in the script _PROCLIB.BAT can be called by executing:

```
call _proclib :KILLALL arg1 arg2
```

This indirect call executes the procedure KILLALL in the script library _PROCLIB.BAT, passing the procedure two arguments, arg1 and arg2.

A skeleton script library, _LIBSKEL.BAT, is shown in the following example:

```
01. @echo OFF
02. @if not "%ECHO%"=="" echo %ECHO%
03. @if not "%OS%"=="Windows_NT" goto DOSEXIT
04. rem $Workfile: MODEL1.BAT $ $Revision: 4 $ $Date: 7/01/97 3:27p $
05. rem $Archive: /SrcSafe/Proto/MODEL1.BAT $
06.
```

```
07. rem If no arguments, show version information and exit
08. if {%1}=={} (
09.     echo Script Library Skeleton [%0] version 1.0
10.     goto :EOF
11. )
12.
13. rem At least one argument, so dispatch to procedure
14. set _PROC=%1
15. shift /1
16. goto %_PROC%
17.
18. rem INIT procedure (all libraries should have this)
19. :INIT
20. .
21. .
22. goto :EOF
23.
24. rem Sample procedure CHECKX86 verifies that we are running on an Intel CPU
25. :CHECKX86
26. if /i "%PROCESSOR_ARCHITECTURE%"=="x86" (set RET=1) else (set RET=0)
27. goto :EOF
28.
29. rem Additional procedures go here...
30.
31. rem These must be the FINAL LINES in the script...
32. :DOSEXIT
33. echo This script requires Windows NT
```

Line 8 handles the display of library version information if the library executes with no arguments. If one or more arguments *have* been supplied, the library *dispatches* to the appropriate procedure. The dispatch code consists of these three lines:

```
1. set _PROC=%1
2. shift /1
3. goto %_PROC%
```

The first line saves the first argument (the name of the procedure to call) in the variable _PROC. The second line shifts all arguments starting at argument 1. This eliminates the first argument from the argument list to be used later by the procedure. Finally, the GOTO command jumps to whatever label is named in the _PROC variable. This indirect GOTO is the key to the indirect CALL convention. When the library executes, by an inter-file CALL, the first argument is the name of the procedure to call. Hence, %1 contains the procedure name, and the command GOTO %_PROC% jumps to the start of this procedure. When the procedure executes a GOTO :EOF command, the inter-file CALL returns.

The SHIFT command in line 15 ensures that arguments accessed in individual procedures are accessed correctly. The first procedure argument actually comes from the *second* argument to the original indirect CALL command (the first is the procedure name). The SHIFT command hides this, and allows the procedure to access the first argument as %1 etc.

Notice that if an attempt is made to call a procedure which does not exist, the GOTO command in line 16 will fail with an error, and script execution will halt.

The IF Command

The IF command provides conditional script command execution. The general syntax of an IF command is:

```
IF condition command
```

The IF command first evaluates the *condition*. If the condition is true, the *command* executes. If the condition is false, the *command* does not execute and control flow continues to the next statement. The *command* can be a compound command in parentheses, which enables several commands to execute, depending upon the result of the conditional test.

The IF command can include an ELSE clause. The syntax of this IF command is:

```
IF condition (true-command) ELSE (false-command)
```

Again, the IF command first evaluates the *condition*. If the condition is true, then the *true-command* executes. If the condition is false, the *false-command* executes. Both the *true-command* and *false-command* can be compound commands, and both require parentheses.

Simple IF Commands

The following IF commands provide ways to test a variety of conditions, including command exit codes, string values, and variable definitions.

The IF ERRORLEVEL Command

The IF ERRORLEVEL command tests the exit code of the previously executed command. The syntax of this command is:

```
IF [NOT] ERRORLEVEL level command
```

The error level test evaluates to true if the previous command returned an exit code with a value greater than or equal to *level*. Commands generally return an exit code of 0 is they are successful and non-zero if they encounter an error. For example:

```
1. dir /*
2. if errorlevel 1 echo Invalid DIR command
```

If the arguments to the DIR command are invalid (as in this case), the IF command displays the error message.

The NOT clause inverts the test performed by the IF ERRORLEVEL command: The *command* executes if the exit code of the previous command was less than *level*.

The IF CMDEXTVERSION Command

The IF CMDEXTVERSION command checks the *command extension* version of the shell. As new command features are added to new versions of the command shell, the command extension version is incremented. For Windows NT 4.0, the command extension version is 1. Scripts can check the command extension version using IF CMDEXTVERSION and modify their processing accordingly.

The IF CMDEXTVERSION command operates like the IF ERRORLEVEL command. The syntax of the command is:

```
IF CMDEXTVERSION version command
```

The test evaluates to true if the command extension version is greater than or equal to *version*. In this case, the *command* executes. For example:

```
if cmdextversion 2 set DIR=%~q1
```

The IF DEFINED Command

The IF DEFINED command tests for the existence of a variable. The syntax of the command is:

```
IF [NOT] DEFINED var-name command
```

If the variable specified by *var-name* is defined, the *command* executes. Do *not* bracket the variable name in percent signs. For example:

```
1. set /a COUNT=0
2. :LOOP
3. set /a COUNT+=1
4. if defined ARRAY_%X%_ goto :LOOP
5. set /a COUNT-=1
```

This example counts the number of entries in the array named ARRAY, assuming the array is not sparsely populated; i.e., the script counts up until the first undefined array entry is reached.

The NOT clause inverts the test performed by the IF DEFINED command: the *command* executes if the specified variable is *not* defined.

The String-Compare IF Command

The string-compare IF command compares two strings for equality or inequality. The syntax of the command is:

```
IF [NOT] [/I] string1==string2 command
```

The two strings *string1* and *string2* are compared. If they are identical (both strings are the same length, and all characters match), the *command* executes.

Use the NOT clause to execute the *command* if the strings are different. The strings to compare are separated by two equal signs.

The strings can have leading and trailing spaces, which are *not* included in the comparison. For example, all these IF commands execute the ECHO command:

```
1. if a==a echo Idential
2. if a ==a echo Identical
3. if a == a echo Identical
```

To include leading and trailing space in the comparison, enclose both strings in double quotes. For example:

```
if "a "=="a " echo Identical
```

The string-compare IF command is typically used to compare a variable to a string or another variable. For example:

```
if "%DEBUG%"=="1" echo Debug enabled
```

When comparing variables, always place both strings in double quotes. If the double quotes are not included, problems can arise. For example:

```
if %DEBUG%==1 echo Debug enabled
```

If the DEBUG variable is not defined, after variable substitution this command is:

```
if ==1 Debug enabled
```

This generates a syntax error. Placing double quotes around both strings avoids this problem. The general rule is to always enclose both strings in double quotes.

A similar problem arises when comparing parameter values. These may be empty, or may already contain double quotes. Therefore, always enclose parameters within braces when they are used in an IF command. For example:

```
if {%1}=={} echo Missing Parameter!
```

For additional information on the use of double quotes in variables and parameters, see the discussion of double quotes at the end of Chapter 3.

The /I switch in a string-compare IF compares the two strings using a case-insensitive comparison. In this case, the strings "abc" and "ABC" are considered identical.

One common use of the string-compare IF command is to process all script arguments sequentially. For example:

```
1. :NEXT_ARG
2. if {%1}=={} goto :DONE
3. call :PROCESS_ARG %1
4. shift /1
5. goto :NEXT_ARG
6. :DONE
```

This script code calls the PROCESS_ARG procedure for each script argument. The code loops until the parameter %1 is empty. Each time the loop executes, the SHIFT command moves the next argument into %1 until no more arguments are available. The loop then terminates.

Advanced IF Commands

The following IF commands provide ways to test for the existence of files and directories and compare values numerically.

The IF EXIST Command

The IF EXIST command tests to see if a file or directory exists. The syntax of the command is:

```
IF [NOT] EXIST file command
```

The *command* executes if the specified *file* exists. For example:

```
if exist temp.txt del temp.txt
```

A drive letter and directory path can be specified along with the file name. If these items are not supplied, the current drive and directory are used.

The NOT clause inverts the test performed by the IF EXIST command: The *command* executes if the specified file does *not* exist.

The IF EXIST command can be used with wild card file names. For example:

```
if exist *.txt echo dir *.txt
```

When used with a wild card, the IF EXIST condition is true if at least one file that matches the wild card exists in the current (or specified) directory.

> **Tip**
>
> *The command shell has more flexible wild card features than those found in MS-DOS. Asterisks may appear anywhere within a wild card pattern. For example, *s.* locates all files with names ending in "s" and D*s.txt locates all .TXT files with names starting with "D" and ending in "s."*

IF EXIST can also be used with directory names. For example:

```
if exist c:\dos echo MS-DOS is installed
```

This example will execute the ECHO command if c:\dos is either a file or a directory. To unambiguously distinguish between a file and directory using IF EXIST, check for the presence of a file named ".". All directories contain a directory named ".". For example:

```
if exist c:\dos\. echo Directory c:\dos exists AND is a directory
```

This IF command only executes the ECHO command if c:\dos exists, and it is a directory.

If the file name or directory name contains spaces or is a variable, enclose the name in double quotes. For example:

```
if exist "c:\Program Files\*.com" echo Programs found
```

The Relational IF Command

The relational IF command compares two values. The syntax of a relational IF command is:

```
IF [/I] value1 relop value2 command
```

The relational IF command compares *value1* and *value2* using the relop operator. If the comparison is true, the *command* executes. Table 4.1 lists the available relational operators.

> *Tip*
>
> *In Windows NT 4.0, relational operators must be specified in upper-case—lowercase operators generate a syntax error. This appears to be a bug.*

Table 4.1. Relational Operators.

Operator	Meaning
EQU	True if values are equal.
NEQ	True if values are not equal.
LSS	True if *value1* is less than *value2*.
LEQ	True if *value1* is less than or equal to *value2*.
GTR	True if *value1* is greater than *value2*.
GEQ	True if *value1* is greater than or equal to *value2*.

If both *value1* and *value2* are numeric values, then the comparison is performed numerically. Otherwise, the comparison is performed lexically, using the ANSI collating sequence (i.e., the Windows character set).

For example:

```
1. if 256 EQU 0x100 echo Numerically equal
2. if "256" EQU "0x100" echo Lexically equal
```

The first IF command evaluates to true because the two values are numerically equal (0x100 hexadecimal is 256 decimal). The second IF command evaluates to false because the string values are lexically different.

When comparing strings lexically, a string is "less than" another string if it is shorter in length or the first non-identical character in the two strings has a numerically smaller ANSI code in the first string.

Multi-Line and Nested IF Commands

The *command* executed by any IF command can be a compound command, including a multi-line command. This enables the commands executed by an IF command to be spread across multiple lines. For example:

```
1. if not "%PROCESSOR_ARCHITECTURE%"=="x86" (
2.     echo Intel x86 compatible CPU required
3.     goto :EOF
4. )
```

The opening parenthesis that begins the multi-line command *must* appear on the same line as the IF command. The closing parenthesis can appear on a line by itself or at the end of the last command. Indenting the commands as shown in the prior example is optional but does improve the readability of the script, as it helps to highlight the control flow through the script.

Multi-line commands can also be used with the ELSE clause of an IF command. For example:

```
1. if defined USERNAME (
2.     echo A user is logged-on
3.     goto :LOGGEDON
4. ) else (
5.     echo A user is not logged-on
6.     goto :NOTLOGGEDON
7. )
```

The first closing parenthesis, the ELSE clause, and the opening parenthesis of the ELSE clause *must* appear together on the same line. As in the previous example, indenting is used to improve readability.

The *command* executed by an IF command can be any valid shell command, including another IF command. For example:

```
1. if not "%PROCESSOR_ARCHITECTURE%"=="x86" (
2.     if not "%PROCESSOR_ARCHITECTURE%"=="MIPS" (
3.         echo Intel or MIPS compatible CPU required
4.         goto :EOF
5.     )
6. )
```

Similarly, each nested IF command can have an ELSE clause. Care should be taken to correctly match ELSE clauses to IF commands: Each ELSE clause binds to the most deeply nested IF command. Statements such as the case (or switch) of other languages can be constructed using multiple IF/ELSE commands. For example:

```
1. if /i "%PROCESSOR_ARCHITECTURE%"=="x86" (
2.     echo Running on Intel CPU
3. ) else if /i "%PROCESSOR_ARCHITECTURE%"=="MIPS" (
4.     echo Running on MIPS CPU
5. ) else if /i "%PROCESSOR_ARCHITECTURE%"=="ALPHA" (
6.     echo Running on Alpha CPU
7. ) else echo Unknown CPU!
```

Interactive Commands

There are several commands that are specifically designed to enable a script to interact with the user. These are:

- The PAUSE command, which waits for a key press before continuing script execution.

- The TIMEOUT [RK] command, which waits for a key press for a specified interval.

- The SLEEP [RK] command, which pauses script execution for a specified interval.

- The CHOICE [RK] command, which gets a single key stroke.

PAUSE

The simplest of these commands is PAUSE, which is typically used to pause execution so that command output can be viewed. The PAUSE command displays the message:

```
Press any key to continue . . .
```

Script execution pauses until a key is pressed, after which it continues normally. Pressing Ctrl+C or Ctrl+Break terminates script execution (after confirmation).

TIMEOUT[RK]

The TIMEOUT [RK] command enhances the PAUSE command by adding a timeout feature. Specify the timeout, in seconds, with the TIMEOUT command. For example:

```
C:\>timeout 5
```

This command pauses until either a key is pressed or the 5-second timeout period expires. During the timeout, the command displays a countdown of the time remaining.

SLEEP[RK]

The SLEEP [RK] command pauses script execution for a specified number of seconds. For example:

```
C:\>sleep 5
```

The SLEEP command is not interactive, but it is frequently used to delay script execution so that results can be displayed, or to "pace" a script so that it does not execute too quickly. While a SLEEP command executes, the thread executing the script is suspended, and therefore does not consume CPU resources.

Script Synchronization Using SLEEP

The SLEEP command is often used to assist in script synchronization issues. Sometimes it is desirable for one script to start another script, perform some additional processing, and then wait for the other script to terminate. This can be achieved by the presence or absence of a key file to flag the script state. For example, here is the script MASTER.BAT:

```
1. if exist lockfile del lockfile
2. start cmd /c slave.bat
3. rem (can do additional processing here)
4. :WAIT_LOOP
5. sleep 1
6. if not exist lockfile goto :WAIT_LOOP
```

Here is the companion SLAVE.BAT script:

```
1. echo Press a key to exit script
2. pause
3. echo . >lockfile
```

The first line of MASTER.BAT deletes the file lockfile if it exists. Line 2 starts the slave script in a new window. Both scripts are now running at the same time. Line 3 indicates that the MASTER script can now perform any additional processing desired. Line 4 marks the start of a wait loop. The MASTER script now spins in the loop from lines 4 to 6 until the file lockfile exists.

The SLEEP command in line 5 is not technically necessary—the loop works without it. But it does make the script thread yield the CPU for 1 second on each loop pass. This makes the loop well behaved in a multi-threaded OS like Windows NT.

The SLAVE script performs any desired processing (in this case, just a PAUSE command) and then indicates completion by creating the lockfile file in line 3. The contents of the lock file are not important—merely that it is created. This triggers the MASTER script to drop out of its wait loop.

The flaw in this scheme is that the MASTER script waits forever for the SLAVE script. If something goes wrong in the SLAVE script, the MASTER script may never terminate. Adding a time-out check to the wait loop can solve this. This example procedure encapsulates a generic "wait for file" loop that incorporates this timeout:

```
01. rem FILEWAIT procedure
02. rem Wait for a file to exist, with a timeout
03. rem    %1=Name of file to check
04. rem    %2=Timeout period, in seconds
05. rem    Returns timeout period (seconds) or -1 if timeout occurred
06. :FILEWAIT
07. setlocal
08. set /a RET=0
09.     :FILEWAIT_LOOP
10. sleep 1
11. set /a RET+=1
12. if %RET% LSS %2 if not exist %1 goto :FILEWAIT_LOOP
13.     if %RET% GEQ %2 set RET=-1
14. endlocal & set RET=%RET%
15. goto :EOF
```

Using a file to synchronize two asynchronous scripts is compact and efficient. The only rule to remember is that the synchronization file *must* be deleted *before* the slave script begins execution. This avoids race conditions that may get the master and slave scripts out of synchronization.

CHOICE

The CHOICE [RK] command waits for the user to type one key from a specified set of choices, and then returns an exit code indicating which key was pressed. This exit code can then be used with the IF ERRORLEVEL command or %ERRORLEVEL% variable to control script execution.

The basic CHOICE command displays a prompt and waits for a Y or N key to be pressed before continuing:

```
C:\>choice Do you wish to continue
Do you wish to continue[Y,N]?
```

Either upper or lower case keys are accepted, unless the /S switch is used, which treats upper and lower case letters as distinct.

The default CHOICE command displays the list of possible keystrokes in brackets, followed by a question mark after the prompt. The /N switch suppresses this. For example:

```
C:\>choice /n Do you wish to continue:
Do you wish to continue:
```

The /C switch specifies allowed keyboard input choices (the default is Y or N). For example:

```
C:\>choice /c:123 Enter adapter card type
Enter adapter card type[1,2,3]?
```

This command accepts the keys 1, 2 or 3 only. Letters specified as choices with the /C switch are not case sensitive, unless the /S switch is used.

Use the /T switch to specify a timeout for the CHOICE command. Follow the switch with a default key and the timeout period (in seconds). For example:

```
C:\>choice /c:123 /t:2,30 Enter adapter card type
Enter adapter card type[1,2,3]?
```

This command automatically enters the "2" key as the choice after 30 seconds.

The CHOICE command returns the position of the chosen key as an exit code. The *exit code* is the index of the chosen key in the list of possible keys. For example, if the switch /C:ABF is used, pressing A returns an exit code of 1, B returns an exit code of 2, and F returns an exit code of 3. The default choices (Y or N) returns 1 for Y and 2 for N.

The exit code is typically used in an IF ERRORLEVEL command to branch based on the choice made. For example:

```
1. choice Do you want to continue
2. if errorlevel 2 goto :EOF
```

The IF ERRORLEVEL command evaluates to true if the exit code (error level) is greater than or equal to the specified value. Therefore, this script code does *not* work as expected:

```
1. choice /c:SPX Enter network card type
2. if errorlevel 1 goto :CARD_S
3. if errorlevel 2 goto :CARD_P
4. if errorlevel 3 goto :CARD_X
```

The first IF command always evaluates as true, because the exit code from the CHOICE command (1, 2 or 3) is *always* greater than or equal to 1. Therefore the GOTO :CARD_S command always executes, presumably not what was desired.

This problem is easily fixed by testing for the *higher* numbered choices first. Alternatively, use the %ERRORLEVEL% variable and make exact IF tests. For example:

```
1. choice /c:SPX Enter network card type
2. if %ERRORLEVEL% EQU 1 goto :CARD_S
3. if %ERRORLEVEL% EQU 3 goto :CARD_X
4. if %ERRORLEVEL% EQU 2 goto :CARD_P
```

The IF ... EQU test performs an exact equality test, and so the GOTO commands execute correctly regardless of the order of the tests.

Another more compact method of branching on the result of a CHOICE command uses carefully constructed label names. For example:

```
1. choice /c:SPX Enter network card type
2. goto :CARD_%ERRORLEVEL%
```

This script code jumps to the label CARD_1 if the choice was S, CARD_2 if the choice was P or CARD_3 if the choice was X. This method is particularly useful if a large number of choices is possible.

Troubleshooting Tip

The version of the CHOICE command in the Windows NT 4.0 Resource Kit supplement 2 has a bug. After executing a CHOICE command, console echo for all line-oriented commands is disabled. To avoid this bug, execute all CHOICE commands within a nested command shell. For example, replace this:

```
choice /n Continue?
```

With this:

```
%COMSPEC% /c choice /n Continue?
```

The exit code of the CHOICE command is correctly passed back from the nested command shell, and console input echo is not disabled in subsequent commands.

COPY

The shell does not offer a command for reading lines of console input. However, the COPY command can be used for this purpose, by reading input from the console into a temporary file. For example:

```
1. echo Enter file name, followed by Ctrl+Z:
2. copy con filename.tmp
```

The COPY command stops reading console input when an end-of-file character (Ctrl+Z) is entered. The temporary file contains the text entered at the keyboard. Typically, this text is then parsed by the FOR command (described in the next section). For example:

```
for /f "delims=~" %i in (filename.tmp) do set FILENAME=%i
```

The FOR Command

The FOR command is probably the most powerful shell script language command. The command is an *iterator*, which repeatedly executes, or iterates, another command. The general syntax of a FOR command is:

```
FOR iterator DO command
```

The *iterator* controls the iteration process. For each step of the iteration, the specific *command* executes once. The *command* can be a compound command, multi-line command, or even a procedure call, allowing multiple commands to be executed at each iteration step.

The *iterator* typically specifies one or more iteration variables. *Iteration variables* are similar to regular variables, but they only exist within the iteration. In interactive mode, iteration variables are specified using a percent sign and a single letter, for example, %I. Within a script, specify the iteration variable by using *two* percent characters, for example, %%I.

Unlike regular environment variables, iteration variables *are* case sensitive: %n and %N are different variables. When the iteration *command* executes, references to iteration variables are replaced with iterator values.

Items that can be iterated by a FOR command include files, directories, numeric ranges, and text files.

The File Iterator FOR Command

The simplest FOR command iterates a set of files. The syntax of this FOR command is:

```
FOR %var IN (set) DO command
```

The %var is the iterator variable. The files to iterate are specified by *set*, which is a file name or wild card file name. The FOR command iterates the current (or specified) directory and executes the *command* for each matching file. For example:

```
C:\>for %I in (*.bat) do echo %I
C:\>echo test.bat
test.bat
C:\>echo master.bat
master.bat
C:\>echo slave.bat
slave.bat
```

This FOR command iterates all .BAT files in the current directory, and executes the ECHO command for each file. Within the ECHO command, the iterator variable %I is replaced with the name of the file. Notice that the FOR command echoes each command before it executes. To eliminate command echo, turn echo off (using the ECHO command), or prefix the *command* with an @ character. For example:

```
C:\>for %I in (*.bat) do @echo %I
test.bat
master.bat
slave.bat
```

By default, the current directory is scanned for matching files. To scan another directory, specify it as part of the *set*. For example:

```
C:\>for %I in (c:\dos\disk*.com) do @echo %I
c:\dos\diskcopy.com
c:\dos\diskcomp.com
```

Iterator variables support the same set of qualifiers as script parameters. (Parameter qualifiers are described in Chapter 3.) For example:

```
C:\>for %I in (c:\dos\disk*.com) do @echo %~nI
diskcopy
diskcomp
```

In this example, the ~n qualifier expands only the file name from the %I variable.

More than one file name is allowed in *set*. Separate each file name with a space, for example:

```
C:\>for %I in (*.com *.exe) do @echo %I
```

This example displays all .COM and .EXE files in the current directory. Since the space character separates file names, enclose a file name with embedded spaces in double quotes. For example:

```
C:\>for %I in ("c:\Program Files\*.*") do @echo %I
```

The Directory Iterator FOR Command

The file iterator FOR command iterates files. The *directory* iterator FOR command iterates directories. The syntax of this FOR command is:

```
FOR /D %var IN (set) DO command
```

The operation of the directory iterator command is identical to the file iterator, except that the *command* executes for each directory that matches the file name *set*. For example:

```
C:\>for /d %I in (c:\winnt\system*) do @echo %I
c:\winnt\system
c:\winnt\system32
```

Troubleshooting Tip

As with all shell commands, the first operation performed on a FOR *command is environment variable substitution. This occurs before the* FOR *command executes, and has certain consequences. For example, this command does* not *work as expected:*

```
C:\>for /d %I in (c:\Apps\*) do @set PATH=%PATH%;%I
```

The intention *of this command is to add all directories in the* C:\APPS *directory to the current search path. However, it does not work, because* %PATH% *is expanded only* once, *before the* FOR *command executes. Then, each iterated* SET *command adds a directory to this fixed path, without accumulating the names.*

To work around this problem, use the FOR *command to call a procedure and execute the* SET *command in the procedure. For example:*

```
1. for /d %%I in (c:\Apps\*) do call :ADDTOPATH %%I
2. goto :EOF
3. :ADDTOPATH
4. set PATH=%PATH%;%1
5. goto :EOF
```

This solution works because the shell rescans the SET *command in the procedure at each iteration, thus allowing the* PATH *variable to correctly accumulate.*

The file and directory FOR commands can be combined. For example:

```
C:\>for /d %I in (c:\winnt\*) do @for %J in ("%I\*.ttf") do @echo %J
```

The first FOR command iterates all sub-directories in the C:\WINNT directory. The second FOR command iterates all .TTF files in each of these directories. Double quotes are used around the second FOR command *set* in case any of the iterated directory names contain spaces. Notice the use of the @ prefix to prevent the ECHO command from being displayed.

The previous example iterated all files in a set of sub-directories, but this search is only one layer deep. Files in sub-directories of sub-directories are not iterated. The tree-iteration FOR command provides a full directory tree iteration. The syntax of this FOR command is:

```
FOR /R [path] %var IN (set) DO command
```

Follow the /R switch with an optional drive and directory path. This FOR command walks the directory tree specified by *path*, and executes the FOR iteration in *each* directory. For example:

```
C:\>for /r c:\ %I in (*.bat *.cmd) do @echo %I
```

This example displays the full path name of all .BAT and .CMD files found anywhere on drive C:.

If the /R switch is not followed by a drive or path, the current drive and directory are assumed. If the *set* is *.*, then all files in all directories of the specified tree are iterated. If the set is a single period, then the special directory name "." in each directory is iterated. For example:

```
C:\>for /r c:\winnt\system32 %I in (.) do @echo %I
c:\winnt\system32\.
c:\winnt\system32\config\.
c:\winnt\system32\drivers\.
Etc.
```

The /R and /D switches can be combined. In this case, the FOR command walks the specified directory tree, and then iterates matching directories in each directory. For example:

```
C:\>for /r c:\winnt /d %I in (system*) do @echo %I
c:\winnt\system
c:\winnt\system32
```

The Numeric Iterator FOR Command

The numeric iterator FOR command increments an iterator variable through a numeric range. It is similar to the FOR command found in other languages such as Basic and C. The syntax of this FOR command is:

```
FOR /L %var IN (start,step,end) DO command
```

The values *start*, *step* and *end* are decimal integers which control the iteration. The iterator variable *var* is initialized to *start*, and then incremented by *step* until the value of the variable is greater than *end*. The *command* executes for each value of the iterator variable. For example:

```
C:\>for /l %I in (1,1,5) do @echo %I
1
2
3
4
5
```

Iteration terminates when the value in the iteration variable is greater than the *end* value (6, in the previous example). This test is made *before* the iteration *command* executes. Therefore, if *start* is greater than *end*, the *command* is not executed at all, and if *start* is equal to *end*, the *command* executes once.

The *step* value can be negative. In this case, the iterator variable decreases in value with each step, and the FOR command ends when the variable value is less than the *end* value. If *start* is less than *end*, the *command* is not executed at all. For example:

```
C:\>for /l %I in (5,-1,3) do @echo %I
5
4
3
```

Numeric iteration is particularly useful when processing arrays. For example, to clear an array to zero:

```
C:\>for /l %I in (1,1,100) do @set ARRAY_%I_=0
```

The Text Parser FOR Command

The text parser FOR command parses text line by line and then executes the iteration command for each line of text. The syntax of this FOR command is:

```
FOR /F ["options"] %var IN (source) DO command
```

The text to parse is specified by *source*, which can be one of the following:

- A set of one or more text file names, separated by spaces. Wild card file names are *not* allowed. The text from each file is read, line by line, and parsed. The *command* executes for each line of text in the source files.

- A string enclosed in double quotes. The string is parsed and the *command* executed once with the parse results. The string can contain environment variables, which are substituted before parsing occurs.

- A command enclosed in single quotes. The source command executes, and all its command output is captured by the FOR command (it is not displayed). This command output is then parsed, line by line, and the *command* executed for each line of output.

Each iteration of the text parser FOR command processes a single line of text from the specified source. Blank lines are skipped by the FOR command; i.e. the iterator *command* is *not* executed for these lines. Non-blank lines are first parsed into individual tokens. A *token* is an arbitrary block of text delimited by special delimiter characters within the line. These tokens are then assigned to one or more iterator variables, and the iterator *command* is then executed using the values of these iterator variables.

To parse a line into tokens, the line is scanned for special delimiter characters. The *delimiters* define how the line is broken into tokens; the default delimiters are space and tab, though others can be specified. For example, this source line contains three tokens:

```
one two three
```

Tokens are numbered, starting at 1 for the left-most token on the line. Once the line is broken into tokens, the tokens are assigned to iterator variables. By default, only the first token is assigned to a variable; all others are discarded. After iterator variable assignment is complete, the iterator *command* executes.

For example, assume the text file USERS.TXT contains:

```
TimHill Admin 400
JohnDoe User 500
KarenVache User 600
```

This example FOR command generates the output shown:

```
C:\>for /f %I in (test.txt) do @echo %I
TimHill
JohnDoe
KarenVache
```

Troubleshooting Tip

The text parser FOR *command has one limitation, which seems to be an oversight by the Windows NT command shell designers. The text parser* FOR *command cannot directly parse the contents of a file if the file name contains one or more spaces. For example:*

```
C:\>for /f %I in (My Document.txt) do @echo %I
```

This FOR *command does not work because the* FOR *command interprets the file set as containing two files:* My *and* Document.txt. *Unfortunately, this cannot be corrected by using double quotes. For example, the following does not work:*

```
C:\>for /f %I in ("My Document.txt") do @echo %I
```

The shell interprets this command as a request to parse the literal text My Document.txt, *rather that the contents of a file by this name. This is one of the few places in the command shell where a file name containing spaces cannot be correctly processed if enclosed in double quotes.*

The work-around for this problem is to parse the text file indirectly. Use the TYPE *command to output the file, and then capture the output of that command. For example:*

```
C:\>for /f %I in ('type "My Document.txt"') do @echo %I
```

Text Parser Options

The default parsing process is modified using the *options* shown in the previous syntax description. Enclose the *options* in double quotes (place all options together in one set of double quotes). Table 4.2 shows the available options. All options are valid regardless of the *source* type.

Table 4.2. Text Parser FOR *Command Options.*

Option	Meaning
eol=c	Specifies *c* as the end-of-line command delimiter character.
skip=nn	Skips *nn* lines of input before starting parsing.
delims=xxx	Specifies *xxx* as the token delimiters to use when parsing each line.
tokens=ttt	Specifies which tokens to assign to iterator variables.

The EOL option specifies an optional end-of-line delimiter character. The parser ignores all text on each line beyond this character. This character therefore acts as a "comment" delimiter character, allowing arbitrary text to be placed on each input line as comments. Lines that begin with a comment delimiter character are treated as blank lines by the parser—they are silently skipped, and the iterator *command* is not executed. Common choices for an end-of-line character are EOL=; or EOL=#. Only a single character is allowed for the end-of-line character.

The SKIP option skips the specified number of input lines before parsing begins. This is a convenient way to skip past header information in text files, or headers generated as part of command output. If multiple text files are specified by *source*, the SKIP option is applied to each file in turn.

The DELIMS option specifies an alternate token delimiter set. The default delimiters are space and tab. Use the DELIMS option to specify an alternate delimiter set. For example, DELIMS=,; uses the semi-colon and comma characters as valid delimiters. In this case, a comma or semi-colon is used to separate tokens on a line. A comma delimiter is often used when parsing comma-delimited files.

Troubleshooting Tip

In Windows NT 4.0, the FOR *command does not correctly process the tab character as a default delimiter. Therefore, if the* source *input contains tab separated tokens, a* DELIMS= *option is needed to explicitly specify a tab character as a separator. Follow the = sign with a single tab character.*

The TOKENS option specifies which tokens are to be assigned to iterator variables. By default, only the first token on each line is assigned to the iterator variable specified in the FOR command (*var*). Use the TOKENS option to explicitly assign specific tokens. Specify a list of tokens to assign, separated by commas.

For example, TOKENS=1,2,4 assigns tokens 1, 2, and 4 to iterator variables, but skips token 3. Ranges of tokens separated by dashes can also be specified. For example, TOKENS=2-4 assigns tokens 2, 3 and 4 but skips token 1. Ranges and lists can be mixed. For example, TOKENS=2,4-6 assigns tokens 2, 4, 5 and 6 only.

If the TOKENS option specifies a single token, its parsed value is assigned to the iterator variable specified in the FOR command. If the TOKENS option specifies multiple tokens, additional iterator variables are automatically created by the FOR command to hold the additional tokens. These are named by incrementing the letter of the specified iterator variable (*var*). For example, if the iterator variable specified is %I, the option TOKENS=2,3 assigns token 2 to %I, and token 3 to %J.

The TOKENS option can also specify the special token number *. This token contains all residual text on the line being parsed (up to the end of the line or the specified EOL character). For example, if the iterator variable is %I, the option TOKENS=2-4* skips token 1, assigns token 2 to %I, assigns token 3 to %J, assigns token 4 to %K, and assigns all residual text after token 4 to %L.

The ordering of token indices in the TOKENS option is not important. Iterator variables are always assigned token values from left to right from the source line. For example, TOKENS=1,2 and TOKENS=2,1 produce identical results; the order or assignment to the two iterator variables is *not* reversed.

For example, suppose the file USERS.TXT contains:

```
; Record of users maximum disk space allowance
TimHill,Admin,400    ; Tim Hill
JaneDoe,User,650     ; Jane
AlexPowers,User,120  ; Alex
```

This example FOR command generates the output shown:

```
C:\>for /f "eol=; tokens=1,3 delims=," %I in (users.txt) do @echo Username=%I
Size=%J
Username=TimHill Size=400
Username=JaneDoe Size=650
Username=AlexPowers Size=120
```

The EOL option eliminates the comments in the file, including the first line, which only contains a comment and is therefore skipped. The DELIMS option specifies a comma separator, and the TOKENS option assigns tokens 1 and 3 only. Token 1 is assigned to the %I variable, and token 3 to the automatically created %J variable. The ECHO command executes three times with the parsed information, resulting in the output shown.

The TOKENS=* option assigns the specified iterator variable all text on the input line, excluding any text after the EOL character (if this option is also specified). This effectively passes *all* processed text lines to the specified command, with the exclusion of blank lines and lines excluded with the SKIP and EOL options. For example:

```
1. C:\>for /f "tokens=*" %I in ('dir *.bat') do @echo %I
2. Volume in drive C is BIGNTFS
3. Volume Serial Number is C095-DBBC
4. Directory of C:\
5. 11/07/97  12:10p                    384 MASTER.BAT
6. 11/07/97  12:08p                    128 SLAVE.BAT
7. 11/05/97  10:46a                    128 TEST.BAT
8. 3 File(s)                640 bytes
9. 571,914,240 bytes free
```

The output of the DIR command is essentially unaltered except that blank lines are eliminated and leading spaces and tabs on lines are eliminated.

Parsing Strings and Command Output

The text parser FOR command can also parse string constants enclosed in double quotes. For example:

```
1. C:\>set ARG=/filename:test.dat
2. C:\>for /f "delims=: tokens=2" %I in ("%ARG%") do @set FILENAME=%I
3. C:\>echo %FILENAME%
4. test.dat
```

This FOR command extracts the file name from the specified argument and stores it in the variable FILENAME. This type of parsing operation lets scripts analyze arguments and extract information using a variety of argument formats.

The output of commands can also be parsed. To parse command output, specify the command to execute as the FOR command *source*. Place the command in *single* quotes. The FOR command executes the specified command and captures its command output, which is *not* displayed. This output is then used as the source for the parsing operation in much the same way that a text file is parsed. For example:

```
C:\>for /f "delims== tokens=2" %I in ('set PROCESSOR_ARCHITECTURE') do @echo %I
x86
```

This use of the FOR command was introduced in Chapter 3 when variable arrays were described. The SET command in single quotes executes, and results in the following command output (which is not actually displayed):

```
PROCESSOR_ARCHITECTURE=x86
```

This single line is then parsed. The DELIMS option breaks the line into two tokens using the = sign as the delimiter. The TOKENS option then assigns the second token (the variable value) to the %I iterator variable.

Any valid shell command can be used as a *source*, even another script. Compound commands are also valid, but the command separators (such as &) must be escaped.

The ability to capture and parse the output of commands is very powerful. Any item of information that can be displayed by a command can also be captured and processed by a script file. For example, the IPCONFIG command displays information about TCP/IP configuration, including the IP address assigned to the NIC. This can be captured and processed using the following command:

```
1. C:\>for /f "delims=: tokens=2" %I in ('ipconfig^¦find "IP Address"') do
@echo %I
2. 207.142.9.99
3. 0.0.0.0
```

The IPCONFIG command executes, and its output is piped to the FIND filter. (The pipe command character is escaped so that it is included in the command to execute.) The FIND command filters lines containing the IP address text. These lines are then parsed by the FOR command, which extracts the IP address from each line and passes it to the ECHO command.

Variable Recursion Using the FOR Command

The FOR command can be used to add recursion to environment variable expansion. As Chapter 3 explained, environment variable substitution is *not* recursive. When variables are substituted into a command, any variable substitutions *within* the variable value are not themselves substituted. For example:

```
1. C:\>set X=
2. C:\>set XX=%X%
3. C:\>set X=Final value
4. C:\>echo %XX%
5. %X%
```

The first SET command deletes variable X. The second command sets variable XX to the value %X%. Since variable X is not defined, the variable XX receives the literal text %X%. The third SET command sets the value of X. The ECHO command shows the lack of recursion; the shell substitutes for the variable %XX% as expected, but the shell does not perform additional substitution. Therefore the ECHO command does not display the contents of variable X, only the text %X%.

The FOR command can be used to provide a general-purpose recursive substitution facility. This script procedure fully expands the RET variable, substituting embedded environment variables to *any* depth:

```
1. rem RESOLVE procedure
2. rem Fully resolves all indirect variable references within RET var, to any depth
3. :RESOLVE
4.     if "%RET%"=="" goto :EOF
```

```
5. set RET1=%RET%
6. for /f "tokens=*" %%I in ('echo %RET%') do set RET=%%I
7. if not "%RET%"=="%RET1%" goto :RESOLVE
8. goto :EOF
```

To see this procedure in operation, add it to this sample script:

```
01. set X=var X
02. set Y=var Y
03. set Z=var Z
04. set XX=%%X%%
05. set YY=%%Y%%
06. set ZZ=%%Z%%
07. set ZZZ=%%ZZ%%
08. set RET=%%XX%% and %%YY%% and %%ZZZ%%
09. echo Before resolve: %RET%
10. call :RESOLVE
11. echo After resolve: %RET%
12. goto :EOF
```

When this script is run, the result is:

```
Before resolve: %XX% and %YY% and %ZZZ%
After resolve: var X and var Y and var Z
```

The initial value of the RET variable contains three indirect references to variables that are not recursively substituted by the first ECHO command. In addition, each of these variables itself contains further indirect variable references. The variable %ZZZ% contains a reference to %ZZ% that in turn references %Z%. The RESOLVE procedure resolves all these references, resulting in the fully substituted output shown.

The RESOLVE procedure operates by repeatedly substituting environment variables via an ECHO command, and then capturing the ECHO command output for additional substitution, if required. The FOR command captures the output of the command ECHO %RET%. This executes the ECHO command, and echoes the current contents of the RET variable. This output is captured by the FOR command, and then the entire output line is parsed into the iterator variable %I. The SET command then assigns this output back into the original RET variable.

The result of the FOR command is thus to provide one level of variable substitution within the RET variable. The FOR command executes in a loop until the value of the RET variable before and after the FOR command execution is identical. This indicates that all variable substitutions are complete.

In the example script, the RET variable starts with:

```
%XX% and %YY% and %ZZZ%
```

After one execution of the FOR command, the new value of the variable is:

```
%X% and %Y% and %ZZ%
```

After the second execution of the FOR command, the new value of the variable is:

```
var X and var Y and %Z%
```

After the third execution of the FOR command, the new value of the variable is:

```
var X and var Y and var Z
```

The FOR command executes once more, and the IF command now detects that there were no more changes to the RET variable, and the procedure exits.

The only restriction on the RESOLVE procedure is that it does not handle recursion loops. If a variable expands to a reference to itself (directly or indirectly), the RESOLVE procedure never exits. This usually indicates a bug in the script, and one solution is to count the number of passes around the RESOLVE loop. If the number of passes reaches a high number (say, 100), then RESOLVE should probably abort and display an error message.

Recursive variable substitution enables scripts to use variable *indirection*. That is, a variable contains, instead of a value, the name of *another* variable that contains a value. Examples of variable indirection include arrays and pointers, both of which are the foundations of nearly all advanced programming techniques. Many of the example scripts in Part III of this book make use of the RESOLVE procedure.

Part **II**

Real-World Scripting

Chapter **5**

A Scripting Toolkit

- **Building scripts**
  Learn the tools and techniques needed to construct robust scripts.

- **Standard script skeleton**
  This section provides a complete script skeleton that can be used as the starting point for any new script project.

- **Standard library skeleton**
  Complete libraries of script procedures can be constructed using the library skeleton described in this section.

- **An example library**
  This sample library provides many useful procedures that are used by the other sample scripts in this book.

Building Scripts

This chapter provides guidelines for using tools to build scripts, and also provides two complete script *skeletons*: templates that can be used as starting points for customized scripts. In addition, the _MTPLIB.BAT script library source code is presented and described in detail. This library contains many useful procedures that can be accessed directly from custom scripts. The sample scripts of Chapter 6 and 7 also make extensive use of the _MTPLIB.BAT script library.

> **Tip**
>
> *The sample scripts in this chapter are available for downloading from the MTP web site at http://www.macmillantech.com.*

Because scripts are text files, the only real tool needed when developing a script is a good text file editor. However, certain special script requirements place two specific constraints on this editor:

- First, some scripts require trailing spaces at the end of a line (for example, the PJCOUNT.BAT script of Chapter 6). Therefore, check that the editor does not automatically strip trailing white space from lines.

- Second, a FOR command bug sometimes requires literal tab characters in the script (for example, the _MTPLIB.BAT script of this chapter). Therefore, make sure that any editor you use does not convert tab characters into spaces (or vice versa).

The Windows Notepad editor correctly handles both trailing spaces and literal tab characters.

The only other (and most important) tool needed to develop a script is good programming discipline. Scripts are often seen as "quick and dirty" solutions to one-off problems. Typically, however, the quick and dirty script takes on a life of its own and is modified and enhanced until it has far outgrown its humble origins. More robust and manageable scripts result when each script, however small, is treated as a simple programming project. The skeleton scripts in this chapter are good starting points for any script and encourage a structured approach to script creation.

The command shell does not offer any built-in script debug facilities, other than the capability to enable and disable script command echo (using the ECHO command). The following techniques may prove helpful when debugging scripts:

- Use the standard preamble shown in the skeleton scripts in this chapter, and disable/enable script tracing using the ECHO variable.

- Use the TRACE variable shown in the skeleton scripts in this chapter.

- Add ECHO commands when developing a script to show intermediate variable values, control flow, and exit codes (via %ERRORLEVEL%). These can be removed when development is complete.

- Add PAUSE commands before a critical part of a script, so that the script can be stopped if something appears to be wrong. These can be removed when development is complete.

- Add ECHO commands to preview complex or "dangerous" commands (such as a command which deletes lots of files) before they are executed. Add a PAUSE command after the ECHO command but before the actual execution of the command.

Most of these techniques are highlighted in the sample script presented in this chapter.

Standard Script Skeleton

Figure 5.1 shows the SKELETON.BAT script. This script does not actually do anything, but instead provides a complete template for script development.

Follow these steps to create a new script based on the SKELETON.BAT template:

1. Copy SKELETON.BAT to a new script file.

2. Add ECHO commands to the HELP procedure to display brief on-line help information.

3. Add the script program logic to the MAIN procedure.

4. If necessary, call any external library INIT procedures following the call to the _MTPLIB.BAT INIT procedure.

5. Create additional procedures used by MAIN following the end of the MAIN procedure and before the DOSEXIT label.

Although SKELETON.BAT does not do anything, it does bring together many of the structural suggestions mentioned in Part I of this book into a complete, ready-to-use script. After some initial setup, the script calls a procedure named MAIN at line 15, and passes to this procedure all of the command line arguments. The MAIN procedure should contain the program logic of the script. When the MAIN procedure exits, the entire script exits. Template code surrounding the MAIN procedure handles all of the logic needed to make the script a "good citizen"—a local scope for variables is created, and the current state is saved.

Before the MAIN procedure is called, the template logic checks to see if the first argument is either /? or /HELP (lines 13 and 14). In this case, the HELP procedure is called instead of MAIN. Typically, this procedure displays a short help message describing the use of the script.

The first two lines of SKELETON.BAT (shown in Figure 5.1) provide the command echo management discussed in Part I. When the script is executed, if the variable ECHO has the value ON, then script command echo is enabled. If the variable ECHO has the value OFF or is not defined, then script command echo is disabled.

The third line checks the operating system type. If the script is run on an OS other than Windows NT, the script jumps immediately to the DOSEXIT label.

This label, located at the very end of the script, simply displays a warning message and then ends script execution by "falling off" the end of the file. Thus, if a script based on this skeleton is run on an OS other than Windows NT, it simply displays:

```
This script requires Windows NT
```

One implication of this code is that the first three lines of the script and all the lines following the DOSEXIT label must be syntax-compatible with MS-DOS, Windows 3.1, Windows 95, and OS/2. This is why, for example, there is no colon character preceding the DOSEXIT label on line 3. Once past that line, however, all of the syntax enhancements provided by Windows NT can be safely used.

```
01. @echo OFF
02. @if not "%ECHO%"=="" echo %ECHO%
03. @if not "%OS%"=="Windows_NT" goto DOSEXIT
04. rem $Workfile: skeleton.bat $ $Revision: 2 $ $Date: 12/04/97 9:51a $
05. rem $Archive: /TimH/Pubs/Books/Macmillan/Windows NT
    Scripting/Scripts/skeleton.bat $
06.
07. rem Set local scope and call MAIN procedure
08. setlocal & pushd & set RET=
09.     set SCRIPTNAME=%~n0
10.     set SCRIPTPATH=%~f0
11.     if "%DEBUG%"=="1" (set TRACE=echo) else (set TRACE=rem)
12.     call _mtplib :INIT %SCRIPTPATH%
13.     if /i {%1}=={/help} (call :HELP %2) & (goto :HELPEXIT)
14.     if /i {%1}=={/?} (call :HELP %2) & (goto :HELPEXIT)
15.     call :MAIN %*
16.     :HELPEXIT
17. popd & endlocal & set RET=%RET%
18. goto :EOF
19.
20. rem //////////////////////////////////////////////////////////////////
21. rem HELP procedure
22. rem Display brief on-line help message
23. rem
24. :HELP
25. if defined TRACE %TRACE% [proc %0 %*]
26.     rem Put help message here...
27.
28. goto :EOF
29.
30. rem //////////////////////////////////////////////////////////////////
31. rem MAIN procedure
32. rem
```

```
33. :MAIN
34. if defined TRACE %TRACE% [proc %0 %*]
35.     rem Put main script code here...
36.
37. goto :EOF
38.
39. rem ////////////////////////////////////////////////////////////////////
40. rem Additional procedures go here...
41.
42. rem These must be the FINAL LINES in the script...
43. :DOSEXIT
44. echo This script requires Windows NT
45.
46. rem ////////////////////////////////////////////////////////////////////
```

Figure 5.1. *The SKELETON.BAT script*

Following the initial setup lines is the main script body. In outline, this is constructed as follows:

```
1. setlocal & pushd & set RET=
2.    .
3.    .
4. popd & endlocal & set RET=%RET%
5. goto :EOF
```

The first line creates a local scope for variables as well as the current drive and directory (via the SETLOCAL and PUSHD commands). After the script body, a corresponding set of commands, ENDLOCAL and POPD, close the local scope. This makes the script "well behaved" and preserves the current drive and directory, as well as all environment variables. It also means that code within the script is free to alter any variable, as any changes made are automatically restored when the script completes.

The RET variable is also initialized by the script body code, and the variable tunneling technique described in Chapter 3 is used to pass the RET value back from the script (SET RET=%RET% on the same line as ENDLOCAL). Thus, after the script executes, the only change in the environment will be the RET value. This means that the SKELETON.BAT script can be used to develop complete script procedures that can be called from other scripts and return results via the RET variable.

The main script body between the local scope "brackets" described previously is as follows:

```
1. set SCRIPTNAME=%~n0
2. set SCRIPTPATH=%~f0
3. if "%DEBUG%"=="1" (set TRACE=echo) else (set TRACE=rem)
```

```
4. call _mtplib :INIT %SCRIPTPATH%
5. if /i {%1}=={/help} (call :HELP %2) & (goto :HELPEXIT)
6. if /i {%1}=={/?} (call :HELP %2) & (goto :HELPEXIT)
7. call :MAIN %*
8. :HELPEXIT
```

The first two lines set two standard variables: SCRIPTNAME and SCRIPTPATH. The SCRIPTNAME variable contains the name of the script (SKELETON, in this case). Uses for the script name include constructing data file names (see the ANI-MAL.BAT script of Chapter 7), and choosing a Registry key name (see the REPL.BAT script of Chapter 7). The second variable, SCRIPTPATH, contains the full path to the script (even if the full path was not entered on the command line). These two variables are set because the program logic in the MAIN procedure does not have direct access to the script name. (The %0 parameter within the MAIN procedure has the value :MAIN, regardless of the script name.)

The third line in the main script body provides trace facilities. The variable TRACE is either set to echo or rem depending upon the value of the DEBUG variable. If the DEBUG variable has the value 1 before the script is executed, then TRACE is defined as echo. If the DEBUG variables has another value or is not defined, then TRACE is defined as rem.

The purpose of the TRACE variable is to provide automatic trace functionality within a script. Consider this script statement:

```
%TRACE% Computing total size...
```

If the DEBUG variable is *not* 1, the TRACE variable is rem, and the statement expands to:

```
rem Computing total size...
```

Obviously, the REM command does nothing. If, however, the DEBUG variable is 1, the TRACE variable is echo, and the statement expands to:

```
echo Computing total size...
```

This displays the text in the console window. Thus, if DEBUG is 1, all %TRACE% prefixed commands display trace information. If DEBUG is not 1, no output is displayed. This allows script trace commands to be embedded throughout a script and enabled or disabled just by changing the DEBUG variable before running the script. All the sample scripts use this technique to display the names of called procedures. Each procedure starts with this line:

```
if defined TRACE %TRACE% [proc %0 %*]
```

This displays the name of the procedure (%0) and all the procedure arguments. To ensure robustness, the line first checks that the variable TRACE is defined (using the IF DEFINED command) before executing the trace statement.

Following the TRACE setup command are one or more library initialization procedure calls. Only one script library, _MTPLIB.BAT, is initialized by the sample skeleton script. If the script uses other libraries, the INIT procedure for each library should be called here. The use of script libraries and the INIT procedure are discussed in Chapter 4.

Finally, when all libraries have been initialized, the main script logic is invoked. Depending upon the first argument, either the HELP or the MAIN procedure is called. The MAIN procedure is passed all script arguments. The HELP procedure is passed only the second argument, allowing a help context to be requested by passing an additional argument following the /? or /HELP switch.

Standard Library Skeleton

Figure 5.2 shows the _LIBSKEL.BAT library script. This library has no function other than to provide a complete template for script library development.

Follow these steps to create a new library based on the _LIBSKEL.BAT template:

1. Copy _LIBSKEL.BAT to a new script file.

2. Change the library name and version number in the first ECHO command after the preamble.

3. Add any necessary library setup logic to the INIT procedure.

4. Add all desired library procedures following the INIT procedure.

5. Place the script library in a directory that is part of the system (not the user) PATH. This ensures that the library is available to all scripts, even if the script is run by the AT command.

6. Document the library! Script logic is not easy to follow, and can be quite obscure even to the script author six months after it was written.

Like SKELETON.BAT, the _LIBSKEL.BAT library script does not do anything, but it does implement the suggestions for script libraries described in Chapter 4. The script contains a *procedure dispatcher* (lines 13 to 16), which automatically vectors to the correct procedure in the library. It also contains an empty INIT procedure, where library initialization code can be added. By convention, any script that makes use of the procedures in a script library should call the INIT procedure in that library first. This allows the library to initialize any resources it needs.

Creating procedures for script libraries is identical to creating procedures for regular scripts. However, as any other script can call the procedures in a script library, some care must be taken to ensure that library procedures are well behaved. Some things to watch out for include:

- Avoid changing state information, such as the current drive or directory (unless that is a desired function of the library procedure). If it is necessary to alter these, use PUSHD and POPD to preserve the caller state.

- Avoid changing global variables. Create a local scope using SETLOCAL and ENDLOCAL if extensive use is made of variables. If only one or two variables are needed, use names prefixed by the name of the library (such as _MYLIB_T1), so that the names do not collide with those used in the caller script.

- Pass return results back to the calling procedure in the RET variable. Pass additional results in additional RET variables (such as RETX, RETV). Document the return results carefully. It is good practice to initialize the RET variable(s) to a default return value immediately upon entry to a procedure.

- Pass arguments to the procedures as parameters. Avoid passing arguments in variables unless there is a special need (for example, if the argument contains a large amount of text). If arguments *are* passed in variables, document this carefully. Also document any standard variables used by the procedure (such as TEMP or PATH).

- Define label names carefully. Labels are global within a script file, so using a label such as :LOOP isn't particularly friendly, as it will quite likely collide with another label of the same name elsewhere in the library. Within a procedure, prefix all label names with the procedure name. (This advice applies equally to procedures in a regular script.)

The _LIBSKEL.BAT script begins with the same preamble lines as the SKELE-TON.BAT script, and ends with the same DOSEXIT label and code. The first line following the preamble checks to see if any arguments are present. If not, the script displays the library name and version information and then exits. If one or more arguments are present, the script falls through into the dispatch code.

As explained in Chapter 4, a library procedure is called using an indirect CALL command, which follows the CALL command with the library name, procedure name, and then procedure arguments. For example:

```
call _libskel :MYPROC arg1 arg2
```

Here, the procedure MYPROC in the _LIBSKEL.BAT library is called with arguments arg1 and arg2. The CALL command calls the _LIBSKEL.BAT library, passing :MYPROC, arg1 and arg2 as three arguments. Eventually, the dispatch code in _LIBSKEL.BAT is reached. This code is:

```
1. set _PROC=%1
2. shift /1
3. goto %_PROC%
```

The first line of the dispatch code saves the first argument (the procedure name, in this case :MYPROC) in the _PROC variable. The second line then shifts the arguments, discarding the procedure name and moving all other arguments down one place in the argument list. In the example above, this moves arg1 to %1 and arg2 to %2. This is where these arguments are expected by the procedure. Finally, the third line jumps to the label specified by the _PROC variable (that is, the procedure name specified in the original CALL command). The result of this processing is that the procedure specified in the original CALL command is called and passed the arguments specified.

The _LIBSKEL.BAT script provides one sample procedure, :CHECKX86, which sets the RET variable to 0 or 1 depending upon whether the script is run on an Intel x86 platform or not. This sample procedure also shows the use of the TRACE variable described previously.

```
01. @echo OFF
02. @if not "%ECHO%"=="" echo %ECHO%
03. @if not "%OS%"=="Windows_NT" goto DOSEXIT
04. rem $Workfile: _libskel.bat $ $Revision: 2 $ $Date: 12/04/97 9:51a $
05. rem $Archive: /TimH/Pubs/Books/Macmillan/Windows NT
Scripting/Scripts/_libskel.bat $
06.
07. rem If no arguments, show version information and exit
08. if "%1"=="" (
09.     (echo Script Library Skeleton [%0] $Revision: 2 $)
10.     (goto :EOF)
11. )
12.
13. rem At least one argument, so dispatch to procedure
14. set _PROC=%1
15. shift /1
16. goto %_PROC%
17.
18. rem ///////////////////////////////////////////////////////////////////////
19. rem INIT procedure
20. rem Must be called in local state before other procs are used
21. rem
22. :INIT
23. if defined TRACE %TRACE% [proc %0 %*]
24.
25. goto :EOF
26.
27. rem ///////////////////////////////////////////////////////////////////////
```

```
28. rem CHECKX86 procedure
29. rem Sample procedure verifies that we are running on an Intel CPU
30. rem
31. rem Returns:    RET=1 if on x86, else RET=0
32. rem
33. :CHECKX86
34. if defined TRACE %TRACE% [proc %0 %*]
35.    if /i "%PROCESSOR_ARCHITECTURE%"=="x86" (set RET=1) else (set RET=0)
36. if defined TRACE %TRACE% [proc %0 returns {%RET%}]
37. goto :EOF
38.
39. rem ///////////////////////////////////////////////////////////////////////
40. rem Additional procedures go here...
41.
42. rem These must be the FINAL LINES in the script...
43. :DOSEXIT
44. echo This script requires Windows NT
45.
46. rem ///////////////////////////////////////////////////////////////////////
```

Figure 5.2. *The _LIBSKEL.BAT script.*

An Example Library

The _MTPLIB.BAT script library shown in Figure 5.3 is a complete sample library based upon the _LIBSKEL.BAT script library described in the previous section. _MTPLIB.BAT contains a number of useful procedures that are used by many of the sample scripts in Chapters 6 and 7, and can also be used by other scripts as desired. To use this library, place it in a directory that is on the system PATH. The SKELETON.BAT script already contains code to call the INIT procedure of this library.

The _MTPLIB.BAT library contains procedures to assist in the following tasks:

- Deleting multiple variables (by variable prefix).
- Parsing a command line for switches and positional arguments.
- Saving and restoring variables to/from the Registry.
- Generating pseudo-random numbers.
- Resolving recursive (nested and indirect) variable references.
- Reading a line of user input to a variable.

- Synchronizing scripts using lock files.

- Generating unique temporary file names.

Tip

The REGGETM *and* REGGETU *procedures in the* _MTPLIB.BAT *library must be entered carefully. The output of the* REG *command is tab-delimited, and (unfortunately) a bug in the* FOR *command means that the* delims= *value for the* FOR *command delimiters must be explicitly set to a tab character. To do this, enter the* delims= *text, and immediately follow the* = *sign with a literal Tab key. The Notepad editor correctly enters literal tab characters into the script file.*

Should _MTPLIB.BAT *ever be edited by an editor that converts tabs to spaces, the functionality of the* REGGETM *and* REGGETU *procedures will be damaged.*

```
001. @echo OFF
002. @if not "%ECHO%"=="" echo %ECHO%
003. @if not "%OS%"=="Windows_NT" goto DOSEXIT
004. rem $Workfile: _mtplib.bat $ $Revision: 2 $ $Date: 12/04/97 9:51a $
005. rem $Archive: /TimH/Pubs/Books/Macmillan/Windows NT
     Scripting/Scripts/_mtplib.bat $
006.
007. rem If no arguments, show version information and exit
008. if "%1"=="" (
009.    (echo Script MTP Script Library [%0] $Revision: 2 $)
010.    (goto :EOF)
011.)
012.
013. rem At least one argument, so dispatch to procedure
014. set _PROC=%1
015. shift /1
016. goto %_PROC%
017.
018. rem ////////////////////////////////////////////////////////////////////
019. rem INIT procedure
020. rem Must be called in local state before other procs are used
021. rem
022. :INIT
023. if defined TRACE %TRACE% [proc %0 %*]
024.
025. goto :EOF
026.
027. rem ////////////////////////////////////////////////////////////////////
```

```
028. rem VARDEL procedure
029. rem Delete multiple variables by prefix
030. rem
031. rem Arguments:    %1=variable name prefix
032. rem
033. :VARDEL
034. if defined TRACE %TRACE% [proc %0 %*]
035.     for /f "tokens=1 delims==" %%I in ('set %1 2^>nul') do set %%I=
036. goto :EOF
037.
038. rem ///////////////////////////////////////////////////////////////////
039. rem PARSECMDLINE procedure
040. rem Parse a command line into switches and args
041. rem
042. rem Arguments:    CMDLINE=command text to parse
043. rem        %1=0 for new parse (def) or 1 to append to existing
044. rem
045. rem Returns:    CMDARG_n=arguments, CMDSW_n=switches
046. rem         CMDARGCOUNT=arg count, CMDSWCOUNT=switch count
047. rem         RET=total number of args processed
048. rem
049. :PARSECMDLINE
050. if defined TRACE %TRACE% [proc %0 %*]
051.     if not {%1}=={1} (
052.         (call :VARDEL CMDARG_)
053.         (call :VARDEL CMDSW_)
054.         (set /a CMDARGCOUNT=0)
055.         (set /a CMDSWCOUNT=0)
056.     )
057.     set /a RET=0
058.     call :PARSECMDLINE1 %CMDLINE%
059.     set _MTPLIB_T1=
060. goto :EOF
061. :PARSECMDLINE1
062.     if {%1}=={} goto :EOF
063.     set _MTPLIB_T1=%1
064.     set _MTPLIB_T1=%_MTPLIB_T1:"=%
065.     set /a RET+=1
066.     shift /1
067.     if "%_MTPLIB_T1:~0,1%"=="/" goto :PARSECMDLINESW
068.     if "%_MTPLIB_T1:~0,1%"=="-" goto :PARSECMDLINESW
069.     set /a CMDARGCOUNT+=1
070.     set CMDARG_%CMDARGCOUNT%=%_MTPLIB_T1%
071.     goto :PARSECMDLINE1
072.     :PARSECMDLINESW
073.     set /a CMDSWCOUNT+=1
074.     set CMDSW_%CMDSWCOUNT%=%_MTPLIB_T1%
075.     goto :PARSECMDLINE1
076. goto :EOF
```

```
077.
078. rem ////////////////////////////////////////////////////////////////////
079. rem GETARG procedure
080. rem Get a parsed argument by index
081. rem
082. rem Arguments:    %1=argument index (1st arg has index 1)
083. rem
084. rem Returns:    RET=argument text or empty if no argument
085. rem
086. :GETARG
087. if defined TRACE %TRACE% [proc %0 %*]
088.     set RET=
089.     if %1 GTR %CMDARGCOUNT% goto :EOF
090.     if %1 EQU 0 goto :EOF
091.     if not defined CMDARG_%1 goto :EOF
092.     set RET=%%CMDARG_%1%%
093.     call :RESOLVE
094. goto :EOF
095.
096. rem ////////////////////////////////////////////////////////////////////
097. rem GETSWITCH procedure
098. rem Get a switch argument by index
099. rem
100. rem Arguments:    %1=switch index (1st switch has index 1)
101. rem
102. rem Returns:    RET=switch text or empty if none
103. rem           RETV=switch value (after colon char) or empty
104. rem
105. :GETSWITCH
106. if defined TRACE %TRACE% [proc %0 %*]
107.     (set RET=) & (set RETV=)
108.     if %1 GTR %CMDSWCOUNT% goto :EOF
109.     if %1 EQU 0 goto :EOF
110.     if not defined CMDSW_%1 goto :EOF
111.     set RET=%%CMDSW_%1%%
112.     call :RESOLVE
113.     for /f "tokens=1* delims=:" %%I in ("%RET%") do (set RET=%%I) & (set
        RETV=%%J)
114. goto :EOF
115.
116. rem ////////////////////////////////////////////////////////////////////
117. rem FINDSWITCH procedure
118. rem Finds the index of the named switch
119. rem
120. rem Arguments:    %1=switch name
121. rem           %2=search start index (def: 1)
122. rem
123. rem Returns:    RET=index (0 if not found)
124. rem           RETV=switch value (text after colon)
```

```
125. rem
126. :FINDSWITCH
127. if defined TRACE %TRACE% [proc %0 %*]
128.     if {%2}=={} (set /a _MTPLIB_T4=1) else (set /a _MTPLIB_T4=%2)
129.     :FINDSWITCHLOOP
130.         call :GETSWITCH %_MTPLIB_T4%
131.         if "%RET%"=="" (set RET=0) & (goto :FINDSWITCHEND)
132.         if /i "%RET%"=="%1" (set RET=%_MTPLIB_T4%) & (goto :FINDSWITCHEND)
133.         set /a _MTPLIB_T4+=1
134.     goto :FINDSWITCHLOOP
135.     :FINDSWITCHEND
136.     set _MTPLIB_T4=
137. goto :EOF
138.
139. rem //////////////////////////////////////////////////////////////////////
140. rem REGSETM and REGSETU procedures
141. rem Set registry values from variables
142. rem
143. rem Arguments:    %1=reg context (usually script name)
144. rem           %2=variable to save (or prefix to save set of vars)
145. rem
146. :REGSETM
147. if defined TRACE %TRACE% [proc %0 %*]
148.     for /f "tokens=1* delims==" %%I in ('set %2 2^>nul') do call :REGSET1
         HKLM %1 %%I "%%J"
149. goto :EOF
150. :REGSETU
151. if defined TRACE %TRACE% [proc %0 %*]
152.     for /f "tokens=1* delims==" %%I in ('set %2 2^>nul') do call :REGSET1
         HKCU %1 %%I "%%J"
153. goto :EOF
154. :REGSET1
155.     set _MTPLIB_T10=%4
156.     set _MTPLIB_T10=%_MTPLIB_T10:\=\\%
157.     reg add %1\Software\MTPScriptContexts\%2\%3=%_MTPLIB_T10% >nul
158.     reg update %1\Software\MTPScriptContexts\%2\%3=%_MTPLIB_T10% >nul
159. goto :EOF
160.
161. rem //////////////////////////////////////////////////////////////////////
162. rem REGGETM and REGGETU procedures
163. rem Get registry value or values to variables
164. rem
165. rem Arguments:    %1=reg context (usually script name)
166. rem           %2=variable to restore (def: restore entire context)
167. rem
168. rem Returns:     RET=value of last variable loaded
169. rem
170. rem WARNING:     The "delims" value in the FOR commands below is a TAB
```

```
171. rem        character, followed by a space. If this file is edited by
172. rem        an editor which converts tabs to spaces, this procedure
173. rem        will break!!!!!
174. rem
175. :REGGETM
176. if defined TRACE %TRACE% [proc %0 %*]
177.     for /f "delims=     tokens=2*" %%I in ('reg query
         HKLM\Software\MTPScriptContexts\%1\%2 ^¦find "REG_SZ"') do call
         :REGGETM1 %%I "%%J"
178. goto :EOF
179. :REGGETU
180. if defined TRACE %TRACE% [proc %0 %*]
181.     for /f "delims=     tokens=2*" %%I in ('reg query
         HKCU\Software\MTPScriptContexts\%1\%2 ^¦find "REG_SZ"') do call
         :REGGETM1 %%I "%%J"
182. goto :EOF
183. :REGGETM1
184.     set _MTPLIB_T10=%2
185.     set _MTPLIB_T10=%_MTPLIB_T10:\\=\%
186.     set _MTPLIB_T10=%_MTPLIB_T10:"=%
187.     set %1=%_MTPLIB_T10%
188.     set RET=%_MTPLIB_T10%
189. goto :EOF
190.
191. rem ///////////////////////////////////////////////////////////////////
192. rem REGDELM and REGDELU procedures
193. rem Delete registry values
194. rem
195. rem Arguments:    %1=reg context (usually script name)
196. rem              %2=variable to delete (def: delete entire context)
197. rem
198. :REGDELM
199. if defined TRACE %TRACE% [proc %0 %*]
200.     call :GETTEMPNAME
201.     echo y >%RET%
202.     reg delete HKLM\Software\MTPScriptContexts\%1\%2 <%RET% >nul
203.     del %RET%
204. goto :EOF
205. :REGDELU
206. if defined TRACE %TRACE% [proc %0 %*]
207.     call :GETTEMPNAME
208.     echo y >%RET%
209.     reg delete HKCU\Software\MTPScriptContexts\%1\%2 <%RET% >nul
210.     del %RET%
211. goto :EOF
212.
213.
214. rem ///////////////////////////////////////////////////////////////////
```

```
215. rem SRAND procedure
216. rem Seed the random number generator
217. rem
218. rem Arguments:    %1=new seed value
219. rem
220. :SRAND
221. if defined TRACE %TRACE% [proc %0 %*]
222.     set /a _MTPLIB_NEXTRAND=%1
223. goto :EOF
224.
225. rem ////////////////////////////////////////////////////////////////////
226. rem RAND procedure
227. rem Get next random number (0 to 32767)
228. rem
229. rem Returns:    RET=next random number
230. rem
231. :RAND
232. if defined TRACE %TRACE% [proc %0 %*]
233.     if not defined _MTPLIB_NEXTRAND set /a _MTPLIB_NEXTRAND=1
234.     set /a _MTPLIB_NEXTRAND=_MTPLIB_NEXTRAND * 214013 + 2531011
235.     set /a RET=_MTPLIB_NEXTRAND ^>^> 16 ^& 0x7FFF
236. goto :EOF
237.
238. rem ////////////////////////////////////////////////////////////////////
239. rem RESOLVE procedure
240. rem Fully resolve all indirect variable references in RET variable
241. rem
242. rem Arguments:    RET=value to resolve
243. rem
244. rem Returns:    RET=as passed in, with references resolved
245. rem
246. :RESOLVE
247. if defined TRACE %TRACE% [proc %0 %*]
248.     :RESOLVELOOP
249.         if "%RET%"=="" goto :EOF
250.         set RET1=%RET%
251.         for /f "tokens=*" %%I in ('echo %RET%') do set RET=%%I
252.     if not "%RET%"=="%RET1%" goto :RESOLVELOOP
253. goto :EOF
254.
255. rem ////////////////////////////////////////////////////////////////////
256. rem GETINPUTLINE procedure
257. rem Get a single line of keyboard input
258. rem
259. rem Returns:    RET=Entered line
260. rem
261. :GETINPUTLINE
262. if defined TRACE %TRACE% [proc %0 %*]
```

```
263.    call :GETTEMPNAME
264.    set _MTPLIB_T1=%RET%
265.    copy con "%_MTPLIB_T1%" >nul
266.    for /f "tokens=*" %%I in ('type "%_MTPLIB_T1%"') do set RET=%%I
267.    if exist "%_MTPLIB_T1%" del "%_MTPLIB_T1%"
268.    set _MTPLIB_T1=
269. goto :EOF
270.
271. rem ////////////////////////////////////////////////////////////////
272. rem GETSYNCFILE procedure
273. rem Get a sync file name (file will not exist)
274. rem
275. rem Returns:    RET=Name of sync file to use
276. rem
277. :GETSYNCFILE
278. if defined TRACE %TRACE% [proc %0 %*]
279.    call :GETTEMPNAME
280. goto :EOF
281.
282. rem ////////////////////////////////////////////////////////////////
283. rem SETSYNCFILE procedure
284. rem Flag sync event (creates the file)
285. rem
286. rem Arguments:    %1=sync filename to flag
287. rem
288. :SETSYNCFILE
289. if defined TRACE %TRACE% [proc %0 %*]
290.    echo . >%1
291. goto :EOF
292.
293. rem ////////////////////////////////////////////////////////////////
294. rem DELSYNCFILE procedure
295. rem Delete sync file
296. rem
297. rem Arguments:    %1=sync filename
298. rem
299. :DELSYNCFILE
300. if defined TRACE %TRACE% [proc %0 %*]
301.    if exist %1 del %1
302. goto :EOF
303.
304. rem ////////////////////////////////////////////////////////////////
305. rem WAITSYNCFILE
306. rem Wait for sync file to flag
307. rem
308. rem Arguments:    %1=sync filename
309. rem          %2=timeout in seconds (def: 60)
310. rem
```

```
311. rem Returns:    RET=Timeout remaining, or 0 if timeout
312. rem
313. :WAITSYNCFILE
314. if defined TRACE %TRACE% [proc %0 %*]
315.     if {%2}=={} (set /a RET=60) else (set /a RET=%2)
316.     if exist %1 goto :EOF
317.     :WAITSYNCFILELOOP
318.         sleep 1
319.         set /a RET-=1
320.     if %RET% GTR 0 if not exist %1 goto :WAITSYNCFILELOOP
321. goto :EOF
322.
323. rem ///////////////////////////////////////////////////////////////////
324. rem GETTEMPNAME procedure
325. rem Create a temporary file name
326. rem
327. rem Returns:    RET=Temporary file name
328. rem
329. :GETTEMPNAME
330. if defined TRACE %TRACE% [proc %0 %*]
331.     if not defined _MTPLIB_NEXTTEMP set /a _MTPLIB_NEXTTEMP=1
332.     if defined TEMP (
333.         (set RET=%TEMP%)
334.     ) else if defined TMP (
335.         (set RET=%TMP%)
336.     ) else (set RET=%SystemRoot%)
337.     :GETTEMPNAMELOOP
338.         set /a _MTPLIB_NEXTTEMP=_MTPLIB_NEXTTEMP * 214013 + 2531011
339.         set /a _MTPLIB_T1=_MTPLIB_NEXTTEMP ^>^> 16 ^& 0x7FFF
340.         set RET=%RET%\~SH%_MTPLIB_T1%.tmp
341.     if exist "%RET%" goto :GETTEMPNAMELOOP
342.     set _MTPLIB_T1=
343. goto :EOF
344.
345. rem These must be the FINAL LINES in the script...
346. :DOSEXIT
347. echo This script requires Windows NT
348.
349. rem ///////////////////////////////////////////////////////////////////
```

Figure 5.3. *The _MTPLIB.BAT script library*

Each procedure available in the _MTPLIB.BAT library is described in the following sections. The procedures are described in the same order that they appear in the script.

VARDEL

Deletes a set of variables by prefix.

Syntax

```
CALL _MTPLIB :VARDEL prefix
```

Arguments

prefix   Prefix of variables to be deleted.

Description

The VARDEL procedure deletes one or more environment variables sharing a common *prefix*. For example, specifying a prefix of JOB_ deletes all variables that begin with JOB_. One common use of VARDEL is deleting all members of an array by specifying the array name as the *prefix*.

Implementation

VARDEL executes a SET command (line 35) with the specified *prefix* without an equal sign following it. This command displays all variables that match this prefix (in the form *name=value*). The output of this SET command is captured by a FOR command and parsed. Each line is parsed for the first token, using = as the delimiter, which yields the variable name. The FOR command then executes the command SET *name=* for each parsed name, thus deleting each variable which matches the *prefix*.

The command error output of the first SET command is redirected to the NUL device (in other words, discarded). This takes care of the situation in which *no* variables match the specified *prefix* (in this case, the SET command displays an error message, which is captured and discarded by this redirection). Notice the use of the escape character (^) before the redirection symbol in the SET command. This ensures that the redirection is processed when the SET command is executed, not when the FOR command is executed.

PARSECMDLINE

Parses a command line(s).

Syntax

```
CALL _MTPLIB :PARSECMDLINE [append]
```

Arguments

CMDLINE   Contains the text of the command line to parse.

append   0 (the default) to perform a new parse, 1 to append to existing parse.

Returns

RET	Total number of arguments parsed.
CMDARGCOUNT	Count of arguments in CMDARG_*n* array.
CMDARG_*n*	Command arguments (CMDARG_1 contains first argument).
CMDSWCOUNT	Count of switches in CMDSW_*n* array.
CMDSW_*n*	Command switches (CMDSW_1 contains the first switch).

Description

The PARSECMDLINE procedure parses a command line, separating the arguments into switches and positional arguments. In most Windows NT commands, a *switch* is a command argument preceded by a / or - character. Switches can generally appear anywhere on a command line, intermixed with regular (positional) arguments. Switches can also contain optional *values*, which follow the switch and are separated by a colon. For example,

```
/SRC:\\transit\files
```

is the /SRC switch with the value \\transit\files.

The PARSECMDLINE procedure parses a command line and separates the arguments into two distinct arrays of arguments: switches and positional arguments. Once the command line has been parsed, the parsed arguments can be accessed directly in the arrays or indirectly via the GETARG, GETSWITCH, and FINDSWITCH procedures.

The command line to parse is passed in the CMDLINE variable, not as an argument. Typically, this variable is initialized with the %* parameter (which contains the entire command line). However, it can also be initialized from other variables or from the contents of a data file. This allows PARSECMDLINE to parse command text from many different sources.

PARSECMDLINE takes one optional argument. If this argument is 0 (the default), a new parse operation is performed, and any previous parse results are discarded. If this argument is 1, the new command line information is appended to any existing parse results. This allows multiple command lines to be merged together and processed as a single line.

Positional (that is, non-switch) arguments parsed by PARSECMDLINE are placed in the CMDARG_*n* array. The first argument is placed in CMDARG_1. A count of all positional arguments is stored in CMDARGCOUNT. Double quotes are stripped from arguments before they are stored in the array. (See Chapter 3 for a discussion of double quotes.) The arguments are stored in the array in the same order as they occurred in the command line.

Switch arguments parsed by PARSECMDLINE are placed in the CMDSW_*n* array. The first switch is placed in CMDSW_1. A count of all switches is stored in CMDSWCOUNT. Double quotes are stripped from switches before they are stored in the array. The switches are stored in the array in the same order as they occurred in the command line.

Implementation

After performing some variable initialization, PARSECMDLINE calls PARSECMDLINE1, passing it the contents of the CMDLINE variable as an argument. The normal command shell parsing mechanism thus performs most of the work of splitting the contents of the CMDLINE variable into individual arguments.

PARSECMDLINE1 then runs a loop to process each parameter (lines 61 to 75). After parameter %1 is processed, the SHIFT command (line 66) shifts the parameters down, and the loop repeats until parameter %1 is empty (line 62), and hence, all parameters have been processed.

Parameter processing begins by removing double quotes via string substitution (lines 63 and 64). The first character of the parameter is then compared to the switch characters / and - (lines 67 and 68). If a match occurs, the parameter is added to the switch array (lines 72 to 75). Otherwise, the parameter is added to the positional argument array (lines 69 to 71).

GETARG

Obtains a positional argument from a parsed command line, by index.

Syntax
```
CALL _MTPLIB :GETARG index
```

Arguments
index   Index of argument to fetch. The first argument is numbered 1.

Returns
RET   Argument text, or empty if index is greater than CMDARGCOUNT.

Description

The GETARG procedure recovers a single positional argument from a command line that has been parsed by the PARSECMDLINE procedure. The single argument specifies the index of the argument to return, which must be between 1 and GETARGCOUNT. The argument is returned in the RET variable. The returned argument will *not* contain double quotes.

Implementation

After performing some basic error checking, the core of the GETARG procedure is a SET command (line 92):

```
set RET=%%CMDARG_%1%%
```

If the index specified is 3, for example, the RET variable contains %CMDARG_3%. This is the name of the variable containing the desired value. GETARG then calls the RESOLVE procedure (described later in this chapter) to convert the name of the variable into its value, which is the desired argument.

GETSWITCH

Obtains a switch argument from a parsed command line, by index.

Syntax

```
CALL _MTPLIB :GETSWITCH index
```

Arguments

index	Index of switch to fetch. The first switch is numbered 1.

Returns

RET	Switch text (name), or empty if index is greater than CMDSWCOUNT.
RETV	Switch value (text following colon) or empty if no value.

Description

The GETSWITCH procedure recovers a single switch and its value (if any) from a command line that has been parsed by the PARSECMDLINE procedure. The single argument, which must be between 1 and GETSWCOUNT, specifies the index of the switch to return.

The argument name is returned in the RET variable (including the / or - character) and the argument value (if any) in the RETV variable. The returned switch and value will *not* contain double quotes.

Implementation

GETSWITCH is similar in implementation to GETARG, except that it contains an additional step after the switch text has been recovered into the RET variable. This step uses a FOR command (line 113) to parse the text into the switch name and value. The name includes all text up to the first colon; the value includes all text after the first colon. Notice that the tokens value in the FOR command is tokens=1* and *not* tokens=1,2. This allows the switch value to contain any text, including additional colon characters.

FINDSWITCH

Finds a switch argument from a parsed command line by name.

Syntax

```
CALL _MTPLIB :FINDSWITCH name [start-index]
```

Arguments

name	Name of switch to locate (with leading / or - character).
start-index	Starting index for search (the default is 1).

Returns

RET	Index of switch, or 0 if not found.
RETV	Switch value (text following colon), or empty if no value or not found.

Description

The FINDSWITCH procedure searches for a switch value by name in a command line that has been parsed by the PARSECMDLINE procedure. The first argument specifies the name of the switch to find (including the leading / or - character). The name is not case-sensitive. The search starts at the first switch unless start-index is present, in which case the search starts at the index specified (start-index must be less than or equal to CMDSWCOUNT). Using start-index allows multiple switches of the same name to be sequentially processed.

The switch index is returned in the RET variable. The value 0 is returned if the switch cannot be located. The value of the switch (if any) is returned in the RETV variable.

Implementation

FINDSWITCH is implemented as a simple loop (lines 129 to 134) that calls GETSWITCH for each index until a matching switch name is found or the end of the switch array is reached. The IF command (line 132), which compares the switch names, uses the /I switch to perform a case-insensitive comparison.

REGSETM and REGSETU

Sets Registry values from variables.

Syntax

```
1. CALL _MTPLIB :REGSETM context prefix
2. CALL _MTPLIB :REGSETU context prefix
```

Arguments

context	Registry context (location). Typically the script name.
prefix	Prefix of variables to be saved in Registry.

Description

The REGSETM and REGSETU procedures save one or more variables in the Registry. These procedures thus provide a way for a script to maintain persistent state information, even across system restarts. The REGSETM procedure stores the variables in the HKEY_LOCAL_MACHINE portion of the Registry, while the REGSETU procedure stores the variables in the HKEY_CURRENT_USER portion of the Registry.

In order to distinguish one script's state from another, each script must specify a *context* for the variables. This same context is used when restoring the variables via the REGETM and REGGETU procedures. Typically, the script uses the script name as the *context* value. If the script is based on the SKELETON.BAT template, the script name is available in the SCRIPTNAME variable.

The variables to save are specified by the *prefix* argument. Like the VARDEL procedure, the REGSETU/REGSETM procedures save all variables that have a prefix that matches *prefix*.

Each variable is stored as a REG_SZ registry value. The values are placed in the key HKEY_LOCAL_MACHINE\Software\MTPScriptContexts*context* for REGSETM and HKEY_CURRENT_USER\Software\MTPScriptContexts*context* for REGSETU.

Implementation

Both REGSETM and REGSETU are similar to the VARDEL procedure. They use a SET command in a FOR command to extract a list of all variables which match the specified *prefix*. The procedures then call the procedure REGSET1 for each matching variable, passing it the root key name (HKLM or HKCU), the name of the variable, and the variable value (in double quotes, as it can contain spaces). REGSET1 then executes a REG command (lines 157 and 158) to store the passed value into the appropriate registry key. Both a REG ADD and a REG UPDATE command are executed, as the procedure has no way of knowing if the variable already exists in the Registry.

The REG command has one undocumented peculiarity. In the value string passed, the backslash character is treated as an escape character to allow special values to be passed. Therefore, before the variable values are stored in the Registry, each backslash character is converted to a double backslash.

REGGETM and REGGETU

Gets variables from the Registry.

Syntax

```
1. CALL _MTPLIB :REGGETM context [variable]
2. CALL _MTPLIB :REGGETU context [variable]
```

Arguments

`context`	Registry context (location). Typically the script name.
`variable`	Name of variable to restore (optional; default restores entire context).

Returns

`RET`	Value of last (or only) variable loaded.

Description

The REGGETM and REGGETU procedures reverse the actions of the REGSETM and REGSETU procedures, and restore one or more variables from the Registry. The REGGETM procedure restores the variables from the HKEY_LOCAL_MACHINE portion of the Registry, while the REGGETU procedure restores the variables from the HKEY_CURRENT_USER portion of the Registry.

The `context` specifies the context from which to restore the variables. It should be the same context name that was used to store the variables. Typically, the script uses the script name as the `context` value. If the script is based on the SKELETON.BAT template, the script name is available in the SCRIPTNAME variable.

To restore an individual variable, specify it using the `variable` argument. To restore all the variables from a context, omit the `variable` argument. When restoring a complete context, only variables that are found in the Registry are altered. Therefore, before calling REGGETM or REGGETU, preset all variables with default values.

Implementation

These procedures use a REG QUERY command (lines 177 and 181) to recover the contents of the variables. The output of this command is somewhat verbose, but by filtering the output by a FIND command, only those lines that actually define a variable are isolated. The entire REG/FIND command is captured by a FOR command and parsed to extract the variable name and value, which is then used in a SET command to restore the variable.

The procedures must also undo the doubled backslash processing performed by the REGSETM and REGSETU procedures. Double quotes are also removed from the variable values.

REGDELM and REGDELU

Delete saved Registry variables or entire context.

Syntax

```
CALL _MTPLIB :REGDELM context [variable]
CALL _MTPLIB :REGDELU context [variable]
```

Arguments

context	Registry context (location). Typically the script name.
variable	Name of variable to delete (optional; the default deletes the entire context).

Description

The REGDELM and REGDELU procedures delete one or more variables from the Registry. The REGDELM procedure deletes the variables from the HKEY_LOCAL_MACHINE portion of the Registry, while the REGDELU procedure deletes the variables from the HKEY_CURRENT_USER portion of the Registry.

The context specifies the context from which to delete the variables. It should be the same context name that was used to store the variables. Typically, the script uses the script name as the context value. If the script is based on the SKELETON.BAT template, the script name is available in the SCRIPTNAME variable.

To delete an individual variable, specify it using the variable argument. To delete all the variables from a context, omit the variable argument.

Implementation

The core of these procedures is a REG DELETE command (lines 202 and 209). Since this command prompts for confirmation before proceeding with the delete operation, a temporary file is created containing the needed response, and the console input of the REG command is redirected to this file. Early versions of the REG command supported the /F switch to skip this confirmation, but newer versions do not, so these procedures avoid the use of this switch.

SRAND

Seeds the random number generator.

Syntax

```
CALL _MTPLIB :SRAND value
```

Arguments

value	New seed value.

Description

The SRAND procedure can be used to re-seed the random number generator used by the RAND procedure. This has the effect of changing the sequence of pseudo-random numbers generated by RAND.

Implementation

The RAND procedure keeps the current seed in the _MTPLIB_NEXTRAND variable. Therefore, all this procedure does is assign a new value to this variable.

RAND

Generates a pseudo-random number.

Syntax

```
CALL _MTPLIB :RAND
```

Returns

RET	Next pseudo-random number.

Description

The RAND procedure returns the next pseudo-random number in the pseudo-random sequence used by the generator. Each call to RAND returns a new value in the RET variable. These values are between 0 and 32767, inclusive.

Implementation

The algorithm used is based upon that recommended by ANSI for the standard C language library. The algorithm is fast and simple, and generates numbers with uniform distribution. It should not, however, be used for serious statistical analysis.

The RAND procedure stores the current seed in the _MTPLIB_NEXTRAND variable, which is updated each time RAND is called. If _MTPLIB_NEXTRAND is not defined, the procedure defines it with an initial value of 1 (line 233). This initialization could be performed by the INIT procedure of the _MTPLIB library, but placing the initialization within the procedure improves the localization and makes the procedure self-contained.

RESOLVE

Resolves recursive and nested variable substitution.

Syntax

```
CALL _MTPLIB :RESOLVE
```

Arguments

RET	Text containing variables to be resolved.

Returns

RET	Text with all variable references resolved.

Description

The RESOLVE procedure implements the technique described in Chapter 3 to handle recursive and nested variable substitutions. The command shell scans all script commands for variable references to expand. However, if the *value* of a variable that is expanded contains additional variables to expand, these are *not* expanded. The RESOLVE procedure overcomes this limitation by providing a fully recursive variable expansion facility.

Before calling RESOLVE, the RET variable should contain the text to be processed. This text can contain any number of variable references (each surrounded by percent signs, as usual). In addition, the value of any of these variables can also contain variable references to resolve and so on to any nesting depth. After RESOLVE has been called, the RET variable contains the original text, with all variable substitutions fully resolved.

RESOLVE is particularly useful when variable information must be accessed indirectly (for example, when arrays of data are accessed), or a variable name must be composed from fragments and then resolved. It is used extensively in the _MTPLIB library and throughout the sample scripts.

Implementation

The key to the RESOLVE procedure is to execute the command ECHO %RET% and capture the output of this command back into the RET variable (line 251). In the process of executing the ECHO command, any variable substitutions within the text of the RET variable are resolved. The new text (with the variable substitutions made) is then stored back into the RET variable, thus resolving one layer of variable indirection.

The FOR command is used to capture the output of the ECHO command. No actual parsing is done, as the entire contents of the ECHO command output are assigned back to the RET variable. To allow any depth of nested substitution to occur, the FOR/ECHO commands are executed in a loop (lines 248 to 252). The loop terminates when the contents of the RET variable before and after the FOR/ECHO commands are unchanged. This indicates that no more variable substitution is required.

GETINPUTLINE

Reads a line of input.

Syntax

```
CALL _MTPLIB :GETINPUTLINE
```

Returns

RET	Line of text read (can be empty).

Description

The GETINPUTLINE procedure reads a single line of text from the keyboard and returns it in the RET variable. This allows a script to prompt for and receive interactive input. To terminate the input line and continue script execution, press Ctrl+Z followed by Enter (or the other way around).

> **Troubleshooting Tip**
>
> *This is a bug in the* CHOICE *command that ships with the resource kit. After a* CHOICE *command executes, all subsequent* COPY *commands that read from the console do not echo typed characters. This therefore disables keyboard echo for the* GETINPUTLINE *procedure. To avoid this problem, execute the* CHOICE *command in a sub-shell (using* CMD /C*).*

Implementation

GETINPUTLINE uses the COPY command (line 265) to capture keyboard input. This means that Ctrl+Z (in addition to Enter) must be typed to terminate the input line. The line is copied to a temporary file, and this file is then parsed by the FOR command to capture the file contents into the RET variable.

The FOR command (line 266) actually parses the results of a TYPE command, rather than parsing the temporary file directly. This is because the FOR command cannot correctly process a file name containing spaces (it mistakenly assumes that the spaces separate multiple file names). Instead, the TYPE command (which can correctly handle file names with spaces) is used, and its output is parsed.

GETSYNCFILE

Obtains the name of a synchronization file.

Syntax

```
CALL _MTPLIB :GETSYNCFILE
```

Returns

RET	Name of the file to use for synchronization.

Description

The GETSYNCFILE procedure returns the name of a file that can be used by the SETSYNCFILE, WAITSYNCFILE, and DELSYNFILE procedures for script synchronization purposes. The file name is returned in the RET variable.

Typically, GETSYNCFILE is called by the "master" script, which then passes the file name to the "slave" script either as a command line argument or in a variable.

Using files for script synchronization is described in Chapter 4.

Implementation
GETSYNCFILE is simply a wrapper procedure for the GETTEMPNAME procedure.

SETSYNCFILE
Sets a synchronization file.

Syntax
```
CALL _MTPLIB :SETSYNCFILE filename
```

Arguments
filename   Name of the file to set. Typically obtained from GETSYNCFILE.

Description
The SETSYNCFILE procedure "sets" the synchronization file. This causes any scripts which are waiting for the file to be set (via the WAITSYNCFILE procedure) to continue execution. A synchronization file is "set" by being created. A slave script typically sets a synchronization file to indicate to a master script(s) that it has completed processing.

The file to set is specified by filename, which is typically a name returned by the GETSYNCFILE procedure.

Using files for script synchronization is discussed in Chapter 4.

Implementation
A file is "set" by being created. Therefore, the procedure simply uses the ECHO command (line 290) to output a single period character to the file.

DELSYNCFILE
Deletes a synchronization file.

Syntax
```
CALL _MTPLIB :DELSYNCFILE filename
```

Arguments
filename   Name of the file to delete. Typically obtained from GETSYNCFILE.

Description

The DELSYNCFILE procedure deletes a synchronization file after it has been used. The file to delete is specified by the *filename* argument. Typically, this file name is obtained using the GETSYNCFILE procedure.

DELSYNCFILE should be called to delete the synchronization file after it has been used. Otherwise, the Windows temporary directory will gradually fill with old synchronization files. After DELSYNCFILE has been called, it is possible to use the same file again for another synchronization event.

Using files for script synchronization is discussed in Chapter 4.

Implementation

DELSYNCFILE is simply a wrapper for the DEL command.

WAITSYNCFILE

Waits for a synchronization file.

Syntax

```
CALL _MTPLIB :WAITSYNCFILE filename [timeout]
```

Arguments

filename	Name of the file to wait for. Typically obtained from GETSYNCFILE.
timeout	Timeout period, in seconds (the default is 60).

Returns

RET	Timeout remaining, or 0 if a timeout occurred.

Description

The WAITSYNCFILE procedure waits for a synchronization file to set. The file upon which to wait is specified by the *filename* argument. The procedure waits for up to *timeout* seconds (the default is 60 seconds) before failing with a timeout. Typically, a master script waits for a slave script to complete by using the WAITSYNCFILE procedure.

Using files for script synchronization is discussed in Chapter 4.

Implementation

WAITSYNCFILE contains a simple loop (lines 317 to 320) that checks for the existence of the specified synchronization file. The loop (and procedure) exits as soon as the file exists. While the file does not exist, the loop continues. Each pass through the loop contains a SLEEP 1 command, which suspends execution for 1 second. Thus, the file is polled every second until it exists. Forcing the script to sleep for one second also yields the CPU while the script is waiting, and the loop thus consumes almost no CPU time while waiting.

Since the loop executes once per second (approximately), the timeout code simply counts down until the *timeout* reaches zero, at which time the loop executes regardless of the state of the synchronization file. Notice the use of the double IF command (line 320) to create an AND condition. This can be interpreted as "if the timeout has not expired *and* the synchronization file does not exist, continue looping."

GETTEMPNAME

Creates a unique temporary file name.

Syntax

```
CALL _MTPLIB :GETTEMPNAME
```

Returns

RET	Temporary file name (can contain spaces).

Description

The GETTEMPNAME procedure creates a temporary file name that can be used for temporary storage of data. The file name is guaranteed not to exist and to be in a location where unrestricted read/write access is permitted.

Implementation

The temporary file name is formed from the prefix ~SH, a pseudo-random number, and the suffix .TMP. The pseudo-random number uses the same algorithm as the RAND procedure, though it uses an independent seed value. If the TEMP variable exists, it is used as the path name for the file. Otherwise, if the TMP variable exists, it is used as the path name. Otherwise, the %SYSTEMROOT% directory is used.

Chapter **6**

User Management Scripts

- **MAKEUSR script**
  This script automates the task of new user account creation.

- **USRQUOTA script**
  Disk quota management can be automated using this sample script.

- **PJCOUNT script**
  This sample script generates a report on print job activity, and can be used as the basis of many other event log analyses scripts.

- **MTPLOGON script**
  This sample logon script can be used as-is or customized for local site requirements.

User Account Creation

This chapter provides sample scripts that offer user management functions, including creating user accounts, disk space quota management, and print job auditing. Also presented is a sample logon script. Each script is first described as a ready-to-use command, and then various implementation details are described to assist you in modifying the script to suit local requirements.

User management is probably the most time-consuming task faced by MIS professionals when managing large Windows NT installations. Maintaining a database of hundreds or even thousands of users can consume large amounts of time, even when all the automation tools in the resource kit are used. Such large, repetitive tasks are ideal candidates for script automation, and this chapter provides several examples of scripts that automate different aspects of user management.

The scripts in this chapter make extensive use of the _MTPLIB.BAT script library described in Chapter 5.

The MAKEUSR Script

Figure 6.1 shows the MAKEUSR.BAT script. This script automates the process of creating a new user account in a typical Windows NT installation. In many cases, the script can be used as-is, while in other cases it can be used as a starting point for a customized user account creation script. In addition to creating the account, MAKEUSR creates a home directory share, populates the home directory, sets permissions on the home directory, and adds the account to any number of local or global groups.

Syntax

MAKEUSR *username* [*password* ¦ *] [*switches*]

Switches

/DOMAIN	Creates the account in the domain (the default is to create the account on the local computer).
/LOCAL:*group*	Adds the user account to the specified local group. More than one /LOCAL switch can be specified.
/GLOBAL:*group*	Adds the user account to the specified global group. More than one /GLOBAL switch can be specified.
/FULLNAME:*name*	Specifies the full user name. Use double quotes if the name contains spaces.
/PROFILEPATH:*path*	Specifies the location of the user profile for this account.
/SCRIPTPATH:*path*	Specifies the name of the logon script for this account.
/HOMEDIR:*path*	Specifies the home directory path for this account.
/HOMECOMPUTER:*computer*	Specifies the home directory computer for this account.
/HOMEPROTO:*uncpath*	Specifies the UNC path to a prototype home directory.
/COMMENT:*text*	Specifies a comment for this user account.

Description

The MAKEUSR script creates a new user account. By default, the account is created in the account database of the computer on which MAKEUSR is executed. Use the /DOMAIN switch to create the account in the domain instead.

The account is given the name specified by *username*, and the password specified by *password*. If an asterisk is used instead of *password*, then the script prompts for the password (which does not echo when entered).

The /FULLNAME switch specifies a full name for the user (enclosed in double quotes if it contains spaces). The /PROFILEPATH switch specifies the profile path for the account, while the /SCRIPTPATH switch specifies a script name for the account. The /COMMENT switch specifies an arbitrary comment for the account. Each of these switches corresponds to a switch of the NET USER command. Additional NET USER switches can be specified using the MUNETUSER variable. This allows switches and settings common to blocks of accounts to be specified once in this variable.

(The /FULLNAME, /PROFILEPATH, /SCRIPTPATH and /COMMENT. switches are normally specified on the command line as these values are typically unique for each user account.)

After the account is created, MAKEUSR automatically adds the account to the local and global groups specified by the /LOCAL and /GLOBAL switches. Enclose the names in double quotes if they contain spaces. Multiple /LOCAL and /GLOBAL switches can be specified, allowing the account to join many groups. In addition, the MULOCAL and MUGLOBAL environment variables can contain additional group names (separated by spaces). Thus, if many similar accounts are being created, set the MULOCAL and MUGLOBAL variables before executing a set of MAKEUSR commands.

The /HOMEDIR switch specifies the home directory for the account. If the /HOMECOMPUTER switch is *not* specified, this home directory path is assumed to be on the local computer, and the path is assumed to be valid on this computer. If the /HOMECOMPUTER switch *is* specified, the home directory is assumed to be relative to the remote computer (for example, C:\ means the root of drive C: on the remote computer). In this case, MAKEUSR automatically creates a new share on the specified home computer, called *username*$, and sets the home directory to \\*computer**username*$.

The /HOMEPROTO switch specifies the UNC name of a prototype home directory. After the home directory is created, the content of the UNC name specified is copied to the new home directory path. This allows a prototype directory and files to be created for all users and then automatically copied into the (new) home directory.

After the prototype directory (if any) is copied to the new home directory, the permissions are set on this directory to grant full access to the new user account. Additional permissions can be specified by adding XCACLS switches to the MUXCACLS variable.

Example

```
makeusr BobMacStart * /global:SalesAdm /global:Marketing
/homedir:e:\users\BobMacStart /homecomputer:CORP1 /domain
```

This example creates a new account called BobMacStart and joins the
SalesAdm and Marketing groups. The home directory is set to the
E:\USERS\BOBMACSTART on the server CORP1. The account is created in
the domain.

The MAKEUSR script can be used either stand-alone or embedded within a
batch processing script. For example:

```
1. set MULOCAL=
2. set MUGLOBAL=Software SrcSafe Pizza
3. for /f "tokens=1,2*" %%I in (newaccts.txt) do call :ADDUSER %%I %%J "%%K"
4. goto :EOF
5. :ADDUSER
6. call makeusr %1 %2 /domain /fullname:%3 /homedir:d:\Users\%1
/homecomputer:SYS-11
7. goto :EOF
```

This simple script reads an account file containing a list of new accounts to
create. Each line in the file must contain three fields, separated by spaces. The
first contains the user name, the second the password, and the third (the rest of
the line) the user's full name. For example:

```
BobDylan Secret1 Bob Dylan
TonyBlair Secret2 Tony Blair
```

The script creates a new account for each name and adds each account to the
Software, SrcSafe, and Pizza global groups. Each account has a new (empty)
home directory created on the SYS-11 server, in the D:\USERS directory on
that computer.

The FOR command in line 3 above uses the `"tokens=1,2*"` option to parse the
text file into arguments. Obviously, the first two tokens are the user name and
password. The third field, however, is captured using the * special token, rather
than token 3. This is done because the last field may contain spaces, and the *
token captures *all* remaining text on the line as the final (third) field.

Implementation

The MAKEUSR.BAT script is based on the SKELETON.BAT script described
in Chapter 5. The MAIN procedure first checks to see if any arguments are present (line 73). If not, then the help text is displayed and the script exits.

If arguments are present, the PARSECMDLINE procedure in _MPTLIB.BAT is called
(line 77) to parse the command line, and the number of positional arguments is
then checked (it must be 2 or more). The command line is then processed.

First, the USERNAME and PASSWORD variables are set from the first two positional arguments (lines 79 to 82). Then all switch variables are preset to default values (lines 85 to 88).

Command line switches are processed in the loop beginning at the :GETSWITCHLOOP label (line 90). This loop (lines 90 to 104) repeatedly calls the GETSWITCH procedure in _MTPLIB.BAT until all switches are processed. The IX variable holds the switch index, which is incremented each time the loop executes. Individual switches are then processed as follows:

- The /DOMAIN switch sets the DOMAINSW variable to "/DOMAIN" (it is empty by default).

- The /HOMEDIR, /HOMECOMPUTER, and /HOMEPROTO switches set corresponding variables to the specified switch value.

- The /FULLNAME, /PROFILEPATH, /SWITCHPATH, and /COMMENT switches are added to the MUNETUSER variable (which can be preset before executing MAKEUSR). These switches, and others supplied by the user, are all passed unaltered to the NET USER command.

- All /LOCAL switch values are appended to the MULOCAL variable. Similarly, all /GLOBAL switch values are appended to the end of the MUGLOBAL variable.

After switch processing is complete, the domain name is then stored in the DOMAINNAME variable by parsing the output of the WHOAMI[RK] command (lines 108 and 109). This is used by the XCACLS command later in the script.

After the setup is complete, the user account is created in a sequence of steps (lines 112 to 116), each of which is handled by an individual procedure, as follows:

- The MAKEHOMEDIR procedure creates the new account home directory. The HOMEDIR variable is passed as an argument, as MAKEHOMEDIR uses the file name qualifiers on this argument to parse various parts of the home directory name (it cannot do this by operating directly on the HOMEDIR variable).

- The CREATEUSER procedure actually creates the user account via a NET USER /ADD command.

- The SECUREHOMEDIR procedure secures the home directory by setting permissions using the XCACLS command. SECUREHOMEDIR assumes that the home directory is located on an NTFS volume.

- The ADDLOCALGROUPS and ADDGLOBALGROUPS procedures add the account to the groups specified by the MULOCAL and MUGLOBAL variables. These are passed as an *unquoted* argument, which makes the command shell do the work of parsing the variables into individual group names.

The first step in account creation is the MAKEHOMEDIR procedure. If no HOMECOMPUTER is specified, MAKEHOMEDIR just creates the required directory locally (line 133). If a HOMECOMPUTER *is* specified, MAKEHOMEDIR must create a new share on that computer and then use this share as the home directory. The share is created using the RMTSHARE command (lines 135 to 138).

Before the directory can be shared, however, it must be created. MAKEHOMEDIR has two items of information: the name of the home computer, and the home directory path *relative to that computer*. To create the directory on the remote computer, MAKEUSR uses the administrative shares on the remote computer. For example, if the home computer is SYS-100 and the home path is e:\Users\ArtfulDodger, then MAKEHOMEDIR must execute the command MD \\ SYS-100\E$\Users\ArtfulDodger. Once the directory exists on the remote computer, the RMTSHARE command is used to create the share, and this share is then used as the home directory. Finally, if a prototype home directory is specified, the XCOPY command (line 142) is used to copy this prototype to the new home directory.

The CREATEUSER procedure creates the user account via the NET USER command. This command is passed the results of the command line parsing, in the following variables:

- USERNAME

- PASSWORD

- MUNETUSER

- DOMAINSW

- HOMEDIRSW

The HOMEDIRSW is either empty (if no home directory is specified) or contains the /HOMEDIR switch and the home directory. Note that the home directory specified to the NET USER command *cannot* be the same value supplied in the MAKEUSR /HOMEDIR switch. If a home computer is specified, the /HOMEDIR switch refers to the share created by the MAKEHOMEDIR procedure.

The SECUREHOMEDIR procedure secures the new home directory by using an XCACLS command (lines 174 and 177) to alter the permissions. The new user account is given full control of the entire home directory tree. The MUXCACLS variable can be used to pass additional switches to the XCACLS command. For example, additional accounts can be given access to the home directory by adding the appropriate XCACLS switches.

The ADDLOCALGROUPS and ADDGLOBALGROUPS procedures add the new user account to one or more local or global groups. Each procedure receives a list of groups as arguments. Both procedures run a loop that executes a NET LOCALGROUP /ADD or NET GROUP /ADD command to add the account to the specified groups. The command arguments are shifted via the SHIFT command during each loop pass, thus making the loop execute once for each passed argument.

```
001. @echo OFF
002. @if not "%ECHO%"=="" echo %ECHO%
003. @if not "%OS%"=="Windows_NT" goto DOSEXIT
004. rem $Workfile: makeusr.bat $ $Revision: 1 $ $Date: 12/04/97 9:51a $
005. rem $Archive: /TimH/Pubs/Books/Macmillan/Windows NT
     Scripting/Scripts/makeusr.bat $
006.
007. rem Set local scope and call MAIN procedure
008. setlocal & pushd & set RET=
009.     set SCRIPTNAME=%~n0
010.     set SCRIPTPATH=%~f0
011.     if "%DEBUG%"=="1" (set TRACE=echo) else (set TRACE=rem)
012.     call _mtplib :INIT %SCRIPTPATH%
013.     if /i {%1}=={/help} (call :HELP %2) & (goto :HELPEXIT)
014.     if /i {%1}=={/?} (call :HELP %2) & (goto :HELPEXIT)
015.     call :MAIN %*
016.     :HELPEXIT
017. popd & endlocal & set RET=%RET%
018. goto :EOF
019.
020. rem //////////////////////////////////////////////////////////////////////
021. rem HELP procedure
022. rem Display brief on-line help message
023. rem
024. :HELP
025. if defined TRACE %TRACE% [proc %0 %*]
026.     echo Syntax: MAKEUSR username [password ^¦ *] [switches]
027.     echo Create a new user NT user account.
028.     echo .
029.     echo /DOMAIN
030.     echo     Create account in domain (def: local computer).
031.     echo /LOCAL:group
032.     echo     Add account to specified local group. Multiple /LOCAL
033.     echo     switches are allowed. In addition, a list of groups
034.     echo     may be supplied in the MULOCAL variable.
035.     echo /GLOBAL:group
036.     echo     Add account to specified global group. Multiple /GLOBAL
037.     echo     switches are allowed. In addition, a list of groups
038.     echo     may be supplied in the MUGLOBAL variable.
039.     echo /FULLNAME:name
040.     echo     Specify full name for account. Use quotes if the name
041,     echo     contains spaces.
042.     echo /PROFILEPATH:path
043.     echo     Profile path for this account.
044.     echo /SCRIPTPATH:path
```

```
045.    echo     Logon script path for this account.
046.    echo /HOMEDIR:path
047.    echo     User home directory. If /HOMECOMPUTER is NOT specified,
048.    echo     this is a local path. If /HOMECOMPUTER is specified, this is
049.    echo     a local path RELATIVE TO THAT COMPUTER (e.g. C: refers to
050.    echo     C: on that computer).
051.    echo /HOMECOMPUTER:name
052.    echo     Computer to contain home directory (def: local computer).
053.    echo /HOMEPROTO:uncpath
054.    echo     UNC name of prototype home directory. Copied to home
055.    echo     directory when created.
056.    echo /COMMENT:text
057.    echo     Text comment for this user name.
058.    echo MUNETUSER
059.    echo     Use this variable to specify additional switches to the
060.    echo     NET USER command. Useful when adding lots of similar
061.    echo     accounts in a batch.
062.    echo MUXCACLS
063.    echo     Use this variable to specify additional switches to the
064.    echo     XCACLS command.
065. goto :EOF
066.
067. rem ////////////////////////////////////////////////////////////////////////
068. rem MAIN procedure
069. rem
070. :MAIN
071. if defined TRACE %TRACE% [proc %0 %*]
072.     rem If no arguments, we default to displaying help
073.     if {%1}=={} (call :HELP) & (goto :EOF)
074.
075.     rem Parse command line and setup variables
076.     set CMDLINE=%*
077.     call _mtplib :PARSECMDLINE 0
078.     if %CMDARGCOUNT% LSS 2 (call :HELP) & (goto :EOF)
079.     call _mtplib :GETARG 1
080.     set USERNAME=%RET%
081.     call _mtplib :GETARG 2
082.     set PASSWORD=%RET%
083.
084.     rem Process command line switches
085.     set DOMAINSW=
086.     set HOMEDIR=
087.     set HOMECOMPUTER=
088.     set HOMEPROTO=
089.     set /a IX=1
090.     :GETSWITCHLOOP
091.         call _mtplib :GETSWITCH %IX%
092.         if "%RET%"=="" goto :GETSWITCHLOOPEND
093.         set /a IX+=1
```

```
094.        if /i "%RET%"=="/domain"  set DOMAINSW=/DOMAIN
095.        if /i "%RET%"=="/homedir" set HOMEDIR=%RETV%
096.        if /i "%RET%"=="/homecomputer" set HOMECOMPUTER=%RETV%
097.        if /i "%RET%"=="/homeproto" set HOMEPROTO=%RETV%
098.        if /i "%RET%"=="/fullname" set MUNETUSER=%MUNETUSER%
            /FULLNAME:"%RETV%"
099.        if /i "%RET%"=="/profilepath" set MUNETUSER=%MUNETUSER%
            /PROFILEPATH:"%RETV%"
100.        if /i "%RET%"=="/scriptpath" set MUNETUSER=%MUNETUSER%
            /SCRIPTPATH:"%RETV%"
101.        if /i "%RET%"=="/comment" set MUNETUSER=%MUNETUSER%
            /COMMENT:"%RETV%"
102.        if /i "%RET%"=="/local" set MULOCAL=%MULOCAL% "%RETV%"
103.        if /i "%RET%"=="/global" set MUGLOBAL=%MUGLOBAL% "%RETV%"
104.    goto :GETSWITCHLOOP
105.    :GETSWITCHLOOPEND
106.
107.    rem Get domain name
108.    set DOMAINNAME=
109.    if not "%DOMAINSW%"=="" for /f "delims=\" %%I in ('whoami') do set
        DOMAINNAME=%%I\
110.
111.    rem Proceed to create the account
112.    call :MAKEHOMEDIR "%HOMEDIR%"
113.    call :CREATEUSER
114.    call :SECUREHOMEDIR
115.    call :ADDLOCALGROUPS %MULOCAL%
116.    call :ADDGLOBALGROUPS %MUGLOBAL%
117. goto :EOF
118.
119. rem ////////////////////////////////////////////////////////////////////
120. rem MAKEHOMEDIR procedure
121. rem Create the home directory/share for the account
122. rem
123. rem Arguments:    HOMEDIR=home directory (local or remote)
124. rem          HOMECOMPUTER=computer name (empty for local)
125. rem
126. :MAKEHOMEDIR
127. if defined TRACE %TRACE% [proc %0 %*]
128.     if "%HOMEDIR%"=="" goto :EOF
129.     set HOMEDRIVE=%~d1%
130.     set HOMEPATH=%~pnx1
131.     set HOMEADMIN=\\%HOMECOMPUTER%\%HOMEDRIVE:~0,1%$%HOMEPATH%
132.     if "%HOMECOMPUTER%"=="" (
133.         (md "%HOMEDIR%")
134.     ) else (
135.         (md "%HOMEADMIN%")
136.         (echo --- rmtshare \\%HOMECOMPUTER%\%USERNAME%$="%HOMEDIR%"
             /remark:"%USERNAME% home directory")
```

```
137.          (rmtshare \\%HOMECOMPUTER%\%USERNAME%$="%HOMEDIR%"
              /remark:"%USERNAME% home directory")
138.          (set HOMEDIR=\\%HOMECOMPUTER%\%USERNAME%$)
139.      )
140.      if not "%HOMEPROTO%"=="" (
141.          (echo --- xcopy "%HOMEPROTO%" "%HOMEDIR%" /e/i/q/r/k)
142.          (xcopy "%HOMEPROTO%" "%HOMEDIR%" /e/i/q/r/k)
143.      )
144.      sleep 2
145. goto :EOF
146.
147. rem ////////////////////////////////////////////////////////////////
148. rem CREATEUSER procedure
149. rem Execute the NET USER command to create the new account
150. rem
151. rem Arguments:    USERNAME=user name
152. rem           PASSWORD=new password or * for interactive
153. rem           MUNETUSER=switches for NET USER
154. rem           DOMAINSW=/DOMAIN switch (if present)
155. rem
156. :CREATEUSER
157. if defined TRACE %TRACE% [proc %0 %*]
158.      if "%HOMEDIR%"=="" (set HOMEDIRSW=) else (set
              HOMEDIRSW=/HOMEDIR:"%HOMEDIR%")
159.      echo --- net user %USERNAME% %PASSWORD% /add %MUNETUSER% %DOMAINSW%
              %HOMEDIRSW%
160,      net user %USERNAME% %PASSWORD% /ADD %MUNETUSER% %DOMAINSW% %HOMEDIRSW%
161.      sleep 2
162. goto :EOF
163.
164. rem ////////////////////////////////////////////////////////////////
165. rem SECUREHOMEDIR procedure
166. rem Secure the home directory for the user
167. rem
168. rem Arguments:    HOMEDIR=path for home directory (may be UNC)
169. rem
170. :SECUREHOMEDIR
171. if defined TRACE %TRACE% [proc %0 %*]
172.      if "%HOMECOMPUTER%"=="" (
173.          (echo --- xcacls %HOMEDIR% /t /g %DOMAINNAME%%USERNAME%:f;f
              %MUXCACLS% 2^>nul)
174.          (xcacls %HOMEDIR% /t /g %DOMAINNAME%%USERNAME%:f;f %MUXCACLS%
              2^>nul)
175.      ) else (
176.          (echo --- xcacls %HOMEADMIN% /t /g %DOMAINNAME%%USERNAME%:f;f
              %MUXCACLS% 2^>nul)
177.          (xcacls %HOMEADMIN% /t /g %DOMAINNAME%%USERNAME%:f;f %MUXCACLS%
              2^>nul)
178.      )
```

```
179. goto :EOF
180.
181. rem ///////////////////////////////////////////////////////////////////////
182. rem ADDLOCALGROUPS procedure
183. rem Add user to each specified local group
184. rem
185. rem Arguments:    %n=names of local groups
186. rem
187. :ADDLOCALGROUPS
188. if defined TRACE %TRACE% [proc %0 %*]
189.     if {%1}=={} goto :EOF
190.     echo --- net localgroup %1 %USERNAME% /add %DOMAINSW%
191.     net localgroup %1 %USERNAME% /add %DOMAINSW%
192.     shift /1
193.     goto :ADDLOCALGROUPS
194. goto :EOF
195.
196. rem ///////////////////////////////////////////////////////////////////////
197. rem ADDGLOBALGROUPS procedure
198. rem Add user to each specified global group
199. rem
200. rem Arguments:    %n=names of global groups
201. rem
202. :ADDGLOBALGROUPS
203. if defined TRACE %TRACE% [proc %0 %*]
204.     if {%1}=={} goto :EOF
205.     echo --- net group %1 %USERNAME% /add %DOMAINSW%
206.     net group %1 %USERNAME% /add %DOMAINSW%
207.     shift /1
208.     goto :ADDGLOBALGROUPS
209. goto :EOF
210.
211. rem ///////////////////////////////////////////////////////////////////////
212. rem Additional procedures go here...
213.
214. rem These must be the FINAL LINES in the script...
215. :DOSEXIT
216. echo This script requires Windows NT
217.
218. rem ///////////////////////////////////////////////////////////////////////
```

Figure 6.1. *The MAKEUSR.BAT script*

The USRQUOTA Script

Figure 6.2 shows the USRQUOTA.BAT script. This script automates per-user disk quota checking, and generates a report of disk space used by each user.

Multiple directories can be totaled and checked, and each user account can be checked against a specified quota value. USRQUOTA can either generate a report on all users, or only those who are over a preset quota amount. Quotas for each account are stored in the user account database.

Syntax

```
USRQUOTA dir-list [/QUOTA] [/DOMAIN] [/OVER]
```

Switches

/QUOTA	Restrict report to user accounts with assigned quotas.
/DOMAIN	Get assigned quota information from the domain (the default is to get quotas from the local computer account database).
/OVER	Restrict report to user accounts that are over their quota limit.

Description

The USRQUOTA script provides a simple but effective quota checking facility for disk space use. The *dir-list* argument specifies one or more directory names (separated by spaces). UNC names can be used, allowing any network share to be included in the report. All directories in the *dir-list* must be on NTFS volumes, as USRQUOTA relies upon the file ownership information maintained by NTFS to compute per-user quotas.

Each directory specified by the *dir-list* argument is scanned, including all sub-directories, and the disk space used by each file found is accumulated on a per-user account basis. The owner of the file is used when decided which account to charge for the space consumed. Also, if the file is compressed, the account is only charged for the physical disk space used. After all directories have been scanned, a report is generated detailing the total space consumed by each user's files (in Mbytes).

Each user account can be assigned a preset disk quota amount. To do this, add the quota limit to the *description* (or *comment*) field of the user account. Using User Manager, place the text #QUOTA:*nnn*# anywhere in this field to set a quota limit of *nnn* Mbytes for this account. By default, USRQUOTA scans the accounts on the local computer for quota information. The /DOMAIN switch instead scans accounts on the domain for quota information. If an account is assigned a quota, USRQUOTA reports these values and also the percentage of the quota consumed by the user.

The /QUOTA switch restricts the report to user accounts which have assigned quotas, that is, those accounts which contain #QUOTA:*nnn*# within the description field of the user account. The /OVER switch further restricts the report to accounts whose actual disk quota exceeds the assigned quota limit for that account.

Example

```
usrquota e:\ h:\ /domain /over /quota
```

This command creates a report of all domain accounts that have exceeded their assigned quota limits.

Implementation

The USRQUOTA.BAT script is based on the SKELETON.BAT script described in Chapter 5. The MAIN procedure first checks to see if any arguments are present (line 49). If not, then the help text is displayed and the script exits.

If arguments are present, the PARSECMDLINE procedure in _MTPLIB.BAT is called (line 53) to parse the command line, and the number of positional arguments is then checked (it must be 1 or more). The command line is then processed. The variable QUOTASW is set to 1 if the /QUOTA switch is present (lines 55 and 56), and the variable OVERSW is set to 1 if the /OVER switch is present (lines 59 and 60). The DOMAINSW variable is either empty (the default) or set to /DOMAIN if the /DOMAIN switch is present (lines 57 and 58). This switch is passed to the NET USER command when extracting user quota limits.

The core of USRQUOTA is a loop which repeatedly executes the DISKUSE[RK] command for each directory specified in *dir-list*. Two temporary files (with names stored in the TEMPONE and TEMPALL variables) are used, both of which are generated by the GETTEMPNAME procedure in _MTPLIB.BAT. The first file (TEMPONE) captures the output of the DISKUSE command (line 75). This file is then processed by a FIND command (line 76) to extract only those lines that contain commas, and the results are accumulated in the second temporary file, TEMPALL. Filtering for lines containing commas eliminates header and other incidental information present in the DISKUSE output.

The final temporary file contains a list of quota charges for each user account. Each line contains one charge for an account, as three fields:

- The domain (or computer) name
- The account name
- The disk charge (in bytes)

Each account name can be listed multiple times in the file, as DISKUSE is run multiple times if more than one directory is specified in *dir-list*.

To tabulate the results and generate the report, the TEMPALL file is filtered by the SORT command (line 84). This command groups together all lines that refer to the same account. The output of the SORT command is then processed by a FOR command, which parses each line into the domain name, user name, and disk charge. The FOR command calls the ADDQUOTA procedure for each line parsed.

The ADDQUOTA procedure (line 99) accumulates the results for each user account. The current user account being accumulated is tracked in the USERNAME variable. As soon as the USERNAME value is different from the user name argument, ADDQUOTA emits a report record for the user account and then resets the counters for the next account (lines 101 to 105). The actual report record is generated by the SHOWUSERINFO procedure, which is called by the ADDQUOTA procedure. SHOWUSERINFO is also called after the FOR command finishes, in order to display the results for the last account.

The ADDQUOTA procedure is passed two arguments. The first consists of the domain name and account name combined using a backslash separator. The second is the disk charge in bytes. ADDQUOTA simply accumulates the disk charge in the MBTOTAL variable (line 106), after converting the charge value from bytes to Mbytes.

Converting each individual total to Mbytes rather than accumulating the exact byte count introduces slight rounding errors, but these are very slight, and converting early avoids any possibility of counter overflow for very large quota charge values.

The SHOWUSERINFO procedure actually generates the report line. The procedure has access to the user name in the USERNAME variable and the total disk charge for that user in the MBTOTAL variable. The procedure must now look up the disk quota limit in the user account database:

1. The USERNAME is parsed using a FOR command (line 123) to extract the user name only (the domain name and user name are separated in USERNAME by a backslash).

2. The extracted user name is then used to execute a NET USER command (line 124), which generates a report on the user account specified (the DOMAINSW is also used here, in order to fetch the account information from the domain if required).

3. The output of the NET USER command is filtered by a FIND command (line 124), which filters lines containing the text #QUOTA:. This command isolates the quota information in the NET USER output.

4. The filter results are passed to another FOR command (line 124), which captures the entire line into the MBQUOTA variable.

After the FOR command completes, the MBQUOTA variable is either empty (no quota is assigned to this account), or it contains the description line including the #QUOTA text. Two additional FOR commands (lines 125 and 126) are used to parse the MBQUOTA text and extract the quota amount. First, the field is parsed for the "#QUOTA:*nnn*# text, using # as a separator. Then, the result of this parse is re-parsed to isolate the *nnn* amount.

The final result of this parsing is that the MBQUOTA field either contains the quota limit for the account (in Mbytes) or is empty if the user account does not specify a quota limit. If the quota limit is *not* empty, the PERCENT variable is computed as the ratio (MBTOTAL*100)/MBQUOTA, which is the amount of disk charge used as a percentage of the user quota (line 127).

Next, the SHOWUSERINFO procedure checks the display criteria. If there is no user quota limit (MBQUOTA is empty) and the /QUOTA switch is specified, then SHOWUSER-INFO exits, as this account is not a candidate for reporting (line 131). Next, if there *is* a user quota limit, *and* the percentage computed is less than or equal to 100, *and* the /OVER switch is specified, then SHOWUSERINFO exits, as this account is not over its quota limit and is not a candidate for reporting (line 132).

Finally, SHOWUSERINFO formats the computed quota information for tabular display. Each of the variables USERNAME, MBTOTAL, MBQUOTA and PERCENT are assigned to a temporary variable using a SET command which has been padded to the end of the line with spaces (lines 137 to 140). Then, each variable is re-assigned to itself using string indexing to limit the length of the variable to the width of each field in the report (lines 143 to 146). By first padding the variable with spaces and then truncating it to a fixed width, a tabular report is generated. Notice the unusual lines where (for example) the USERNAME variable is assigned to the T1 variable:

```
set T1=%USERNAME%
```

Although not obvious from the printed copy, the SET command is padded after the last percent sign with spaces all the way to the end of the line. This is important, as these spaces contribute to the contents of the T1 variable. Then, the T1 variable is assigned to itself, as follows:

```
set T1=%T1:~0,30%
```

This SET command (which is *not* space padded) assigns the T1 variable with the first 30 characters of itself. In other words, the T1 variable is truncated to 30 characters or less. Since the first SET command added sufficient spaces to T1 such that it is *always* greater than 30 characters, the T1 variable now contains *exactly* 30 characters and is comprised of the contents of the USERNAME variable plus extra spaces to pad it to a width of 30. This is how the fixed column report is generated by SHOWUSERINFO.

```
001. @echo OFF
002. @if not "%ECHO%"=="" echo %ECHO%
003. @if not "%OS%"=="Windows_NT" goto DOSEXIT
004. rem $Workfile: usrquota.bat $ $Revision: 1 $ $Date: 12/04/97 9:51a $
005. rem $Archive: /TimH/Pubs/Books/Macmillan/Windows NT
     Scripting/Scripts/usrquota.bat $
006.
007. rem Set local scope and call MAIN procedure
008. setlocal & pushd & set RET=
009.     set SCRIPTNAME=%~n0
010.     set SCRIPTPATH=%~f0
011.     if "%DEBUG%"=="1" (set TRACE=echo) else (set TRACE=rem)
012.     call _mtplib :INIT %SCRIPTPATH%
013.     if /i {%1}=={/help} (call :HELP %2) & (goto :HELPEXIT)
014.     if /i {%1}=={/?} (call :HELP %2) & (goto :HELPEXIT)
015.     call :MAIN %*
016.     :HELPEXIT
017. popd & endlocal & set RET=%RET%
018. goto :EOF
019.
020. rem ////////////////////////////////////////////////////////////////////
021. rem HELP procedure
022. rem Display brief on-line help message
023. rem
024. :HELP
025. if defined TRACE %TRACE% [proc %0 %*]
026.     echo Syntax: USRQUOTA dir-list [/QUOTA] [/DOMAIN] [/OVER]
027.     echo Check disk quota usage per user.
028.     echo .
029.     echo dir-list
030.     echo    One or more directories to check (UNC names are ok).
031.     echo /QUOTA
032.     echo    Only report on users with restricted quotas.
033.     echo /DOMAIN
034.     echo    Gets quota info from domain (def: local computer).
035.     echo /OVER
036.     echo    Only display users over quota limit.
037.     echo .
038.     echo To specify a quota for a user account, add the text #QUOTA:nnn#
039.     echo to the comment (description) field of the user account, where
040.     echo nnn in the user quota in megabytes.
041. goto :EOF
042.
043. rem ////////////////////////////////////////////////////////////////////
044. rem MAIN procedure
```

```
045. rem
046. :MAIN
047. if defined TRACE %TRACE% [proc %0 %*]
048.     rem If no arguments, we default to displaying help
049.     if {%1}=={} (call :HELP) & (goto :EOF)
050.
051.     rem Parse command line and setup variables
052.     set CMDLINE=%*
053.     call _mtplib :PARSECMDLINE 0
054.     if %CMDARGCOUNT% LSS 1 (call :HELP) & (goto :EOF)
055.     call _mtplib :FINDSWITCH /quota
056.     if not "%RET%"=="0" (set QUOTASW=1) else (set QUOTASW=0)
057.     call _mtplib :FINDSWITCH /domain
058.     if not "%RET%"=="0" (set DOMAINSW=/DOMAIN) else (set DOMAINSW=)
059.     call _mtplib :FINDSWITCH /over
060.     if not "%RET%"=="0" (set OVERSW=1) else (set OVERSW=0)
061.
062.     rem Get temporary filenames
063.     call _mtplib :GETTEMPNAME
064.     set TEMPALL=%RET%
065.     call _mtplib :GETTEMPNAME
066.     set TEMPONE=%RET%
067.
068.     rem Accumulate disk usage results into temporary file
069.     set /a IX=1
070.     :DISKUSELOOP
071.         call _mtplib :GETARG %IX%
072.         if "%RET%"=="" goto :DISKUSELOOPEND
073.         set /a IX+=1
074.         if exist "%TEMPONE%" del "%TEMPONE%"
075.         diskuse "%RET%" /T /S /F:%TEMPONE% >nul
076.         type %TEMPONE% ¦ find "," >>"%TEMPALL%"
077.     goto :DISKUSELOOP
078.     :DISKUSELOOPEND
079.
080.     rem Now parse the results file
081.     set USERNAME=
082.     echo Username                        Used     Quota    Percent
083.     echo --------------------------- -------- -------- --------
084.     for /f "tokens=1-3 delims=," %%I in ('type %TEMPALL% ^¦ sort') do call
         :ADDQUOTA %%I\%%J %%K
085.     call :SHOWUSERINFO
086.
087.     rem Delete temporary files
088.     del %TEMPALL%
089.     del %TEMPONE%
090. goto :EOF
091.
092. rem ////////////////////////////////////////////////////////////////////
```

```
093. rem ADDQUOTA procedure
094. rem Add a line of quota information
095. rem
096. rem Arguments:    %1=user name
097. rem         %2=quota bytes
098. rem
099. :ADDQUOTA
100.    rem Handle switch to new username
101.    if not {%1}=={%USERNAME%} (
102.        (call :SHOWUSERINFO)
103.        (set USERNAME=%1)
104.        (set /a MBTOTAL=0)
105.    )
106.    set /a MBTOTAL+=%2/1048576
107. goto :EOF
108.
109. rem /////////////////////////////////////////////////////////////////////
110. rem SHOWUSERINFO procedure
111. rem Display accumulated results for one user
112. rem
113. rem Arguments:    USERNAME=user name
114. rem         MBTOTAL=total mbytes for this user
115. rem
116. :SHOWUSERINFO
117. if defined TRACE %TRACE% [proc %0 %*]
118.    if "%USERNAME%"=="" goto :EOF
119.
120.    rem Get quota information for user
121.    set MBQUOTA=
122.    set /a PERCENT=0
123.    for /f "tokens=2 delims=\" %%I in ("%USERNAME%") do set USER=%%I
124.    for /f "tokens=*" %%I in ('net user %USER% %DOMAINSW% 2^>nul ^| find
     /i "#QUOTA:"') do set MBQUOTA=%%I
125.    for /f "tokens=2 delims=#" %%I in ("%MBQUOTA%") do set MBQUOTA=%%I
126.    for /f "tokens=2 delims=:" %%I in ("%MBQUOTA%") do set MBQUOTA=%%I
127.    if not "%MBQUOTA%"=="" set /a PERCENT=MBTOTAL*100/MBQUOTA
128.
129.    rem Filter display based upon switches
130.    set T5=
131.    if "%MBQUOTA%"=="" if "%QUOTASW%"=="1" goto :EOF
132.    if not "%MBQUOTA%"=="" if %PERCENT% LEQ 100 if "%OVERSW%"=="1" goto
     :EOF
133.    if not "%MBQUOTA%"=="" if %PERCENT% GTR 100 set T5=***
134.    if "%MBQUOTA%"=="" set PERCENT=---
135.
136.    rem The following SET commands are all space-padded to here ------->
137.    set T1=%USERNAME%
138.    set T2=%MBTOTAL%
139.    set T3=%MBQUOTA%
```

```
140.    set T4=%PERCENT%%%
141.
142.    rem Do not pad these SET commands
143.    set T1=%T1:~0,30%
144.    set T2=%T2:~0,8%
145.    set T3=%T3:~0,8%
146.    set T4=%T4:~0,8%
147.    echo %T1% %T2% %T3% %T4% %T5%
148. goto :EOF
149.
150. rem /////////////////////////////////////////////////////////////////////
151. rem Additional procedures go here...
152.
153. rem These must be the FINAL LINES in the script...
154. :DOSEXIT
155. echo This script requires Windows NT
156.
157. rem /////////////////////////////////////////////////////////////////////
```

Figure 6.2. *The USRQUOTA.BAT script*

The PJCOUNT Script

Figure 6.3 shows the PJCOUNT.BAT script. This script audits print job activity by generating a report showing the print jobs, pages, and bytes printed by each user account. The script generates this information by analyzing information in the system event log on a computer. This script can easily be modified to audit other user activity, such as logon/logoff activity or RAS (dial-in) activity.

Also, the sample script generates the report based upon "live" information in the actual event log. The script can easily be modified to process a saved event log file by altering the arguments to the DUMPEL command.

Syntax
```
PJCOUNT [computer]
```

Description
The PJCOUNT script analyzes the system event log on the specified *computer* (or the local computer if none is specified) and generates a report showing all print activity for each user. The report includes the number of jobs printed, the number of pages printed, and the number of bytes sent to the printer for each user.

> ### Tip
>
> *The* DUMPEL *output format was altered between the initial release of the resource kit and the Supplement 2 release. This script requires the version of* DUMPEL *that ships with Supplement 2 or later.*

Windows 95 clients do not provide page count information, so the page count is only accurate if all the clients are Windows NT computers.

Example

```
pjcount SOCRATES
```

This command generates a report on all print jobs submitted to the SOCRATES computer (that is, all print jobs sent to printers attached to SOCRATES).

Implementation

The PJCOUNT.BAT script is based on the SKELETON.BAT script described in Chapter 5. The core of the PJCOUNT script is a DUMPEL command (line 42). The output of this command is analyzed and a report is generated based upon this analysis.

In the MAIN procedure, if a computer name is specified as the (only) argument, the COMPUTER variable is set to the text /S plus the name of the computer (line 38). Otherwise, the COMPUTER variable is left empty. This provides the required computer name switch for the DUMPEL[RK] command.

The script then executes a DUMPEL command (line 42), passing switches to filter the system event log for print jobs only. The COMPUTER variable is passed as an argument, so that DUMPEL analyzes the event log on the required computer. The DUMPEL output is formatted so that it contains only the user name and print description string. This output is passed to the SORT command to be sorted by user name. Finally, each line of sorted output is passed to the SCANJOB procedure.

The SCANJOB procedure (line 53) analyzes each print job. As with the ADDQUOTA procedure of the USRQUOTA script (see the previous section in this chapter), the SCANJOB procedure accumulates results for each user account and then outputs a report for each user by calling the SHOWUSERINFO procedure. Results are accumulated in the JOBCOUNT, PAGECOUNT, and BYTECOUNT variables.

Unfortunately, the output of the DUMPEL command cannot easily be split into fields (one reason is that the name of the file printed is not quoted, and so cannot be distinguished syntactically in the report). Therefore, SCANJOB analyzes the line (which is passed as a set of arguments to SCANJOB) for keyword information. SCANJOB loops, processing each argument until it locates a keyword. It then uses the keyword to extract the required information.

For example, the number of bytes in a print job is always preceded by the keyword bytes:. Therefore, as soon as SCANJOB sees the bytes: keyword, it extracts the byte count from the next argument.

The SHOWUSERINFO procedure actually generates a line in the print job report. The operation of this procedure is similar to the identically named procedure in the USRQUOTA script, and it uses the same techniques to generate a tabular report.

```
001. @echo OFF
002. @if not "%ECHO%"=="" echo %ECHO%
003. @if not "%OS%"=="Windows_NT" goto DOSEXIT
004. rem $Workfile: pjcount.bat $ $Revision: 1 $ $Date: 12/04/97 9:51a $
005. rem $Archive: /TimH/Pubs/Books/Macmillan/Windows NT
     Scripting/Scripts/pjcount.bat $
006.
007. rem Set local scope and call MAIN procedure
008. setlocal & pushd & set RET=
009.     set SCRIPTNAME=%~n0
010.     set SCRIPTPATH=%~f0
011.     if "%DEBUG%"=="1" (set TRACE=echo) else (set TRACE=rem)
012.     call _mtplib :INIT %SCRIPTPATH%
013.     if /i {%1}=={/help} (call :HELP %2) & (goto :HELPEXIT)
014.     if /i {%1}=={/?} (call :HELP %2) & (goto :HELPEXIT)
015.     call :MAIN %*
016.     :HELPEXIT
017. popd & endlocal & set RET=%RET%
018. goto :EOF
019.
020. rem /////////////////////////////////////////////////////////////////
021. rem HELP procedure
022. rem Display brief on-line help message
023. rem
024. :HELP
025. if defined TRACE %TRACE% [proc %0 %*]
026.     echo Syntax: PJCOUNT [computer]
027.     echo Collate and count print jobs per user.
028,     echo .
029.     echo Counts print jobs and pages for each user, using event log
030.     echo of specified or local computer.
031. goto :EOF
032.
033. rem /////////////////////////////////////////////////////////////////
034. rem MAIN procedure
035. rem
036. :MAIN
037. if defined TRACE %TRACE% [proc %0 %*]
038.     if not {%1}=={} (set COMPUTER=/S %1) else (set COMPUTER=)
```

```
039.    set USERNAME=
040.    echo Username                      Jobs    Pages    Bytes
041.    echo --------------------------- -------- -------- ------------
042.    for /f "tokens=*" %%I in ('dumpel /l system %COMPUTER% /e 10 /m Print
        /format "us" 2^>nul ^¦ sort') do call :SCANJOB %%I
043.    call :SHOWUSERINFO
044. goto :EOF
045.
046. rem ////////////////////////////////////////////////////////////////////
047. rem SCANJOB procedure
048. rem Collate information from one print job
049. rem
050. rem Arguments:    %1=username (sorted)
051. rem         %n=rest of arguments
052. rem
053. :SCANJOB
054. if defined TRACE %TRACE% [proc %0 %*]
055.     rem Handle switch to new username
056.     if not {%1}=={%USERNAME%} (
057.         (call :SHOWUSERINFO)
058.         (set USERNAME=%1)
059.         (set /a JOBCOUNT=0)
060.         (set /a PAGECOUNT=0)
061.         (set /a BYTECOUNT=0)
062.     )
063.
064.     set /a JOBCOUNT+=1
065.     :SCANJOBLOOP
066.         if {%2}=={} goto :SCANJOBLOOPEND
067.         if /i {%2}=={bytes:} set /a BYTECOUNT+=%3
068.         if /i {%2}=={printed:} set /a PAGECOUNT+=%3
069.         shift /2
070.     goto :SCANJOBLOOP
071.     :SCANJOBLOOPEND
072. goto :EOF
073.
074. rem ////////////////////////////////////////////////////////////////////
075. rem SHOWUSERINFO procedure
076. rem Display accumulated results for one user
077. rem
078. rem Arguments:    USERNAME=user name
079. rem         JOBCOUNT=job count
080. rem         PAGECOUNT=page count
081. rem         BYTECOUNT=byte count
082. rem
083. :SHOWUSERINFO
084. if defined TRACE %TRACE% [proc %0 %*]
085.     if "%USERNAME%"=="" goto :EOF
086.
```

```
087.      rem The following SET commands are all space-padded to here ------->
088.      set T1=%USERNAME%
089.      set T2=%JOBCOUNT%
090.      set T3=%PAGECOUNT%
091.      set T4=%BYTECOUNT%
092.
093.      rem Do not pad these SET commands
094.      set T1=%T1:~0,30%
095.      set T2=%T2:~0,8%
096.      set T3=%T3:~0,8%
097,      set T4=%T4:~0,12%
098.      echo %T1% %T2% %T3% %T4%
099. goto :EOF
100.
101. rem ///////////////////////////////////////////////////////////////////
102. rem Additional procedures go here...
103.
104. rem These must be the FINAL LINES in the script...
105. :DOSEXIT
106. echo This script requires Windows NT
107.
108. rem ///////////////////////////////////////////////////////////////////
```

Figure 6.3. *The PJCOUNT.BAT script*

The MTPLOGON.BAT Script

Figure 6.4 shows the MTPLOGON.BAT script. This is a sample logon script, which is executed as part of the logon sequence during client logon.

Logon scripts can execute any legal script commands, but they are restricted by two basic constraints:

- Because they execute at logon time, they must complete rapidly. Users will not be pleased if they have to wait extra time while a complex logon script executes.

- The logon script executes on the client OS. This means that the logon script must be able to execute on MS-DOS, Windows 95, or Windows NT. This restricts the operations allowed in the script to those compatible with MS-DOS.

Implementation

The MTPLOGON.BAT script illustrates many of the typical actions performed by a logon script, and has been structured to allow easy modification to suit local system requirements. The script performs the following actions:

1. Sets the local computer clock from a timeserver computer. This ensures that all computers are correctly synchronized, which is important for some shared file applications that use timestamps to compare file versions.

2. Maps a global share to a local drive letter for all users.

3. Maps one or more "group" shares depending upon the user's group membership.

4. Maps the user's home directory to a local drive letter.

5. Executes special per-user and per-machine logon script extensions.

6. Dumps debug information to a trace file.

The logon script is also self-installing. Executing the script from the command line with the /INSTALL switch installs the script into a target directory on a target network share. Typically, the target is the \WINNT\SYSTEM32\REPL \EXPORT\SCRIPTS directory or the IMPORT\SCRIPTS directory if replication is not being used.

Tip

Logon script replication sometimes causes confusion among new system administrators. When a client connects to a domain controller to load a logon script, it connects to the NETLOGON share on that server. By default, Windows NT assigns the \WINNT\SYSTEM32\REPL\IMPORT\SCRIPTS directory to this share. Therefore, logon scripts must be placed in this directory.

When several domain controllers exist, it is customary to set up the replication service to automatically replicate the logon scripts to all servers. In this case, the master *logon script is placed in the \WINNT\SYSTEM32\REPL\EXPORT\SCRIPTS directory, and this directory is exported by the replication service to all other domain controller's IMPORT\SCRIPTS directories, from where it is subsequently executed during client logon.*

The primary domain controller (PDC) is typically set up to replicate the EXPORT\SCRIPTS directory back to itself. So on the PDC, the logon script exists both in the EXPORT\SCRIPTS directory (the master copy) and the IMPORT\SCRIPTS directory (the copy accessed via the NETLOGON share).

Customization

The logon script operation can be customized by altering the following variables, which are set at the start of the script:

INSTALLSHARE	Target share to use when installing the logon script, in *server**share* format.
INSTALLDIR	Target directory to use when installing the logon script, relative to the INSTALLSHARE share.
DUMPFILE	The full path name of the file used to hold logon script dump information, or (if empty) to suppress dump file output.
TIMESERVER	The name of the server used for time synchronization, in *server* format.
GLOBALDRIVE	The drive letter used when mapping the global (all users) network share, followed by a colon.
GLOBALSHARE	The name of the global (all users) share, in *server**share* format.
GROUPDRIVE	The drive letter used when mapping a group network share, followed by a colon.
GROUPSERVER	The server name containing the group shares, in *server* format.
GROUP*n*	Up to four group names, which are used for group mapping.
HOMEDRIVE	The drive letter used when mapping the home directory, followed by a colon.

The MTPLOGON.BAT script begins by checking for an install request (line 23). The /INSTALL switch copies the script to the target location specified by the INSTALLSHARE and INSTALLDIR variables. Installation is only possible under Windows NT, and so this code is skipped if the OS is not Windows NT.

Next, options are set for the NET USE command (lines 35 and 36). This command is used to map network shares to local drive letters. Unfortunately, the /PERSISTENT switch is not supported by Windows 95. Therefore, the /PERSISTENT:NO option switch is placed in the NETSW variable only if the operating system is Windows NT.

If the TIMESERVER variable is set to the name of a timeserver, the NET TIME command (line 41) is used to synchronize the time of the local computer to that at the specified server. This ensures that all computers have synchronized clocks.

After the time has been set, various network shares are mapped to local drive letters. Before each share is mapped, however, a NET USE /DELETE command is used to ensure that no conflicts exist between the logon script and any locally requested mappings. This means that the logon script over-rides any locally mapped shares.

A single global share is mapped in the sample script (lines 44 to 49), though obviously others can be added as needed. The GLOBALSHARE specifies the share name, and the GLOBALDRIVE specifies the local drive to map.

Up to four group shares are also mapped by the sample script. Group share mapping relies upon the IFMEMBER command, which only operates under Windows NT. Therefore, the script does not attempt group share mapping if the operating system on the client is not Windows NT. Membership in each group is checked using the IFMEMBER command. If the user account is a member of the group, the GROUPDRIVE drive letter is mapped to the appropriate GROUP share on the GROUPSERVER server. This sample code assumes that the name of the share on the server is the same as the name of the group.

The final drive mapping performed by the sample script maps the user's home directory to the HOMEDRIVE drive letter (lines 81 to 86).

After all drives are mapped, the logon script checks to see if two additional scripts exist, and executes them if they are present. First, drive C: is checked for an additional script named MTPLOGON.BAT in the root (line 89). If this is present, it is executed. Next, drive U: (the user home directory drive) is checked in the same manner (line 93). The drive C: script can provide "per-machine" initialization; that is, initialization unique to a particular computer, but independent of the user. The drive U: script can provide "per-user" initialization; that is, initialization unique to the user but independent of the machine.

The final action performed by the logon script creates a dummy file called lmscript.$$$ in the C:\WINDOWS or C:\WIN95 directory. This is a bug fix that is recommended by Microsoft to correct certain problems associated with Windows 3.x and Windows 95 clients. These clients can fail to recognize the end of logon script execution under certain conditions. Creating this dummy file corrects this condition.

After the logon script is complete, the script generates a dump file containing a report of all current network drive mappings and the current user environment. This can be useful when debugging logon script problems.

```
001. @echo OFF
002. @if not "%ECHO%"=="" echo %ECHO%
003. rem $Workfile: mtplogon.bat $ $Revision: 2 $ $Date: 12/06/97 6:35p $
004. rem $Archive: /TimH/Pubs/Books/Macmillan/Windows NT
     Scripting/Scripts/mtplogon.bat $
005.
006. rem Alter these settings to customize the logon script
007. set INSTALLSHARE=\\SERVER\SHARE
```

```
008. set INSTALLDIR=\winnt\system32\repl\export\scripts
009. set DUMPFILE=c:\mtplogon.dmp
010. set TIMESERVER=\\SERVER
011. set GLOBALDRIVE=h:
012. set GLOBALSHARE=\\SERVER1\GLOBAL
013. set GROUPDRIVE=g:
014. mset GROUPSERVER=\\SERVER
015. set GROUP1=SalesMarketing
016. set GROUP2=HumanRes
017. set GROUP3=
018. set GROUP4=
019. set HOMEDRIVE=u:
020.
021. rem Process INSTALL request
022. if not "%OS%"=="Windows_NT" goto NOTNT1
023. if /i "%1"=="/install" (
024.     echo Installing script on server...
025.     xcopy %0 %INSTALLSHARE%%INSTALLDIR% /R
026.     goto :EOF
027. )
028. :NOTNT1
029.
030. rem Start of logon script
031. echo --- LOGON SCRIPT START $Revision: 2 $ ---
032. set MTPLOGONVER=$Revision: 2 $
033.
034. rem Set OS specific switches
035. set NETSW=/yes
036. if "%OS%"=="Windows_NT" set NETSW=/persistent:no %NETSW%
037.
038. rem Set the computer clock from the time-server clock
039. if "%TIMESERVER%"=="" goto NOTIMES
040.     echo --- Set computer time from %TIMESERVER% ---
041.     net time %TIMESERVER% /set /yes
042. :NOTIMES
043.
044. rem Map global drives
045. if "%GLOBALDRIVE%"=="" goto NOGLOBAL
046.     echo --- Map %GLOBALDRIVE% to %GLOBALSHARE% ---
047.     if exist %GLOBALDRIVE%*.* net use %GLOBALDRIVE% /delete
048.     net use %GLOBALDRIVE% %GLOBALSHARE% %NETSW%
049. :NOGLOBAL
050.
051. rem Map group drives
052. if not "%OS%"=="Windows_NT" goto NOGROUPS
053. if "%GROUPDRIVE%"=="" goto NOGROUPS
054.     if exist %GROUPDRIVE%*.* net use %GROUPDRIVE% /delete
055.     if "%GROUP1%"=="" goto NOGROUP1
056.     ifmember %GROUP1%
057.     if not errorlevel 1 goto NOGROUP1
058.         echo --- Map %GROUPDRIVE% to %GROUPSERVER%\%GROUP1%
059.         net use %GROUPDRIVE% %GROUPSERVER%\%GROUP1% %NETSW%
```

```
060.    :NOGROUP1
061.    if "%GROUP2%"=="" goto NOGROUP2
062.    ifmember %GROUP2%
063.    if not errorlevel 1 goto NOGROUP2
064.        echo --- Map %GROUPDRIVE% to %GROUPSERVER%\%GROUP2%
065.        net use %GROUPDRIVE% %GROUPSERVER%\%GROUP2% %NETSW%
066.    :NOGROUP2
067.    if "%GROUP3%"=="" goto NOGROUP3
068.    ifmember %GROUP3%
069.    if not errorlevel 1 goto NOGROUP3
070.        echo --- Map %GROUPDRIVE% to %GROUPSERVER%\%GROUP3%
071.        net use %GROUPDRIVE% %GROUPSERVER%\%GROUP3% %NETSW%
072.    :NOGROUP3
073.    if "%GROUP4%"=="" goto NOGROUP4
074.    ifmember %GROUP4%
075.    if not errorlevel 1 goto NOGROUP4
076.        echo --- Map %GROUPDRIVE% to %GROUPSERVER%\%GROUP4%
077.        net use %GROUPDRIVE% %GROUPSERVER%\%GROUP4% %NETSW%
078.    :NOGROUP4
079. :NOGROUPS
080.
081. rem Map users home directory
082. if "%HOMEDRIVE%"=="" goto NOHOME
083.     echo --- Map %HOMEDRIVE% to home directory ---
084.     if exist %HOMEDRIVE%*.* net use %HOMEDRIVE% /delete
085.     net use %HOMEDRIVE% /home %NETSW%
086. :NOHOME
087.
088. rem Execute logon script extensions
089. if not exist c:\mtplogon.bat goto NOTCEXT
090.     echo --- Execute machine-specific logon extension ---
091.     call c:\mtplogon.bat
092. :NOTCEXT
093. if not exist u:\mtplogon.bat goto NOTUEXT
094.     echo --- Execute user-specific logon extension ---
095.     call u:\mtplogon.bat
096. :NOTUEXT
097.
098. rem Special fix for Windows logon script end bugs
099. if exist c:\windows\*.* echo . >c:\windows\lmscript.$$$
100. if exist c:\win95\*.* echo . >c:\windows\lmscript.$$$
101.
102. rem End of logon script
103. echo --- LOGON SCRIPT END $Revision: 2 $ ---
104. if not "%DUMPFILE%"=="" net use >%DUMPFILE%
105. if not "%DUMPFILE%"=="" set >>%DUMPFILE%
106. u:
```

Figure 6.4. *The MTPLOGON script*

Chapter 7

Miscellaneous Scripts

- **UNCBACK script**
  This script adds UNC filename support to the Windows NT backup application.

- **XCPTEST script**
  This script can provide a thorough machine test/burn-in to validate new hardware.

- **REPL script**
  The most complete sample script in the book, this script provides a complete peer-to-peer file replication facility.

- **ANIMAL script**
  To close this part of the book, a classic computer game is implemented as a script.

Ready-to-Use Scripting Techniques

This chapter includes scripts to enhance the NT Backup utility, a machine "health" test, a complete replication facility, and finally, a simple game. Each script is first described as a ready to use command, and then various implementation details are described to assist you in modifying the script to suit local requirements.

The previous chapter focused on scripts which assist in user account management. However, scripts can do far more than this, and this chapter provides some additional sample scripts which assist in other areas of Windows NT management. On a lighter note, the final script in this book presents a classic computer science game implemented as a script.

The scripts in this chapter make extensive use of the _MTPLIB.BAT script library described in Chapter 5.

The UNCBACK Script

Figure 7.1 shows the UNCBACK.BAT script. This script enhances the NTBACKUP utility by providing support for UNC names. NTBACKUP provides a complete backup facility, but does not fully support UNC names (that is, network shares in the form *server**share*). UNCBACK enhances NTBACKUP by adding support for UNC names. This allows an NTBACKUP session to back up UNC shares without their being mapped to local network drives.

Syntax

```
UNCBACK [dir-list] [switches]
```

Description

The UNCBACK script executes an NTBACKUP backup command. The `dir-list` argument is one or more directory names to back up, separated by spaces. Following `dir-list` are zero or more switches. These switches are passed, unedited, to the NTBACKUP command. Thus, any valid NTBACKUP switch can be placed on the command line of UNCBACK.

In addition, any switches placed in the NTBACKUPSW variable are also passed to the NTBACKUP command. These switches (if any) are inserted in the command *before* any switches placed on the UNCBACK command line.

Items in the `dir-list` can be either local or mapped network drives, or UNC names (in the form *server**share*). If the directory name is a UNC name, the share is temporarily mapped to a drive letter for the duration of the backup operation.

Example

```
uncback c:\ d:\ \\PLX14\Users /hc:on /v
```

This example backs up the local drives C: and D:, and the network share \\PLX14\Users. The /HC:ON and /V switches are passed to the NTBACKUP command, thus enabling hardware compression and verifying the backup.

Implementation

The UNCBACK.BAT script is based on the SKELETON.BAT script described in Chapter 5. The MAIN procedure first checks to see if any arguments are present (line 51). If not, then the help text is displayed and the script exits.

If one or more arguments are present, the command line is parsed. The command line is comprised of two parts: the *dir-list* directory list, followed by any switches. First, all directory names in the *dir-list* are placed in the PATH-LIST variable (liens 59 to 72). Each directory name is placed in double quotes, and they are separated from each other by spaces. This processing is performed by the loop beginning at the :PATHLISTLOOP label. The loop ends when either all arguments have been processed, or the first switch (an argument that begins with a / or - character) is encountered.

Individual directory names are processed as follows: First, surrounding double quotes (if any) are removed (line 62). Then, the first two characters of the name are checked. If they are \\, the name is assumed to be a UNC name (line 65). If a UNC name is encountered, the following commands are executed:

```
1. pushd "%T1%"
2. set /a UNCCOUNT+=1
3. for /f "tokens=*" %%I in ('cd') do set T1=%%I
```

Since the PUSHD command is passed a UNC name, it automatically maps the UNC name to a drive letter. Using PUSHD is superior to the NET USE command for this purpose, as PUSHD automatically assigns drive letters, choosing unused letters. The variable UNCCOUNT is then incremented, which tracks the number of UNC names that have been assigned using the PUSHD command.

The script now needs to discover which drive letter was mapped by the PUSHD command, so this can be passed to the NTBACKUP command instead of the UNC name. To do this, a CD command is executed with no arguments (which therefore displays the current drive and directory). This output is captured by a FOR command and placed in the T1 variable. Thus, the lines shown above start with a UNC name in the variable T1, and end with an equivalent mapped drive letter and path in T1 instead. Therefore, when the T1 variable is added to the PATHLIST variable, a mapped drive letter replaces the UNC name.

After the directory names are accumulated, a similar loop (beginning at the :SWITCHLISTLOOP label, line 76) builds a list of all switch arguments. These are placed, separated by spaces, in the SWITCHLIST variable.

Once all command arguments have been processed, the NTBACKUP command is executed (line 85). The command is passed the PATHLIST, NTBACKUPSW, and SWITCHLIST variables as arguments. This constructs the required NTBACKUP command.

After NTBACKUP completes, the temporary drive mappings assigned by the PUSHD commands must be removed. This is done by executing zero or more POPD commands. The number of POPD commands to execute is controlled by UNCCOUNT, and therefore a FOR iterator command (line 88) is used to execute the required number of POPD commands.

```
01. @echo OFF
02. @if not "%ECHO%"=="" echo %ECHO%
03. @if not "%OS%"=="Windows_NT" goto DOSEXIT
04. rem $Workfile: uncback.bat $ $Revision: 2 $ $Date: 12/04/97 9:51a $
05. rem $Archive: /TimH/Pubs/Books/Macmillan/Windows NT
       Scripting/Scripts/uncback.bat $
06.
07. rem Set local scope and call MAIN procedure
08. setlocal & pushd & set RET=
09.     set SCRIPTNAME=%~n0
10.     set SCRIPTPATH=%~f0
11.     if "%DEBUG%"=="1" (set TRACE=echo) else (set TRACE=rem)
12.     call _mtplib :INIT %SCRIPTPATH%
13.     if /i {%1}=={/help} (call :HELP %2) & (goto :HELPEXIT)
14.     if /i {%1}=={/?} (call :HELP %2) & (goto :HELPEXIT)
15.     call :MAIN %*
16.     :HELPEXIT
17. popd & endlocal & set RET=%RET%
18. goto :EOF
19.
20. rem //////////////////////////////////////////////////////////////////////
21. rem HELP procedure
22. rem Display brief on-line help message
23. rem
24. :HELP
25. if defined TRACE %TRACE% [proc %0 %*]
26.     echo Syntax: UNCBACK [dir-list] [switches]
27.     echo Invokes NTBACKUP for the specified dir-list.
28.     echo .
29.     echo All switches at the end of the command line are passed unaltered to
30.     echo NTBACKUP. The contents of the NTBACKUPSW variable is prefixed before
31.     echo these switches.
32.     echo .
33.     echo Directory names in the dir-list can be UNC names, which are mapped
34.     echo to drive letters for the duration of the backup operation.
35.     echo .
36.     echo Example:
37.     echo    UNCBACK C:\ D:\ \\SERVER\FILES1 /A /B /V
38. goto :EOF
39.
40.
41. rem //////////////////////////////////////////////////////////////////////
42. rem MAIN procedure
43. rem
44. rem Arguments:   path(s)=path names to backup (incl. UNC names)
45. rem            /...=first switch marks start of switches passed to NTBACKUP
46. rem          NTBACKUPSW=additional switches passed before cmdline ones
47. rem
48. :MAIN
49. if defined TRACE %TRACE% [proc %0 %*]
```

```
50.     rem If no arguments, we default to displaying help
51.     if {%1}=={} (call :HELP) & (goto :EOF)
52.
53.     rem Clear variables
54.     set PATHLIST=
55.     set SWITCHLIST=
56.     set /a UNCCOUNT=0
57.
58.     rem Build list of paths, mapping UNC names
59.     :PATHLISTLOOP
60.         if {%1}=={} goto :PATHLISTLOOPEND
61.         set T1=%1
62.         set T1=%T1:"=%
63.         if "%T1:~0,1%"=="/" goto :PATHLISTLOOPEND
64.         if "%T1:~0,1%"=="-" goto :PATHLISTLOOPEND
65.         if "%T1:~0,2%"=="\\" (
66.             (pushd "%T1%")
67.             (set /a UNCCOUNT+=1)
68.             (for /f "tokens=*" %%I in ('cd') do set T1=%%I)
69.         )
70.         set PATHLIST=%PATHLIST% "%T1%"
71.         shift /1
72/     goto :PATHLISTLOOP
73.     :PATHLISTLOOPEND
74.
75.     rem Append residual switches to SWITCHLIST
76.     :SWITCHLISTLOOP
77.         if {%1}=={} goto :SWITCHLISTLOOPEND
78.         set SWITCHLIST=%SWITCHLIST% %1
79.         shift /1
80.     goto :SWITCHLISTLOOP
81.     :SWITCHLISTLOOPEND
82.
83.     rem Execute the NTBACKUP command
84.     echo -- ntbackup backup %PATHLIST% %NTBACKUPSW% %SWITCHLIST%
85.     ntbackup backup %PATHLIST% %NTBACKUPSW% %SWITCHLIST%
86.
87.     rem Delete all temporary UNC drive maps
88.     for /l %%I in (1,1,%UNCCOUNT%) do popd
89. goto :EOF
90.
91. rem ////////////////////////////////////////////////////////////////////////
92. rem Additional procedures go here...
93.
94. rem These must be the FINAL LINES in the script...
95. :DOSEXIT
96. echo This script requires Windows NT
97.
98. rem ////////////////////////////////////////////////////////////////////////
```

Figure 7.1. *The UNCBACK.BAT script*

The XCPTEST Script

Figure 7.2 shows the XCPTEST.BAT script. This script provides a burn-in test-bed for computers running Windows NT. The test itself is very simple: a set of files is repeatedly copied from one directory to another. However, if the file set is large enough the test actually exercises virtually all major hardware components, including memory (via the Windows NT cache), disk controller, disk drives, I/O busses, and (if one of the paths is on the network) the network connection.

Frequently, running this script overnight can highlight subtle problems on a machine that other testing does not reveal. Conversely, if the script runs for many hours without an error, the hardware can be assumed to be functioning correctly.

Syntax

```
XCPTEST ref-dir test-dir [...] [/PASSES:n] [/CHECK:m] [/NOSTOP] [/NOCONFIRM]
```

Switches

/PASSES:n	Sets the number of test passes to perform to *n* (the default is infinite).
/CHECK:m	Sets the pass count between file integrity checks (the default is 10).
/NOSTOP	Don't stop on a file copy error.
/NOCONFIRM	Skips the confirmation before erasing the test directory contents.

Description

The XCPTEST script provides a simple burn-in (or *soak test*) for computers running Windows NT. XCPTEST can frequently detect hardware errors that go undetected by other testing methods.

XCPTEST works by copying a set of files from one directory to another in round-robin fashion. That is, if three directories, A, B and C, are specified, the test copies from A to B, then B to C and finally from C to A. This constitutes a single "pass" by the test loop.

By default, XCPTEST executes an infinite number of passes. The /PASSES switch limits the number of passes to *n*. In addition, the test prompts with a Continue? request at the end of each pass. If no response is entered within five seconds, testing continues. This allows the test to run unattended, but to be interrupted gracefully.

The set of files to copy is obtained from a known good source, the *ref-dir*. A good source for the *ref-dir* is a CD-ROM. To ensure accurate testing, make sure that the total size of all the files in the *ref-dir* is larger than the amount of physical memory present in the machine under test. Sub-directories of the *ref-dir* are *not* included in the set of test files. A good choice for *ref-dir* is the \I386 directory on the Windows NT distribution CD-ROM.

The test directories are specified on the command line following *ref-dir*. If only one *test-dir* is specified, XCPTEST creates two sub-directories within this directory, called TEST1 and TEST2, and uses these for copying the files back and forth. If more than one *test-dir* is specified, the named directories are used for file copying. Any number of test directories can be specified, in any valid location. Local drives and network drives can be used, and UNC names are allowed *except* for the first *test-dir*.

The test directories are created if they do not already exist. If they *do* already exist, all files in the directories are deleted. Therefore, take great care when choosing test directories. Unless the /NOCONFIRM switch is used, the script prompts for confirmation before deleting the test directories.

Gross hardware errors that occur during testing usually manifest themselves as system hangs or Windows NT STOP screens. More subtle hardware errors typically result in corruption of the file data copied by the test. To check for this corruption, XCPTEST periodically verifies the contents of the test directories against the reference directory. By default, the file contents are checked every 10 passes, and once again before the test finally terminates. The /CHECK switch changes the number of passes between file verification checks. If the checking detects a file corruption, the test terminates with an error. The /NOSTOP switch over-rides this behavior, and allows testing to continue regardless of the number of errors which occur.

In addition to hardware testing, XCPTEST can be used to stress-test networks and disk sub-systems. Running multiple copies of XCPTEST (using separate sets of test directories) can also exercise SMP (that is, multi-CPU) systems quite effectively.

Example

```
xcptest g:\i386 c:\test d:\test f:\test /nostop
```

This example obtains test files from the G:\I386 directory. The files are then copied between the directories C:\TEST, D:\TEST and F:\TEST repeatedly. The /NOSTOP switch stops the test from terminating on an error.

Implementation

The MAKEUSR.BAT script is based on the SKELETON.BAT script described in Chapter 5. The MAIN procedure first checks to see if any arguments are present. If not, then the help text is displayed and the script exits.

If arguments are present, the PARSECMDLINE procedure in _MTPLIB.BAT is called to parse the command line, and the number of positional arguments is then checked (it must be 2 or more). The command line is then processed. The /PASSES switch sets the PASSES variable to the pass count, and the /CHECK switch sets the CHECKEVERY variable to the number of passes between integrity checks. The /NOSTOP switch sets the NOSTOP variable to 1 and the /NOCONFIRM switch sets the NOCONFIRM switch to 1.

The REFDIR variable is set to the reference directory, which is obtained from the first positional argument. The DIRLIST variable is then set to the list of test directories (each placed in double quotes), separated by spaces. If there is only one test directory specified, the DIRLIST variable is assigned two entries: the TEST1 and TEST2 subdirectories below this directory. If there is more than one test directory specified, each test directory is added directly to the DIRLIST variable.

Before proceeding, the script confirms that it is okay to delete the specified test directory contents (unless the /NOCONFIRM switch was specified). The DELETETEST-DIRS procedure is called to delete the contents of the test directories, and the COPYREFDIR is called to copy the reference directory into the first test directory.

The main test loop logic begins at the MAINPASSLOOP label. The PASS variable contains the pass number, and the CHECK variable is a down counter that is used to control the calls to the CHECKDIR procedure:

1. First, the pass count is checked and then incremented. A pass count of zero is interpreted to mean an infinite pass count. The COPYDIRLIST procedure is called to perform a single round-robin file copy operation (that is, a single test pass).

2. The CHECK counter is then decremented. If this is zero, a file integrity check is needed, and the CHECKDIR procedure is called to perform this. The CHECK counter is then reset.

3. Finally, the error counter (the ERRORS variable) is checked. If this is non-zero, and the /NOSTOP switch is *not* specified, testing immediately terminates. Otherwise, the CHOICE command is used to confirm that testing should continue (with a five second timeout).

After all test passes are complete, a final CHECKDIR is performed and DELETEDIRS is called again to cleanup the test directories. If errors have occurred, the test directories are *not* deleted, allowing additional analysis of the error data to be made.

The DELETETESTDIRS procedure is called to delete the contents of all the test directories. The procedure is passed the DIRLIST variable, and so receives the complete list of test directories as procedure arguments. DELETETESTDIRS then processes each argument (directory) in a loop. If the directory exists, all files are deleted. If it does not exist, it is created.

The COPYREFDIR procedure is a wrapper for an XCOPY command, which copies the contents of the reference directory into the first test directory.

The COPYDIRLIST procedure provides the actual round robin file copying. Like DELETETESTDIRS, it is passed the DIRLIST variable and so receives the list of test directories as arguments. The procedure enters a loop at the COPYDIRLISTLOOP label until there are fewer than two arguments remaining. For each pass of the loop, an XCOPY command copies one test directory to the next. Finally, an additional XCOPY command copies the last directory in the list back to the first, completing the round robin loop.

The CHECKDIR procedure verifies the integrity of the test files against the reference directory. The core of this procedure is an FC /B command that compares all reference directory files to those in the first test directory. The FC command does not return a valid exit code, and so the report output produced by the command is analyzed for errors. The output of the FC command is passed to a FIND command, which removes all lines containing the text Comparing. The output of this FIND command is then passed to another FIND which removes all lines containing FC: no. After these two filter commands, the residual output consists of empty lines and error lines. The output is then captured by a FOR command and parsed. The FOR command filters all blank lines, leaving only lines containing errors. The ERRORS counter is then incremented for each of these lines.

```
001. @echo OFF
002. @if not "%ECHO%"=="" echo %ECHO%
003. @if not "%OS%"=="Windows_NT" goto DOSEXIT
004. rem $Workfile: xcptest.bat $ $Revision: 1 $ $Date: 12/04/97 9:51a $
005. rem $Archive: /TimH/Pubs/Books/Macmillan/Windows NT
     Scripting/Scripts/xcptest.bat $
006.
007. rem Set local scope and call MAIN procedure
008. setlocal & pushd & set RET=
009.     set SCRIPTNAME=%~n0
010.     set SCRIPTPATH=%~f0
011.     if "%DEBUG%"=="1" (set TRACE=echo) else (set TRACE=rem)
012.     call _mtplib :INIT %SCRIPTPATH%
013.     if /i {%1}=={/help} (call :HELP %2) & (goto :HELPEXIT)
014.     if /i {%1}=={/?} (call :HELP %2) & (goto :HELPEXIT)
015.     call :MAIN %*
016.     :HELPEXIT
017. popd & endlocal & set RET=%RET%
018. goto :EOF
```

```
019.
020. rem ////////////////////////////////////////////////////////////////////
021. rem HELP procedure
022. rem Display brief on-line help message
023. rem
024. :HELP
025. if defined TRACE %TRACE% [proc %0 %*]
026.     echo Syntax: XCPTEST ref-dir test-dir [...] /PASSES:n /CHECK:m
027.     echo Ping-pong XCOPY machine soak test.
028.     echo .
029.     echo Copies a reference directory in round-robin fashion among
030.     echo two or more test dirs, checking for file corruption or loss.
031.     echo .
032.     echo The source dir is ref-dir. If two or more test-dirs are
033.     echo specified, these are used round-robin. If one test-dir is
034.     echo specified, two sub-dirs (test1 and test2) are used in this
035.     echo test-dir. ALL FILES IN THE TEST DIRECTORIES ARE DELETED!!!
036.     echo .
037.     echo Use /PASSES to specify the number of passes (def: infinite).
038.     echo Use /CHECK to specify pass counts between each file check.
039.     echo (def: 10). Use /NOSTOP to prevent test stopping on error(s).
040. goto :EOF
041.
042. rem ////////////////////////////////////////////////////////////////////
043. rem MAIN procedure
044. rem
045. :MAIN
046. if defined TRACE %TRACE% [proc %0 %*]
047.     rem If no arguments, we default to displaying help
048.     if {%1}=={} (call :HELP) & (goto :EOF)
049.
050.     rem Parse command line and setup variables
051.     set CMDLINE=%*
052.     call _mtplib :PARSECMDLINE 0
053.     if %CMDARGCOUNT% LSS 2 (call :HELP) & (goto :EOF)
054.     call _mtplib :FINDSWITCH /passes
055.     if "%RET%"=="0" (set /a PASSES=0) else (set /a PASSES=RETV)
056.     call _mtplib :FINDSWITCH /check
057.     if "%RET%"=="0" (set /a CHECKEVERY=10) else (set /a CHECKEVERY=RETV)
058.     call _mtplib :FINDSWITCH /nostop
059.     if "%RET%"=="0" (set /a NOSTOP=0) else (set /a NOSTOP=1)
060.     call _mtplib :FINDSWITCH /y
061.     if "%RET%"=="0" (set NOCONFIRM=0) else (set NOCONFIRM=1)
062.     call _mtplib :GETARG 1
063.     set REFDIR="%RET%"
064.     if %CMDARGCOUNT% GTR 2 goto :USERLIST
065.         call _mtplib :GETARG 2
066.         set DIRLIST="%RET%\test1" "%RET%\test2"
067.     goto :DIRLISTDONE
068.     :USERLIST
069.         set DIRLIST=
```

```
070.        set ARG=2
071.        :USERLISTLOOP
072.            if %ARG% GTR %CMDARGCOUNT% goto :USERLISTLOOPEND
073.            call _mtplib :GETARG %ARG%
074.            set DIRLIST=%DIRLIST% "%RET%"
075.            set /a ARG+=1
076.        goto :USERLISTLOOP
077.        :USERLISTLOOPEND
078.    :DIRLISTDONE
079.
080.    rem Verify everything is ok before starting
081.    if not "%NOCONFIRM%"=="1" (
082.        echo All files in these directories will be deleted:
083.        echo    %DIRLIST%
084.        %COMSPEC% /c choice /n "Delete all files?"
085.        if errorlevel 2 goto :EOF
086.    )
087.
088.    rem Copy reference directory
089.    call :DELETETESTDIRS %DIRLIST%
090.    call :COPYREFDIR %REFDIR% %DIRLIST%
091.
092.    rem Now process each test pass
093.    set /a PASS=0
094.    set /a ERRORS=0
095.    set /a CHECK=CHECKEVERY
096.    :MAINPASSLOOP
097.        if %PASSES% NEQ 0 if %PASS% GEQ %PASSES% goto :MAINPASSLOOPEND
098.        set /a PASS+=1
099.        echo XCPTEST: Pass %PASS% of %PASSES%, %ERRORS% errors
100.        call :COPYDIRLIST %DIRLIST%
101.        set /a CHECK-=1
102.        if %CHECK% GTR 0 goto :SKIPCHECK
103.            call :CHECKDIR %REFDIR% %DIRLIST%
104.            set /a CHECK=CHECKEVERY
105.        :SKIPCHECK
106.        if %NOSTOP% EQU 0 if %ERRORS% GTR 0 goto :MAINPASSLOOPEND
107.        %COMSPEC% /c choice /n /T:Y,5 "Continue testing?"
108.        if errorlevel 2 goto :MAINPASSLOOPEND
109.    goto :MAINPASSLOOP
110.    :MAINPASSLOOPEND
111.    if %ERRORS% EQU 0 call :CHECKDIR %REFDIR% %DIRLIST%
112.    if %ERRORS% EQU 0 call :DELETETESTDIRS %DIRLIST%
113.    echo XCPTEST: End of test, %PASS% passes, %ERRORS% errors
114. goto :EOF
115.
116. rem ///////////////////////////////////////////////////////////////
117. rem CHECKDIR procedure
118. rem Check test dir against refdir
119. rem
120. rem Arguments:    %1=ref directory
```

```
121. rem        %2=test directory
122. rem
123. :CHECKDIR
124.     set D1=%1
125.     set D2=%2
126.     set D1=%D1:"=%
127.     set D2=%D2:"=%
128.     for /f "tokens=*" %%I in ('fc /b %D1%\*.* %D2%\*.* ^¦ find /v
"Comparing" ^¦ find /v "FC: no"') do (set /a ERRORS+=1) & (echo %%I)
129. goto :EOF
130.
131. rem ///////////////////////////////////////////////////////////////////
132. rem DELETETESTDIRS procedure
133. rem Delete test directories
134. rem
135. rem Arguments:    %n=list of all directories
136. rem
137. :DELETETESTDIRS
138.     echo Deleting directory %1...
139.     if {%1}=={} goto :EOF
140.     if exist %1 del %1 /f/q
141.     if not exist %1 md %1
142.     shift /1
143.     goto :DELETETESTDIRS
144. goto :EOF
145.
146. rem ///////////////////////////////////////////////////////////////////
147. rem COPYREFDIR procedure
148. rem Copy reference directory to 1st test directory
149. rem
150. rem Arguments:    %1=refdir
151. rem        %2=first test dir
152. rem
153. :COPYREFDIR
154.     echo Copying reference directory...
155.     xcopy %1 %2 /r
156. goto :EOF
157.
158. rem ///////////////////////////////////////////////////////////////////
159. rem COPYDIRLIST procedure
160. rem Copy directories in round-robin list
161. rem
162. rem Arguments:    %n=list of all directories
163. rem
164. :COPYDIRLIST
165.     if {%2}=={} goto :EOF
166.     set FIRST=%1
167.     :COPYDIRLISTLOOP
168.         if {%2}=={} goto :COPYDIRLISTLOOPEND
169.         xcopy %1 %2 /r/q
170.         shift /1
```

```
171.      goto :COPYDIRLISTLOOP
172.      :COPYDIRLISTLOOPEND
173.      xcopy %1 %FIRST% /r/q
174. goto :EOF
175.
176. rem ///////////////////////////////////////////////////////////////////////
177. rem Additional procedures go here...
178.
179. rem These must be the FINAL LINES in the script...
180. :DOSEXIT
181. echo This script requires Windows NT
182.
183. rem ///////////////////////////////////////////////////////////////////////
```

Figure 7.2. *The XCPTEST.BAT script*

The REPL Script

Figure 7.3 shows the REPL.BAT script. This script provides an automatic file replication facility that is similar to the replication service provided by Windows NT. The REPL script differs from this facility, however, by providing a peer-to-peer replication, instead of the master-slave replication provided by the replication service. In addition, the REPL script is more flexible and can support Windows 95 target computers as well as Windows NT computers.

The REPL.BAT script is the most complex of the scripts presented in this book. It demonstrates that scripts can provide facilities equal to native Windows NT commands, and can significantly enhance the operating system with new features.

Syntax

```
1. REPL [site-name]
2. REPL site-name [/ADD:dir ...] [/DELETE:dir ...]
3. REPL site-name /DELALL [/Y]
4. REPL site-name [/ENABLE ¦ /DISABLE]
5. REPL /RESET [/Y]
6. REPL /START [/INTERVAL:nnn] [/FIRST:nnn] [/LOG:log-file]
7. REPL /STOP
8. REPL /RUN [/LOG:log-file]
```

Switches

/ADD:*dir*	Adds a directory to a replication site.
/DELETE:*dir*	Deletes a directory from a replication site.
/DELALL	Deletes all directories from a replication site.

/ENABLE	Enables a replication site.
/DISABLE	Disables a replication site.
/RESET	Resets REPL, and deletes *all* replication sites.
/START	Starts automatic replication.
/INTERVAL:*nnn*	Sets the interval between replications to *nnn* minutes (the default is 60 minutes).
/FIRST:*nnn*	Sets the interval before the first replication to *nnn* minutes (default: 1).
/LOG:*log-file*	Sends replication results to the specified log file.
/STOP	Stops automatic replication.
/RUN	Runs a manual replication pass.
/Y	Skips confirmation prompts for the /RESET and /DELALL switches.

Description

The REPL script provides a general-purpose file and directory replication facility for Windows NT. Unlike the Windows NT replication service, all replication directories managed by REPL are "peers." That is, there are no "master" and "slave" (or export/import) directories. Instead, REPL treats all directories as export *and* import directories.

REPL manages sets of directories known as *sites*. A *site* is a set of one or more directory trees that are to be synchronized by the REPL facility. Sites are given arbitrary names to identify them, and REPL can support any number of sites, each containing any number of directories. Directories can be specified as local drive paths or UNC names. For example, a site named SAMPLE could contain the directories C:\Source, E:\Users\Source and \\LIBRARY\Archive\Source. When REPL updates the SAMPLE site, all the directories are synchronized so that the contents of each tree are identical. The full directory trees are synchronized, including all sub-directories.

Using UNC names for directories is recommended. REPL can perform replication runs with no user logged-in. In this case, networked drives may not be mapped as expected, and the replication can fail. Using UNC names avoids this problem, as the name is always valid, regardless of user logon state.

REPL synchronizes the directories within a site by performing a round robin copy of files from one directory tree to the next. Thus, if a site contains three directories, A, B, and C, the REPL script copies directory A to B, then B to C, and then C back to A. In this way, a file placed in *any* of the directories A, B or C will eventually be propagated to all three directories (although it can take up to two replication passes to complete the copy).

Actual directory replication is performed by the ROBOCOPY command. Since this command only copies changed or new files, replication of directory trees is very efficient, and consumes a minimal amount of system bandwidth.

Replication occurs when a replication "run" is initiated. Runs can be executed manually, using the /RUN switch, or automatically at predetermined intervals, using the /START switch. Once automatic replication is started, it continues while the Windows NT computer is running (it is not necessary for a user to be logged in). In addition, all replication information is persistent (it is stored in the system registry), and replication automatically restarts whenever the Windows NT computer is restarted. Automatic replication relies upon the Windows NT Schedule Service, and so this service must be running for replication to proceed.

Use REPL(1) to display the status of the replication site named *site-name*. If *site-name* is absent, all replication sites are detailed. This command also displays the status of automatic replication (running or stopped).

Use REPL(2) and REPL(3) to edit the contents of a site, or create a new site. The /DELALL switch deletes an entire replication site, the /ADD switch adds the specified *dir* to the site, and the /DELETE switch deletes the specified *dir*. Multiple /ADD and /DELETE commands can be specified on a single REPL command line.

Use REPL(4) to enable or disable a site. Replication runs do not replicate disabled sites, but they can still be edited. New sites are always enabled by default.

Use REPL(5) to reset the entire replication facility, and delete all sites. The run/stop state of automatic replication is *not* changed by this command.

Use REPL(6) to start automatic replication, and REPL(7) to stop automatic replication. The /INTERVAL switch specifies the interval between replication runs (in minutes). The default is 60 minutes. The /FIRST switch specifies the interval to the first replication run after the facility is started. The default is one minute. Automatic replication uses the Scheduler Service on the local Windows NT computer, and so this must be running before automatic replication can be used. The /LOG switch specifies a log file. This file, if specified, accumulates the replication results (actually the report generated by the ROBOCOPY command).

Use REPL(8) to perform a manual replication run. This is useful when testing a replication setup before starting automatic replication, or to perform an immediate update of all replicated information. As a result of the algorithm used, two REPL(8) commands should be issued to ensure that complete peer replication has occurred.

Example

```
repl Scripts /add:c:\Scripts /add:e:\SrcSafe\Scripts /add:\\
SRV-USERS\Users\TimH\Scripts /enable
```

This example adds three directories to the Scripts site and enables the site. The Scripts site is created if it does not already exist.

```
repl /start /interval:30 /log:c:\repl.log
```

This example starts automatic replication, with an interval of 30 minutes. Replication results are logged to the file C:\REPL.LOG.

Implementation

The REPL.BAT script is based on the SKELETON.BAT script described in Chapter 5. All state and site information managed by REPL is maintained in the registry in the HKEY_LOCAL_MACHINE key (this key is used so that the information is available when REPL executes under the control of the Scheduler service). REPL functionality can be broken into two parts:

- The interactive functions that edit the state information

- The actual replication functions that interpret the state information.

Replication state information for a site is maintained in the variable RSENABLE_*sitename* and the array RSDIR_*sitename_n_*, where *n* is the array index. This information is moved to and from the registry using the LOADREG and SAVEREG procedures, which are wrappers for the REGSETM and REGGETM procedures in _MTPLIB.BAT. These procedures load the state information for all sites at once. To simplify coding, one specific site is designated as the *working* site. The working site is maintained in the variables WORKENABLE, WORKDIR_*n_* and WORKCOUNT. The procedures LOADSITE and SAVESITE move state information in the site variables to/from the working site variables. Therefore, to edit a site, the following operations must be performed:

1. Load the state information from the registry using LOADREG.

2. Load the required site to the working site using LOADSITE.

3. Edit the working site.

4. Save the working site back into the site variables.

5. Save all site variables in the registry.

The SAVESITE procedure also provides a packing function. When the working site is edited, one or more directories can be deleted. Deletions are processed by deleting entries in the WORKDIR_*n_* array. Thus, this array can have "holes" when SAVESITE is called. The procedure therefore re-packs the site before it is saved back to the site variables.

The MAIN procedure begins by parsing the command line using the PARSECMDLINE procedure from the _MTPLIB.BAT script library (line 59). The variable SITE-NAME is then set to the first positional argument (line 63). Then, depending upon the command-line switches, MAIN dispatches (lines 66 to 76) to a handler routine as follows:

1. If no switches are present, REPLSHOW is called to display the current replication status.

2. If the /RESET switch is found, REPLRESET is called to reset (clear) all replication sites.

3. If the /START switch is found, REPLSTART is called to start automatic replication.

4. If the /STOP switch is found, REPLSTOP is called to stop automatic replication.

5. If the /RUN switch is found, REPLRUN is called to perform a single replication run.

6. REPLEDIT is called to handle all other switches and edit the site information.

The REPLSHOW procedure (line 85) displays site information. The registry information is loaded using LOADREG, and REPLSHOW1 is called to display information on each site. If a *site-name* is present on the command line, REPLSHOW1 is called once for this site (line 89). Otherwise, a FOR command (line 90) is used to iterate all sites, and REPLSHOW1 is called for each site. Finally, the current automatic replication state is displayed.

REPLSHOW1 displays the details for a specified site. The site is loaded using LOAD-SITE (line 104), and then the list of directories replicated by the site is displayed, along with the enabled state of the site.

The REPLRESET procedure (line 118) resets all replication sites. After confirming this operation with the user, the procedure simply deletes the entire replication registry state (line 127). This resets all replication information.

The REPLSTART procedure (line 139) starts automatic replication, while the REPLSTOP replication stops automatic replication. Automatic replication is actually initiated by the Windows NT schedule service. An AT command is submitted which executes a REPL /RUN command. Additional switches to the REPL command cause an additional REPL /RUN command to be submitted for later execution. This ensures that REPL executes regularly at the specified interval.

REPLSTART begins by disabling any existing automatic replication. It calls GETRE-PLJOBID (line 141) to get the schedule service job ID of any REPL.BAT command. This command is then deleted using the AT /DELETE command (line 143). A new schedule service command is then constructed using the command line switches, and this is then passed to the SOON[RK] command (line 161), which schedules the command for later execution.

The REPLRUN procedure (line 187) performs the actual replication. Before starting any replication work, REPLRUN regenerates a new schedule service command and submits it via the SOON command (line 200). This only occurs if the current run request is an automatic run (indicated by the presence of the /INTERVAL switch). Each time an automatic replication operation is run, the next periodic command is re-scheduled to start after the appropriate interval. The interval value is passed from command to command using the /INTERVAL switch.

After scheduling another command, REPLRUN proceeds to perform the actual file and directory replication. All sites are loaded via LOADREG, and the REPLRUN1 procedure (line 210) is called for each site (by iterating each variable named RSEN-ABLE_*sitename*). The REPLRUN1 procedure loads the site into the working site via the LOADSITE procedure (line 212), and then enters the REPLRUNLOOP, which processes each directory in the directory list. Directory pairs are then passed to the REPLRUN2 procedure (line 226), which executes the ROBOCOPY command (line 234) to replicate one directory into the next. REPLRUN1 completes by calling REPLRUN2 one more time (line 224) , to copy the last directory in the list back to the first, thus closing the round robin loop.

The REPLEDIT procedure (line 247) edits a site. The site is first loaded using the LOADREG and LOADSITE procedures. Then each command switch is processed by using a numeric iterator FOR command. Finally, the edited site is saved using the SAVESITE and SAVEREG procedures. Each command switch invokes the appropriate edit procedure (for example, /ADD invokes the REPLEDITADD procedure).

The REPLEDITADD procedure (line 275) adds a new directory to a site. To ensure that duplicate directories do not exist in a site, REPLEDITADD begins by deleting the directory from the site, and then appends the directory to the end of the site directory list.

The REPLEDITDELETE procedure (line 282) deletes a directory from the site. The list of directories is searched, and any matching directories are deleted by clearing the appropriate array entry. This leaves "holes" in the working directory array, which must be packed by the SAVESITE procedure.

The REPLEDITDELALL procedure (line 294) deletes all directories from a site, simply by deleting the entire working site.

```
001. @echo OFF
002. @if not "%ECHO%"=="" echo %ECHO%
003. @if not "%OS%"=="Windows_NT" goto DOSEXIT
004. rem $Workfile: repl.bat $ $Revision: 1 $ $Date: 12/04/97 9:51a $
005. rem $Archive: /TimH/Pubs/Books/Macmillan/Windows NT
     Scripting/Scripts/repl.bat $
006.
007. rem Set local scope and call MAIN procedure
008. setlocal & pushd & set RET=
009.    set SCRIPTNAME=%~n0
010.    set SCRIPTPATH=%~f0
011.    if "%DEBUG%"=="1" (set TRACE=echo) else (set TRACE=rem)
012.    call _mtplib :INIT %SCRIPTPATH%
013.    if /i {%1}=={/help} (call :HELP %2) & (goto :HELPEXIT)
014.    if /i {%1}=={/?} (call :HELP %2) & (goto :HELPEXIT)
015.    call :MAIN %*
016.    :HELPEXIT
017. popd & endlocal & set RET=%RET%
018. goto :EOF
019.
020. rem /////////////////////////////////////////////////////////////////////
021. rem HELP procedure
022. rem Display brief on-line help message
023. rem
024. :HELP
025. if defined TRACE %TRACE% [proc %0 %*]
026.    echo Syntax: REPL [switches]
027.    echo Automates peer-to-peer directory and file replication.
028.    echo .
29.     echo REPL [site-name]
030.    echo     Display current replication status for all sites or for
031.    echo     specified site.
032.    echo REPL site-name /ADD:dir [...]
033.    echo     Add specified directories to replication site.
034.    echo REPL site-name /DELETE:dir [...]
035.    echo     Delete specified directories from replication site.
036.    echo REPL site-name /DELALL [/Y]
037.    echo     Delete all directories from specified site. /Y skips confirm.
038.    echo REPL site-name /ENABLE ^| /DISABLE
039.    echo     Enable or disable an individual site.
040.    echo REPL /RESET [/Y]
041.    echo     Delete all sites. /Y skips confirm.
042.    echo REPL /START [/INTERVAL:nnn] [/FIRST:nnn] [/LOG:log-file]
043.    echo     Start automatic replication to run every nnn minutes. The
044.    echo     default is once per hour. The first will occur in nnn
                minutes.
045.    echo REPL /STOP
046.    echo     Stop automatic replication.
047.    echo REPL /RUN [/LOG:log-file]
048.    echo     Execute a manual replication run.
049. goto :EOF
```

```
050.
051. rem /////////////////////////////////////////////////////////////////////
052. rem MAIN procedure
053. rem
054. :MAIN
055. if defined TRACE %TRACE% [proc %0 %*]
056.     rem Parse command line and check for basic switches etc
057.     set CONTEXT=%SCRIPTNAME%.BAT
058.     set CMDLINE=%*
059.     call _mtplib :PARSECMDLINE 0
060.     call _mtplib :FINDSWITCH /y
061.     if "%RET%"=="0" (set NOCONFIRM=0) else (set NOCONFIRM=1)
062.     call _mtplib :GETARG 1
063.     set SITENAME=%RET%
064.
065.     rem Dispatch to handler based upon arguments and switches
066.     if "%CMDSWCOUNT%"=="0" (call :REPLSHOW) & (goto :EOF)
067.     call _mtplib :FINDSWITCH /reset
068.     if not "%RET%"=="0" (call :REPLRESET) & (goto :EOF)
069.     call _mtplib :FINDSWITCH /start
070.     if not "%RET%"=="0" (call :REPLSTART) & (goto :EOF)
071.     call _mtplib :FINDSWITCH /stop
072.     if not "%RET%"=="0" (call :REPLSTOP) & (goto :EOF)
073.     call _mtplib :FINDSWITCH /run
074.     if not "%RET%"=="0" (call :REPLRUN) & (goto :EOF)
075.     if "%SITENAME%"=="" (echo repl: site name required) & (goto :EOF)
076.     call :REPLEDIT
077. goto :EOF
078.
079. rem /////////////////////////////////////////////////////////////////////
080. rem REPLSHOW procedure
081. rem Show status of one or all sites
082. rem
083. rem Arguments:    SITENAME=name of site to display, empty for all sites
084. rem
085. :REPLSHOW
086. if defined TRACE %TRACE% [proc %0 %*]
087.     rem Load site information and display it
088.     call :LOADREG
089.     if not "%SITENAME%"=="" (call :REPLSHOW1 RSENABLE_%SITENAME%) & (goto
         :REPLSHOW9)
090.     for /f "tokens=1 delims==" %%I in ('set RSENABLE_ 2^>nul') do call
         :REPLSHOW1 %%I
091.     :REPLSHOW9
092.
093.     rem Display run status
094.     call :GETREPLJOBID
095.     if "%RET%"=="NONE" (
096.         echo Replication is not running.
097.     ) else (
098.         echo Replication is running.
```

```
099.      )
100. goto :EOF
101. :REPLSHOW1
102.      if not defined %1 goto :EOF
103.      for /f "tokens=2 delims=_" %%J in ("%1") do set T1=%%J
104.      call :LOADSITE %T1%
105.      if "%WORKENABLE%"=="1" (set RET=enabled) else (set RET=disabled)
106.      echo Replication site %T1% (%WORKCOUNT% dirs) is %RET%:
107.      for /l %%J in (1,1,%WORKCOUNT%) do call :REPLSHOW2 %%J
108. goto :EOF
109. :REPLSHOW2
110.      set RET=%%WORKDIR_%1_%%
111.      call _mtplib :RESOLVE
112.      echo      %RET%
113. goto :EOF
114.
115. rem /////////////////////////////////////////////////////////////////////
115. rem REPLRESET procedure
116. rem Reset (delete) all replication sites (requires confirmation)
117. rem
118. :REPLRESET
119. if defined TRACE %TRACE% [proc %0 %*]
120.      rem Confirm deletion is ok
121.      if not "%NOCONFIRM%"=="1" (
122.          %COMSPEC% /c choice /n "Delete all sites?"
123.          if errorlevel 2 goto :EOF
124.      )
125.
126.   -  rem Delete all registry contents for script
127.      call _mtplib :REGDELM %CONTEXT%
128.      echo All sites deleted.
129. goto :EOF
130.
131. rem /////////////////////////////////////////////////////////////////////
132. rem REPLSTART procedure
133. rem Start automatic replication
134. rem
135. rem Arguments:    /interval:nnn=set interval to nnn minutes (def: 60)
136. rem         /first:nnn=do first run in nnn minutes (def: 1)
137. rem         /log:file=send o/p to log-file (def: none)
138. rem
139. :REPLSTART
140. if defined TRACE %TRACE% [proc %0 %*]
141.      rem First, stop any current replication
142.      call :GETREPLJOBID
143.      if not "%RET%"=="NONE" at %RET% /delete
144.
145.      rem Get logfile info
146.      set LOGFILE=
147.      set LOGCMD=
148.      call _mtplib :FINDSWITCH /log
```

```
149.    if not "%RET%"=="0" (set LOGFILE=%RETV%) & (set LOGCMD=/log:%RETV%)
150.
151.    rem Get values for interval and first run delay
152.    set /a INTERVAL=60
153.    call _mtplib :FINDSWITCH /interval
154.    if not "%RET%"=="0" set /a INTERVAL=RETV
155.    set /a FIRST=1
156.    call _mtplib :FINDSWITCH /first
157.    if not "%RET%"=="0" set /a FIRST=RETV
158.
159.    rem Schedule the first AT command via SOON
160.    set /a FIRST*=60
161.    soon %FIRST% "%COMSPEC% /c %SCRIPTPATH% /run /interval:%INTERVAL%
        %LOGCMD%" >nul
162.    echo Replication started.
163. goto :EOF
164.
165. rem //////////////////////////////////////////////////////////////////////
166. rem REPLSTOP procedure
167. rem Stop automatic replication
168. rem
169. :REPLSTOP
170. if defined TRACE %TRACE% [proc %0 %*]
171.    call :GETREPLJOBID
172.    if "%RET%"=="NONE" (
173.        echo Replication is not running.
174.    ) else (
175.        at %RET% /delete
176.        echo Replication stopped.
177.    )
178. goto :EOF
179.
180. rem //////////////////////////////////////////////////////////////////////
181. rem REPLRUN procedure
182. rem Perform a replication run (may be invoked from AT)
183. rem
184. rem Arguments:    /interval:nnn=set interval to nnn minutes (def: 60)
185. rem        /log:file=send o/p to log-file (def: none)
186. rem
187. :REPLRUN
188. if defined TRACE %TRACE% [proc %0 %*]
189.    rem Get logfile info
190.    set LOGFILE=
191.    set LOGCMD=
192.    call _mtplib :FINDSWITCH /log
193.    if not "%RET%"=="0" (set LOGFILE=%RETV%) & (set LOGCMD=/log:%RETV%)
194.
195.    rem Regenerate next run if required
196.    call _mtplib :FINDSWITCH /interval
197.    if "%RET%"=="0" goto :NOREGEN
198.        set /a INTERVAL=RETV
```

```
199.          set /a RETV*=60
200.          soon %RETV% "%COMSPEC% /c %SCRIPTPATH% /run /interval:%INTERVAL%
              %LOGCMD%" >nul
201.   :NOREGEN
202.
203.       rem Load all sites and replicate them
204.       if "%LOGFILE%"=="" (set LOGCMD=^>nul) else (set LOGCMD=^>^>%LOGFILE%)
205.       date /t %LOGCMD%
206.       time /t %LOGCMD%
207.       call :LOADREG
208.       for /f "tokens=1 delims==" %%I in ('set RSENABLE_ 2^>nul') do call
              :REPLRUN1 %%I
209.  goto :EOF
210.  :REPLRUN1
211.       for /f "tokens=2 delims=_" %%J in ("%1") do set T1=%%J
212.       call :LOADSITE %T1%
213.       if %WORKENABLE%==0 goto :EOF
214.       if %WORKCOUNT% LEQ 1 goto :EOF
215.       set /a SRCIX=1
216.       set /a DSTIX=2
217.       :REPLRUNLOOP
218.           if %DSTIX% GTR %WORKCOUNT% goto :REPLRUNLOOPEND
219.           call :REPLRUN2 %SRCIX% %DSTIX%
220.           set /a SRCIX+=1
221.           set /a DSTIX+=1
222.       goto :REPLRUNLOOP
223.       :REPLRUNLOOPEND
224.       call :REPLRUN2 %SRCIX% 1
225.  goto :EOF
226.  :REPLRUN2
227.       set RET=%%WORKDIR_%1_%%
228.       call _mtplib :RESOLVE
229.       set SRC=%RET%
230.       set RET=%%WORKDIR_%2_%%
231.       call _mtplib :RESOLVE
232.       set DST=%RET%
233.       echo --- robocopy "%SRC%" "%DST%" /e %LOGCMD%
234.       robocopy "%SRC%" "%DST%" /e %LOGCMD%
235.  goto :EOF
236.
237.  rem ////////////////////////////////////////////////////////////////////
238.  rem REPLEDIT procedure
239.  rem Edit a site contents
240.  rem
241.  rem Arguments:    /add:dir=add specified directory to site
242.  rem          /delete:dir=delete specified directory from site
243.  rem          /delall=delete entire site (requires confirm)
244.  rem          /enable=enable site
245.  rem          /disable=disable site
246.  rem
247.  :REPLEDIT
```

```
248. if defined TRACE %TRACE% [proc %0 %*]
249.     rem Load site information
250.     call :LOADREG
251.     call :LOADSITE %SITENAME%
252.
253.     rem Process all command switches
254.     for /l %%I in (1,1,%CMDSWCOUNT%) do call :REPLEDIT1 %%I
255.
256.     rem Save edited site information
257.     call :SAVESITE %SITENAME%
258.     call :SAVEREG
259. goto :EOF
260. :REPLEDIT1
261.     call _mtplib :GETSWITCH %1
262.     if "%RET%"=="/add" (
263.         (call :REPLEDITADD)
264.     ) else if "%RET%"=="/delete" (
265.         (call :REPLEDITDELETE)
266.     ) else if "%RET%"=="/delall" (
267.         (call :REPLEDITDELALL)
268.     ) else if "%RET%"=="/enable" (
269.         (set WORKENABLE=1)
270.     ) else if "%RET%"=="/disable" (
271.         (set WORKENABLE=0)
272.     )
273. goto :EOF
274.
275. :REPLEDITADD
276.     if "%RETV%"=="" goto :EOF
277.     call :REPLEDITDELETE
278.     set /a WORKCOUNT+=1
279.     set WORKDIR_%WORKCOUNT%_=%RETV%
280. goto :EOF
281.
282. :REPLEDITDELETE
283.     if "%RETV%"=="" goto :EOF
284.     set /a IX=1
285.     :REPLEDITDELETELOOP
286.         if %IX% GTR %WORKCOUNT% goto :EOF
287.         set RET=%%WORKDIR_%IX%_%%
288.         call _mtplib :RESOLVE
289.         if /i "%RET%"=="%RETV%" set WORKDIR_%IX%_=
290.         set /a IX+=1
291.     goto :REPLEDITDELETELOOP
292. goto :EOF
293.
294. :REPLEDITDELALL
295.     if not "%NOCONFIRM%"=="1" (
296.         %COMSPEC% /c choice /n "Delete all site directories?"
297.         if errorlevel 2 goto :EOF
298.     )
```

```
299.     set /a WORKENABLE=0
300.     set /a WORKCOUNT=0
301.     call _mtplib :VARDEL WORKDIR_
302. goto :EOF
303.
304, rem /////////////////////////////////////////////////////////////////////
305. rem GETREPLJOBID procedure
306. rem
307. rem Returns:    RET=job ID of REPL command, or "NONE" if not found
308. rem
309. :GETREPLJOBID
310. if defined TRACE %TRACE% [proc %0 %*]
311.     set RET=NONE
312.     for /f "tokens=1" %%I in ('at ^¦ find "%SCRIPTNAME%"') do set RET=%%I
313. goto :EOF
314.
315. rem /////////////////////////////////////////////////////////////////////
316. rem LOADREG procedure
317. rem Load registry information into variables
318. rem
319. :LOADREG
320. if defined TRACE %TRACE% [proc %0 %*]
321.     rem Delete existing site information
322.     call _mtplib :VARDEL RSENABLE_
323.     call _mtplib :VARDEL RSDIR_
324.
325.     rem Load site data from the registry
326.     call _mtplib :REGGETM %CONTEXT%
327. goto :EOF
328.
329. rem /////////////////////////////////////////////////////////////////////
330. rem SAVEREG procedure
331. rem Save registry information from variables
332, rem
333. :SAVEREG
334. if defined TRACE %TRACE% [proc %0 %*]
335.     rem Save site data to the registry
336.     call _mtplib :REGDELM %CONTEXT%
337.     call _mtplib :REGSETM %CONTEXT% RSENABLE_
338.     call _mtplib :REGSETM %CONTEXT% RSDIR_
339. goto :EOF
340.
341. rem /////////////////////////////////////////////////////////////////////
342. rem LOADSITE procedure
343. rem Load site into working vars
344. rem
345. rem Arguments:    %1=site name
346. rem
347. rem Returns:    WORKENABLE=0/1 for site enable
348. rem            WORKDIR_n_=list of directories (1 based)
349. rem            WORKCOUNT=count of directories in list
```

```
350. rem
351. :LOADSITE
352. if defined TRACE %TRACE% [proc %0 %*]
353.     rem Clear existing working site
354.     set /a WORKENABLE=1
355.     set /a WORKCOUNT=0
356.     call _mtplib :VARDEL WORKDIR_
357.     if not defined RSENABLE_%1 goto :EOF
358.
359.     rem Load site into working site
360.     set /a WORKENABLE=RSENABLE_%1
361.     for /f "tokens=1 delims==" %%I in ('set RSDIR_%1_ 2^>nul') do call
         :LOADSITE1 %1 %%I
362. goto :EOF
363. :LOADSITE1
364.     for /f "tokens=3 delims=_" %%J in ("%2") do set IX=%%J
365.     set RET=%%%2%%
366.     call _mtplib :RESOLVE
367.     set WORKDIR_%IX%_=%RET%
368.     set /a WORKCOUNT+=1
369. goto :EOF
370..
371. rem //////////////////////////////////////////////////////////////////////
372. rem SAVESITE procedure
373. rem Save site from working vars, with site compaction
374. rem
375. rem Arguments:     %1=site name
376. rem
377. :SAVESITE
378. if defined TRACE %TRACE% [proc %0 %*]
379.     rem Clear existing site data
380.     set RSENABLE_%1=
381.     call _mtplib :VARDEL RSDIR_%1_
382.     if not defined WORKENABLE goto :EOF
383.     if not defined WORKCOUNT goto :EOF
384.     if %WORKCOUNT% EQU 0 goto :EOF
385.
386.     rem Save working site
387.     set /a RSENABLE_%1=WORKENABLE
388.     set /a NEWCOUNT=0
389.     for /l %%I in (1,1,%WORKCOUNT%) do call :SAVESITE1 %1 %%I
390. goto :EOF
391. :SAVESITE1
392.     if not defined WORKDIR_%2_ goto :EOF
393.     set RET=%%WORKDIR_%2_%%
394.     call _mtplib :RESOLVE
395.     set /a NEWCOUNT+=1
396.     set RSDIR_%1_%NEWCOUNT%_=%RET%
397. goto :EOF
398.
399. rem //////////////////////////////////////////////////////////////////////
```

```
400. rem Additional procedures go here...
401.
402. rem These must be the FINAL LINES in the script...
403. :DOSEXIT
404. echo This script requires Windows NT
405.
406. rem ///////////////////////////////////////////////////////////////
```

Figure 7.3. *The REPL.BAT script*

The ANIMAL Script

Figure 7.4 shows the ANIMAL.BAT script. This is the final sample script in this book, and is rather less serious in intent than the other samples. It does, however, illustrate several useful techniques, including interactive text input, and simple database file manipulation.

Description

The ANIMAL.BAT script plays the classic Animal computer game, which was originally developed during the 1970s as a demonstration of simple artificial intelligence. Animal is a very simple but surprisingly challenging game. The computer maintains a database of animal species, and an additional database of yes/no answer questions.

The game begins by the (human) player thinking of an animal. The computer then asks a series of yes/no questions until either it correctly guesses the animal, or it runs out of questions. What makes the game interesting is that the computer then asks what animal you are thinking of, and also asks for a *new* yes/no question so it can distinguish this animal from its best guess. This information is then added to the database maintained by the game. This database is stored in a data file, and so each time the computer plays the game, it increases its knowledge of fauna.

Eventually, it can become quite challenging to think of an animal that the computer cannot guess. Many years ago, one of the computers at MIT is rumored to have amassed a database of several thousand animals, and prizes were offered to anyone who could think of a new animal.

To play the Animal game, simply execute the script. The game has a built-in database of only two animals: dog and duck. New animals are stored in the data file ANIMAL.DAT, which is stored in the same directory as ANIMAL.BAT.

Implementation

The core of the ANIMAL script is a database of known animals and questions about those animals. This database is structured as a binary tree, in which each interior node contains a yes/no question, and each leaf contains an animal name. Interior nodes maintain a Yes and a No branch which each point to another (lower) node. The initial built-in tree contains one question: "Does it have a beak?" and two animals: "Dog" and "Duck." The root node of the tree contains the question. The "Yes" leaf contains "Duck" and the "No" leaf contains "Dog." Leaves are distinguished from interior nodes by having no pointer in the yes and no branches.

In the script, the tree is represented as an array of nodes. Each node is comprised of one entry in each of three arrays:

- ANIMAL_TEXT_*n*_ contains the question (for interior nodes) or the name of an animal (for leaf nodes).

- ANIMAL_YES_*n*_ contains the index of the node for a yes answer, or 0 if the node is a leaf node.

- ANIMAL_NO_*n*_ contains the index of the node for a no answer, or 0 if the node is a leaf node.

The ANIMAL.DAT file provides persistent storage for the array, which is stored in node index order (the actual node indices are not stored). Each line in the file comprises a single node in the tree. The first two fields contain the yes and no branches, and the final fields contain the node text.

To play the game, the computer simply starts at the root node, which is the array entry at index 1. If the node is not a leaf, it asks the question stored at the node, and then moves down through either the Yes or No pointer (depending upon the response to the question) to the next node. This continues until the script reaches a leaf node. When this happens, the computer asks Is it a ..., where ... is the animal name stored at the leaf.

If the answer to this final question is yes, the game is over. If the answer is no, the computer has been defeated. In this case, the computer adds new information about the new animal:

1. The computer gets the name of the new animal.

2. The computer gets a yes/no question to distinguish its best-guess animal from the new animal.

3. The computer then creates two new leaf nodes to contain the best-guess animal and the new animal, and places the new question in the current leaf.

4. Finally, the current leaf is converted to an interior node by adding the two new leaves to the yes and no pointers of the node.

```
001. @echo OFF
002. @if not "%ECHO%"=="" echo %ECHO%
003. @if not "%OS%"=="Windows_NT" goto DOSEXIT
004. rem $Workfile: animal.bat $ $Revision: 2 $ $Date: 12/04/97 9:51a $
005. rem $Archive: /TimH/Pubs/Books/Macmillan/Windows NT
     Scripting/Scripts/animal.bat $
006.
007. rem Set local scope and call MAIN procedure
008. setlocal & pushd & set RET=
009.     set SCRIPTNAME=%~n0
010.     set SCRIPTPATH=%~f0
011.     set DATAFILENAME=%~dpn0.DAT
012.     if "%DEBUG%"=="1" (set TRACE=echo) else (set TRACE=rem)
013.     call _mtplib :INIT %SCRIPTPATH%
014.     if /i {%1}=={/help} (call :HELP %2) & (goto :HELPEXIT)
015.     if /i {%1}=={/?} (call :HELP %2) & (goto :HELPEXIT)
016.     call :MAIN %*
017.     :HELPEXIT        .
018. popd & endlocal & set RET=%RET%
019. goto :EOF
020.
021. rem /////////////////////////////////////////////////////////////////
022. rem HELP procedure
023. rem Display brief on-line help message
024. rem
025. :HELP
026. if defined TRACE %TRACE% [proc %0 %*]
027.     echo Syntax: ANIMAL
028.     echo Plays the ancient and well-known animal computer game.
209. goto :EOF
030.
031. rem /////////////////////////////////////////////////////////////////
032. rem MAIN procedure
033. rem
034. rem Arguments:    DATAFILENAME=name of data file for dynamic animal
database
035. rem
036. :MAIN
307. if defined TRACE %TRACE% [proc %0 %*]
308.     rem Load the tree from the datafile
039.     echo One moment please...
040.     call :LOADDATAFILE "%DATAFILENAME%"
041.     set /a NEWANIMALCOUNT=0
042.
043.     rem Main game loop
044.     :MAINLOOP
045.         set /a IX=1
046.         %COMSPEC% /c choice /n Are you thinking of an animal?
```

```
047.          if errorlevel 2 goto :MAINLOOPEND
048.
049.          rem Work down the tree
050.          :TREELOOP
051.              call :GETANIMALNODE %IX%
052.              if %NODE_YES% EQU 0 goto :TREELOOPEND
053.              %COMSPEC% /c choice /n %NODE_TEXT%
054.              if errorlevel 1 set /a IX=NODE_YES
055.              if errorlevel 2 set /a IX=NODE_NO
056.          goto :TREELOOP
057.          :TREELOOPEND
058.
059.          rem We're at a leaf: the end-game
060.          %COMSPEC% /c choice /n Is it a %NODE_TEXT%?
061.          if errorlevel 2 (
062.              (call :ADDNEWANIMAL)
063.          ) else (
064.              (echo I guessed it!)
065.          )
066.      goto :MAINLOOP
067.      :MAINLOOPEND
068.
069.      rem Game wrap-up
070.      if %NEWANIMALCOUNT% GTR 0 (
071.          (echo One moment please...)
072.          (call :SAVEDATAFILE "%DATAFILENAME%")
073.          if %NEWANIMALCOUNT% EQU 1 (
074.              (echo I learned about a new animal!)
075.          ) else (
076.              (echo I learned about %NEWANIMALCOUNT% new animals!)
077.          )
078.      )
079.      echo Thanks for playing!
080. goto :EOF
081.
082. rem ///////////////////////////////////////////////////////////////////
083. rem ADDNEWANIMAL procedure
084. rem Adds a new animal to the tree
085. rem
086. rem Arguments:    NODE=var loaded with current node
087. rem          IX=current node index
088. rem
089. :ADDNEWANIMAL
090. if defined TRACE %TRACE% [proc %0 %*]
091.      rem Get the new animal name
092.      echo I give up! What is the animal you are thinking of?
093.      :GETANIMALLOOP
094.      echo (type the name and Ctrl+Z)
095.      call _mtplib :GETINPUTLINE
096.      set NEWANIMAL=%RET%
097.      if "%NEWANIMAL%"=="" (
```

```
098.          (echo Please type an animal name)
099.          (goto :GETANIMALLOOP)
100.      )
101.
102.      rem Get the distinguishing question
103.      echo Type a yes/no question to distinguish a %NODE_TEXT% from a
          %NEWANIMAL%:
104.      :GETQUESTIONLOOP
105.      echo (type the question and Ctrl+Z)
106.      call _mtplib :GETINPUTLINE
107.      set NEWQUESTION=%RET%
108.      if "%NEWQUESTION%"=="" (
109.          (echo Please type a question)
110.          (goto :GETQUESTIONLOOP)
111.      )
112.      if "%NEWQUESTION%"=="%NEWQUESTION:?=%" (
113.          (echo Please type a question ^(with a question mark^))
114.          (goto :GETQUESTIONLOOP)
115.      )
116.
117.      rem Get the answer for the NEW animal
118.      %COMSPEC% /c choice /n For a %NEWANIMAL%, the answer to this question
          would be?
119.      set NEWANSWER=%ERRORLEVEL%
120.
121.      rem Allocate the new nodes
122.      set /a NEWNODE_YES=ANIMALCOUNT+1
123.      set /a NEWNODE_NO=ANIMALCOUNT+2
124.      set /a ANIMALCOUNT+=2
125.      set /a NEWANIMALCOUNT+=1
126.
127.      rem Fill existing node with the new question
128.      set /a ANIMAL_YES_%IX%_=NEWNODE_YES
129.      set /a ANIMAL_NO_%IX%_=NEWNODE_NO
130.      set ANIMAL_TEXT_%IX%_=%NEWQUESTION%
131.
132.      rem Swap node indexes if new answer is NO
133.      if "%NEWANSWER%"=="2" (
134.          set /a T1=NEWNODE_YES
135.          set /a NEWNODE_YES=NEWNODE_NO
136.          set /a NEWNODE_NO=T1
137.      )
138.
139.      rem Install the new animal in the YES node
140.      set /a ANIMAL_YES_%NEWNODE_YES%_=0
141.      set /a ANIMAL_NO_%NEWNODE_YES%_=0
142.      set ANIMAL_TEXT_%NEWNODE_YES%_=%NEWANIMAL%
143.
144.      rem Install the old animal in the NO node
145.      set /a ANIMAL_YES_%NEWNODE_NO%_=0
146.      set /a ANIMAL_NO_%NEWNODE_NO%_=0
```

```
147.     set ANIMAL_TEXT_%NEWNODE_NO%_=%NODE_TEXT%
148.
149.     echo Thank you!
150. goto :EOF
151.
152. rem ////////////////////////////////////////////////////////////////////
153. rem LOADDATAFILE procedure
154. rem Load animal data from specified file
155. rem
156. rem Arguments:    %1=filename to load
157. rem
158. :LOADDATAFILE
159. if defined TRACE %TRACE% [proc %0 %*]
160.     set /a ANIMALCOUNT=0
161.     if exist %1 (
162.         (for /f "eol=; tokens=1,2* delims=," %%I in ('type %1') do call
             :LOADDATARECORD %%I %%J 163. "%%K")
164.     ) else (
165.         (call :LOADDATARECORD 2 3 "Does it have a beak?")
166.         (call :LOADDATARECORD 0 0 "duck")
167.         (call :LOADDATARECORD 0 0 "dog")
168.     )
169. goto :EOF
170.
171. rem ////////////////////////////////////////////////////////////////////
172. rem LOADDATARECORD procedure
173. rem Load animal data from
174. rem
175. rem Arguments:    %1=yes answer index (or 0)
176. rem          %2=no answer index (or 0)
177. rem          %3=question or animal name (in double quotes)
178. rem
179. :LOADDATARECORD
180. if defined TRACE %TRACE% [proc %0 %*]
181.     set T1=%3
182.     set /a ANIMALCOUNT+=1
183.     set /a ANIMAL_YES_%ANIMALCOUNT%_=%1
184.     set /a ANIMAL_NO_%ANIMALCOUNT%_=%2
185.     set ANIMAL_TEXT_%ANIMALCOUNT%_=%T1:"=%
186. goto :EOF
187.
188. rem ////////////////////////////////////////////////////////////////////
189. rem SAVEDATAFILE procedure
190. rem Save animal data to specified file
191. rem
192. rem Arguments:    %1=filename
193. rem
194. :SAVEDATAFILE
195. if defined TRACE %TRACE% [proc %0 %*]
196.     echo ;ANIMAL data (%ANIMALCOUNT%) >%1
197.     for /l %%I in (1,1,%ANIMALCOUNT%) do call :SAVEDATARECORD %1 %%I
```

```
198. goto :EOF
199.
200. rem /////////////////////////////////////////////////////////////////
201. rem SAVEDATARECORD procedure
202. rem Save specified record in file
203. rem
204. rem Arguments:    %1=file name to save
205. rem              %2=index into array
206. rem
2097. :SAVEDATARECORD
208. if defined TRACE %TRACE% [proc %0 %*]
209.     call :GETANIMALNODE %2
210.     echo %NODE_YES%,%NODE_NO%,%NODE_TEXT%>>%1
211. goto :EOF
212.
213. rem /////////////////////////////////////////////////////////////////
214. rem GETANIMALNODE procedure
215. rem Get a node into the working node
216. rem
217. rem Arguments:    %1=index into animal array
218. rem
219. rem Returns:     NODE_...=working node loaded
220. rem
221. :GETANIMALNODE
222. if defined TRACE %TRACE% [proc %0 %*]
223.     set /a NODE_YES=ANIMAL_YES_%1_
224.     set /a NODE_NO=ANIMAL_NO_%1_
225.     set RET=%%ANIMAL_TEXT_%1_%%
226.     call _mtplib :RESOLVE
227.     set NODE_TEXT=%RET%
228. goto :EOF
229.
230. rem /////////////////////////////////////////////////////////////////
231. rem Additional procedures go here...
232.
233. rem These must be the FINAL LINES in the script...
234. :DOSEXIT
235. echo This script requires Windows NT
236.
237. rem /////////////////////////////////////////////////////////////////
```

Figure 7.4. *The ANIMAL.BAT script*

A Final Word on Scripting

The Animal script is the final sample script in this book. The code and techniques shown in the sample scripts in Chapters 5, 6, and 7 can be easily adapted to many script projects. In particular, the _MTPLIB.BAT script library can be used directly by virtually any script.

Scripts are not a perfect solution (by any means) to many of the everyday problems facing managers and users of Windows NT installations. But, as this book has tried to show, they can at least be used to manage the complexity of these problems, by hiding complex command syntax, and automating many repetitive and error-prone management tasks.

Happy scripting!

Part III

Scripting Command Reference

Command Reference

Alphabetical Listing of Commands

Command Reference

The tables in this section provide categorized lists of commands that enable you to quickly access the complete reference information in the alphabetical command section.

Account Management Commands

These commands manage the local or domain user account database.

Command	Description
ADDUSERS [RK]	Creates, updates, and deletes user accounts.
AUDITPOL [RK]	Displays or alters Windows NT auditing policies.
DISKUSE [RK]	Displays file usage statistics by user.
DUMPEL [RK]	Dumps a formatted event log.
GLOBAL [RK]	Displays the names of members of a global group.
IFMEMBER [RK]	Tests group membership.
LOCAL [RK]	Displays the names of members of a local group.
NET ACCOUNTS	Manages user account database policies.
NET COMPUTER	Adds or deletes computers from a Windows NT domain.
NET GROUP	Manages global groups.
NET LOCALGROUP	Manages local groups.
NET USER	Manages user accounts.
PULIST [RK]	Displays process and user accounts.
USRSTAT [RK]	Displays user statistics for a domain.
WHOAMI [RK]	Displays the current user name and domain name.

System Management Commands

These commands provide general computer and system management.

Command	Description
AT	Schedules commands to execute at a specified time and date.
CMD	Executes the default Windows NT command shell.
COMMAND	Executes the MS-DOS command shell.
DATE	Displays or sets the system date.
DUMPEL [RK]	Dumps a formatted event log.
EXIT	Exits the current command shell.
INSTSRV [RK]	Installs or removes a Windows NT service executable.
KILL [RK]	Kills a process.
LOGEVENT [RK]	Logs an event in the application event log.
LOGOFF [RK]	Logs off the current Windows NT session.
NET COMPUTER	Adds or deletes computers from a Windows NT domain.
NET CONFIG SERVER	Configures the server service.
NET CONFIG WORKSTATION	Configures the workstation service.
NET CONTINUE	Continues services.
NET NAME	Manages messenger service names.
NET PAUSE	Pauses services.
NET SEND	Sends a messenger service message.
NET SESSION	Manages server computer connections.
NET SHARE	Manages printer and directory shares.
NET START	Starts services.
NET STATISTICS	Displays server and workstation service statistics.
NET STOP	Stops services.
NET TIME	Displays and synchronizes to remote computer time.
NET USE	Manages remote connections.
NET VIEW	Displays available network resources.
NTBACKUP	Automatic volume backup.
PERMCOPY [RK]	Copies share permissions.
PULIST [RK]	Displays process and user accounts.
REG [RK]	Manipulates the Windows NT registry.
RMTSHARE [RK]	Manages shares on a remote computer.
SC [RK]	Manages Windows NT services.
SCLIST [RK]	Displays services on specified computer.

SCOPY [RK]	Copies files and security information.
SHUTDOWN [RK]	Initiates Windows NT shutdown on the specified computer.
SOON [RK]	Executes a scheduled command in the near future.
SRVINFO [RK]	Displays general computer and server information.
SUBST	Creates virtual drive mappings.
TIME	Displays or sets the system time.
TRANSLATE [RK]	Translates a Windows NT error code to text.
USRSTAT [RK]	Displays user statistics for a domain.
VER	Displays Windows NT version information.
WINAT	Schedules commands to execute at a specified time and date.

Application Control Commands

These commands provide application control.

Command	Description
ASSOC	Displays and alters file associations.
ASSOCIATE [RK]	Creates or deletes file associations.
AT	Schedules commands to execute at a specified time and date.
ATTRIB	Displays or changes the attributes of one or more files.
CMD	Executes the default Windows NT command shell.
COMMAND	Executes the MS-DOS command shell.
EXIT	Exits the current command shell.
FTYPE	Displays and alters file types.
KILL [RK]	Kills a process.
LOCAL [RK]	Displays the names of members of a local group.
LOGOFF [RK]	Logs off the current Windows NT session.
PULIST [RK]	Displays process and user accounts.
REG [RK]	Manipulates the Windows NT registry.
SCLIST [RK]	Displays services on specified computer.
SHUTDOWN [RK]	Initiates Windows NT shutdown on the specified computer.
SLEEP [RK]	Pauses execution for a specified period of time.
SOON [RK]	Executes a scheduled command in the near future.
START	Executes a command in a new window or console window.
WINAT	Schedules commands to execute at a specified time and date.

Network Management Commands

These commands provide network control and management.

Command	Description
DUMPEL [RK]	Dumps a formatted event log.
NET COMPUTER	Adds or deletes computers from a Windows NT domain.
NET FILE	Manages open files on a server.
NET NAME	Manages messenger service names.
NET SEND	Send a messenger service message.
NET SESSION	Manages server computer connections.
NET SHARE	Manages printer and directory shares.
NET TIME	Displays and synchronizes to remote computer time.
NET USE	Manages remote connections.
NET VIEW	Displays available network resources.
PERMCOPY [RK]	Copies share permissions.
RMTSHARE [RK]	Manages shares on a remote computer.
SHUTDOWN [RK]	Initiates Windows NT shutdown on the specified computer.
SRVINFO [RK]	Displays general computer and server information.
USRSTAT [RK]	Displays user statistics for a domain.
WHOAMI [RK]	Displays the current user name and domain name.

File and Directory Commands

These commands provide file and directory control and management.

Command	Description
ATTRIB	Displays or changes the attributes of one or more files.
CACLS	Displays and modifies access control lists of files.
CD	Changes or displays the current directory.
CHDIR	Changes or displays the current directory.
COPY	Copies files.
DEL	Deletes files.
DIR	Lists files in a directory.
DIRUSE [RK]	Displays directory and file space usage statistics.
DISKUSE [RK]	Displays file usage statistics by user.
ERASE	Deletes files.
FC	Compares files.

FIND	Filters text files for matching lines.
FINDSTR	Searches for strings in files.
MD	Creates directories.
MKDIR	Creates directories.
MORE	Filters text files into pages.
MOVE	Moves files from one directory to another.
NET FILE	Manages open files on a server.
NTBACKUP	Automatic volume backup.
RD	Deletes directories and their contents.
REN	Renames files and directories.
RENAME	Renames files and directories.
REPLACE	Replaces files with updated versions.
RMDIR	Deletes directories and their contents.
ROBOCOPY [RK]	Replicates file and directory trees.
SCOPY [RK]	Copies files and security information.
SORT	Sorts text lines.
SUBST	Creates virtual drive mappings.
TYPE	Displays a text file in the console window.
XCACLS	Displays and modifies access control lists of files.
XCOPY	Copies files and directories.

Scripting Language Commands

These commands comprise the core shell scripting language.

Command	Description
CALL	Invokes another script file or script label as a procedure.
CHOICE [RK]	Obtains keyboard input for script.
CLIP [RK]	Captures command input to the clipboard.
CLS	Clears the console window.
CMD	Executes the default Windows NT command shell.
COLOR	Sets the console window foreground and background colors.
COMMAND	Executes the MS-DOS command shell.
DOSKEY	Manages command editing, history, and macros.
ECHO	Controls command output to console window.
ENDLOCAL	Ends localized scope for environment variable changes.
EXIT	Exits the current command shell.

FOR	Iterates commands.
GOTO	Transfers control to a script label.
IF	Executes commands conditionally.
PATH	Sets the command search path.
PAUSE	Pauses script execution.
POPD	Restores previously saved drive and directory.
PROMPT	Sets the command shell prompt.
PUSHD	Saves current directory and changes to new drive/directory.
REM	Comments.
SET	Sets environment variables and performs arithmetic computations.
SETLOCAL	Begins localized scope for environment variable changes.
SHIFT	Accesses additional command arguments.
START	Executes a command in a new window or console window.
TITLE	Sets the title text of the console window.
VER	Displays Windows NT version information.

Alphabetical Listing
of Commands

The rest of this part provides a complete alphabetical command reference for all Windows NT shell commands. In addition, the following topics in this section provide summary information on various aspects of shell scripting:

Command Line Editing   Standard Variables

Command Line Syntax   Variable Syntax

Parameter Syntax

The formatting used in the syntax descriptions accompanying each command is described in the introduction of this book. Some of the more common syntax elements used in commands are shown in the following table.

Syntax	Description
.ext	A file extension, typically of 1 to 3 letters, prefixed with a period.
args	An arbitrary list of command arguments, typically separated by spaces.
command	Any valid Windows NT scripting command, possibly including arguments.
command-name	Any valid Windows NT script command name, without arguments.
computer	A NetBIOS computer name, typically prefixed with \\.
drive:	A drive letter followed by a colon character.
file	A combination of a drive letter, path and file name.
filename	A file name only, without a drive or directory path. This can be a long file name, possibly including spaces, unless noted otherwise.
filetype	A registry defined file type name.
label	A script label.

nn	A decimal number.
path	A directory path. One or more directory names separated by backslash characters. Paths that begin with a backslash are *absolute* paths that start at the root directory. Paths that begin with a directory name are relative to the current directory.
switches	If a command has a large number of optional switches, these are all represented by *switches* in the command syntax.
uncname	A UNC name, such as \\server\share\path.
var	An environment variable name.
Reserved shell character	Any of the special characters &, ¦, (,) or ^.

Where a command has several syntax variations, these are numbered in the syntax description. The text then refers to a specific variation by this number. For example, ASSOC(2) refers to syntax variant 2 of the ASSOC command.

Command examples follow the conventions used throughout this book. Commands are shown in lowercase except for variable names and script labels, which are shown in uppercase.

ADDUSERS [RK]

Creates, updates and deletes user accounts.

Syntax:

```
1. ADDUSERS [\\computer] /D [drive:][path]filename [/S:c]
2. ADDUSERS [\\computer] /C [drive:][path]filename [/S:c]
3. ADDUSERS [\\computer] /E [drive:][path]filename [/S:c]
```

Switches:

/D	Dumps user accounts to *filename*.
/C	Creates accounts as specified by the contents of *filename*.
/E	Deletes accounts as specified by the contents of *filename*.
/S:c	Sets the field delimiter character to *c*.

The ADDUSERS command creates, updates, or deletes user accounts on the specified *computer*. The local account database is used if no computer is specified. Account information is accessed via a text file, allowing large numbers of accounts to be rapidly processed.

The account file used by ADDUSERS is a text file containing comma-delimited records suitable for processing with a spreadsheet program. If required, the /S switch changes the delimiter character used in the file.

Use ADDUSERS(1) to dump the account database of the specified *computer* (or, by default, the local computer) to the specified *filename*. This records account information for later restore, if needed. It also creates a prototype account file to assist in the preparation of a new file for ADDUSERS(2) and ADDUSERS(3). All information about accounts, local groups and global groups is saved *except* account password information.

Use ADDUSERS(2) to create accounts, local groups and global groups. Information for the accounts to create is taken from the specified account file. Passwords for newly created accounts are left blank.

Use ADDUSERS(3) to delete accounts, local groups and global groups. Information for the accounts to delete is taken from the specified account file. Take care when deleting accounts—the Windows NT security model does not allow an account to be recreated once deleted.

The account file is a text file that is divided into three sections: for user accounts, local groups and global groups. Each section begins with a header, which is [User] for the user account section, [Global] for global groups, and [Local] for local groups. Not all sections need be present in the account file.

Following the appropriate header are individual records for each user, global group, or local group, one record per line. For user accounts, the record is organized as follows:

> *User Name, Full Name, Password, Home Drive, Home Path, Profile, Script*

For global groups, the record is organized as follows.

> *Global Group Name, Comment, UserName, ...*

For local groups, the record is organized as follows.

> *Local Group Name, Comment, UserName, ...*

For both global and local groups, the *UserName* element is repeated as often as needed for each user in the group.

ASSOC

Displays and alters file associations.

Syntax:

```
1. ASSOC
2. ASSOC .ext
3. ASSOC .ext=
4. ASSOC .ext=filetype
```

The ASSOC command displays and alters the mapping between file extensions and file types. A *file type* is a named registry entry describing a type of file and how to launch its associated application. Use ASSOC to connect a file type to one or more file extensions (and hence to an application). File types are manipulated by the FTYPE command.

Use ASSOC(1) to display all current associations, and ASSOC(2) to display a specific association. Use ASSOC(3) to delete an existing association, and ASSOC(4) to create a new association or change an existing one.

After you create an association, you can automatically invoke an application by opening a file with the associated extension. You can also use the PATHEXT standard variable to further automate the association.

Example:

```
ftype NotePad=notepad.exe "%1"
assoc .abc=NotePad
set PATHEXT=%PATHEXT%;.abc
```

These commands first create a new file type called NotePad, which will execute NOTEPAD.EXE. Then the file extension .ABC is associated with this type. Finally, the .ABC extension is added to the path extension list. Once these commands are executed, entering DATA at the command prompt opens the file DATA.ABC in Notepad.

Notes:

File type information and file extension associations are stored in the HKEY_CLASSES_ROOT section of the registry. Therefore, changes made using the ASSOC command are retained across system shutdowns and will affect all users.

See also: ASSOCIATE, FTYPE, Standard Variables, START

ASSOCIATE [RK]

Creates or deletes file associations.

```
1. ASSOCIATE .ext
2. ASSOCIATE .ext /D [/F]
3. ASSOCIATE .ext [drive:][path]filename [/F]
```

Switches:

/D	Deletes association.
/F	Forces operation without a confirmation.

The ASSOCIATE command displays and alters the associations between file extensions and an application. ASSOCIATE combines the ASSOC and FTYPE commands into a single step process.

Use ASSOCIATE(1) to display the association for a file extension. Use ASSOCI-ATE(2) to delete an existing association. The /F switch forces the deletion without prompting for confirmation. Use ASSOCIATE(3) to create an association or change an existing association. The /F switch forces the change without confirmation, should an existing association already exist.

ASSOCIATE automatically creates an intermediate *file type* to connect the specified file extension and application. This type is named *extfile*, where *ext* is taken from the file extension specified.

Notes:

Although ASSOCIATE is easier to use, ASSOC and FTYPE are preferred, as they are more flexible, and provide a finer grained control of file type associations.

File type information and file extension associations are stored in the HKEY_CLASSES_ROOT section of the registry. Therefore, changes made using the ASSOCIATE command are retained across system shutdowns and will affect all users.

See also: ASSOC, FTYPE

AT, WINAT [RK]

Schedules commands to execute at a specified time and date.

Syntax:

```
1. AT [\\computer]
2. AT [\\computer] /DELETE [/YES]
3. AT [\\computer] id /DELETE
4. AT [\\computer] time [/INTERACTIVE] "command"
5. AT [\\computer] time [/INTERACTIVE] /NEXT:date[,...] "command"
6. AT [\\computer] time [/INTERACTIVE] /EVERY:date[,...] "command"
```

Switches:

/DELETE	Deletes either the specified command or all commands.
/YES	Deletes all commands without prompting for confirmation.
/INTERACTIVE	Allows the scheduled command to interact with the desktop.
/NEXT	Specifies that the command executes once on the specified date.
/EVERY	Specifies that the command executes repeatedly on the specified date.

The AT command schedules a Windows NT command for later execution. The WINAT command offers a GUI to the AT command. By default, the AT command schedules commands on the local computer. Specify *computer* to schedule commands on remote computers.

Use AT(1) to display a list of all currently scheduled commands. This also provides a list of command identifiers (ID numbers). Use AT(2) to delete all scheduled commands. The /YES switch skips the confirmation prompt. Use AT(3) to delete a specific command by command ID number.

Use AT(4) to schedule a command to execute once at the specified time. If the time specified is later than the current clock time, the command will execute later the same day. If the time is earlier than the specified time, the command will execute at that time the next day. After the command executes it is automatically deleted from the scheduled command list.

Use AT(5) to execute a command once at a specified time and date. The *date* value is either the name of a day of the week or a day of the month. If omitted, the current day of the month is assumed. If the day or date is earlier in the week or month than the current day or date, the command is scheduled for the next week or month. If the day or date is the same as the current day or date, the command may execute today, next week, or next month, depending upon the value of *time*.

Use AT(6) to execute a command repeatedly at the specified time and date, or time and day of the week. The syntax is identical to AT(5) except for the use of the /EVERY switch instead of /NEXT.

For all command forms, specify *time* using either am/pm or a 24-hour clock format. Spaces are not permitted in the time string.

The /INTERACTIVE switch allows the command to interact with the Windows NT desktop when executed.

Example:

```
at 3:00am /every:Saturday "backup c: d:"
at 15:00 /next:15 /interactive "reminder birthday"
```

Notes:

The AT command relies upon the Windows NT Schedule service to execute scheduled commands. If necessary, start this service using Windows NT Control Panel or the WINAT [RK] command. The service must execute in an account with sufficient rights to access the resource needed by the command, such as shared directories.

Commands can execute when no interactive user is logged on. Therefore, do not rely on interactive drive mappings to network shares. Either use UNC names in commands, or include the necessary NET USE commands to map the shares to drives.

Administrator rights are required to schedule commands. Scheduled commands are preserved across system restarts.

See also: SOON

ATTRIB

Displays or changes the attributes of one or more files.

Syntax:

```
1. ATTRIB [/S]
2. ATTRIB [drive:][path]filename [/S]
3. ATTRIB [+R ¦ -R] [+A ¦ -A] [+S ¦ -S] [+H ¦ -H] [drive:][path]filename [/S]
```

Switches:

+R ¦ -R	Sets or resets the read-only attribute.
+A ¦ -A	Sets or resets the archive attribute.
+S ¦ -S	Sets or resets the system attribute.
+H ¦ -H	Sets or resets the hidden attribute.
/S	Searches for matching files in all sub-directories.

The ATTRIB command sets or resets the attributes of specified files. Attributes include R for read-only files, A for archived files, S for system files, and H for hidden files. Use the "+" form to set the attribute, and the "-" form to reset it.

Use ATTRIB(1) to display the attributes of all files in the current directory. The /S switch displays attributes of files in the current directory and all sub-directories. Use ATTRIB(2) to display the attributes for a single file or a set of files matching a wildcard file name. Use ATTRIB(3) to alter attributes of the specified file or files. You can specify multiple attributes to alter by placing a space between each attribute.

Use the filename argument to specify the files to alter or display. Wildcards can be used. If no file name is specified, *.* is assumed. Note that ATTRIB requires a space between the end of the file name and the /S switch, if present.

Example:

```
attrib +r +s +h c:\boot.ini
```

See also: DIR, DEL.

AUDITPOL [RK]

Displays or alters Windows NT auditing policies.

Syntax:

```
1. AUDITPOL [\\computer]
2. AUDITPOL [\\computer] [/ENABLE ¦ /DISABLE] [/cat:opt] [...]
```

Switches:

/ENABLE	Enables auditing (default).
/DISABLE	Disables auditing.
/cat:opt	Sets auditing options for audit category cat to opt.

The AUDITPOL command displays or alters Windows NT auditing policies. By default, the AUDITPOL command processes policies on the local computer. Specify computer to process policies on remote computers

Use AUDITPOL(1) to display current policies for the specified computer or the local computer. Use AUDITPOL(2) to alter auditing policies. The /ENABLE or /DISABLE switches enable or disable auditing. Each category switch (/cat:opt) sets specific policies for the computer.

The categories used for cat are as follows:

- System   Audit system events.
- Logon   Audit logon/logoff events.
- Object   Audit object access.
- Privilege   Audit use of privileges.
- Process   Audit process creation and termination.
- Policy   Audit security policy changes.
- Sam   Audit SAM changes.

Each category is followed by an opt option to control the auditing for that category. The options used for opt are as follows:

- Success   Audit success events.
- Failure   Audit failure events.
- All   Audit all events in this category.
- None   Do not audit this category.

Example:

```
auditpol \\transfer-4 /enable /logon:failure
```

AUTOEXEC.BAT

The MS-DOS startup script.

Windows NT does not process AUTOEXEC.BAT in the same way as MS-DOS. The script file is not processed at system startup. Instead, Windows NT scans C:\AUTOEXEC.BAT during logon. During scanning, any SET and PATH commands are processed, thus adding to or modifying the user environment variables. Environment variables set through AUTOEXEC.BAT are set *after* those defined for the system and the user through Control Panel. These variables are then available to all applications, including Windows NT command shell sessions.

Windows NT only scans AUTOEXEC.BAT; it does not execute it. If the script contains conditional statements (IF, GOTO, etc.) that are used to control the setting of environment variables, the results can be unpredictable.

The PATH variable is treated specially. Any PATH commands or SET PATH commands in AUTOEXEC.BAT append the path value to the current path, rather than over-writing it.

You can disable the processing of AUTOEXEC.BAT at logon using the following registry value:

HKEY_CURRENT_USER\Software\Microsoft\
Windows NT\CurrentVersion\Winlogon\ParseAutoexec

Set this value to a type of DWORD and a value of 1 to enable parsing, or 0 to disable parsing. Note that this value is per-user, not per-system.

Notes:

The Windows NT Resource Kit ships with a tool, AUTOEXNT, which enables Windows NT to execute an equivalent to AUTOEXEC.BAT at startup.

CACLS, XCACLS [RK]

Displays and modifies access control lists of files.

Syntax:

```
1. CACLS [drive:][path]filename [/T]
2. XCACLS [drive:][path]filename [/T]
3. CACLS [drive:][path]filename [switches]
4. XCACLS [drive:][path]filename [switches]
```

Switches:

/T	Processes files in the current directory and all sub-directories.
/E	Edits ACLs instead of replacing them.

/C	Continues on access denied errors.
/G *user*:*perm*;*sp*	Grants user-specified permission (*sp* is valid for XCACLS only).
/R *user*	Revokes specified users access rights.
/P *user*:*perm*;*sp*	Replaces specified users access rights (*sp* is valid for XCACLS only).
/D *user*	Denies specified user access.
/Y	Skips confirmation and prompt when replacing access rights (XCACLS only).

The CACLS command displays and alters the access permissions on files and directories. The XCACLS[RK] command is an extended form of the CACLS command. Both commands operate only on files stored on NTFS partitions.

Use CACLS(1) or XCACLS(2) to display the current permissions for one or more files or directories. Use the /T switch to include subdirectories. Wildcards may be specified for *filename*.

The output of CACLS(1) and XCACLS(2) differs depending on the type of object being displayed. For files, the commands display the name of the file and the associated permissions. Each permission is displayed as the name of a user of group, followed by the permission granted to that user or group. For example, BUILTIN\Guests:F indicates that the Guests group has full permission on the file.

When directory permissions are displayed, the output consists of two lines for each user or group granted access to the directory. The first line shows file permissions, while the second shows directory permissions. Each permission type is identified by a two letter code as follows:

Permission Code	Permission Type	Description
(OI)	Object Inherit	Specifies the permissions that are inherited by files copied into or created in this directory.
(IO)	Inherit Only	Specifies that the OI or CI permissions apply only to created or copied files, and not to the directory itself.
(CI)	Container Inherit	Specifies the permissions that are inherited by directories copied into or created in this directory.
(NP)	No Propagation	Specifies that the listed permissions are not be to propagated into new ACLs.

Use CACLS(3) or XCACLS(4) to modify or replace the permissions for the files and directories specified. These commands edit or replace the access control lists (ACLs) that are used to control access rights to files and directories. By default, CACLS/XCACLS replaces the entire ACL with a new one based on the supplied switches. Use the /E switch to edit the existing ACL instead (that is, the existing ACL is altered by the CACLS/XCACLS command, rather then being replaced by a new one).

The /R switch removes all ACL entries (ACEs) for the specified *user* from the ACL, thus revoking all rights for that user. This makes sense only when editing the ACL (with the /E switch), since replacing the ACL will revoke all existing permissions anyway. Multiple user names can be specified following the /R switch.

The /D switch adds an access denied ACE to the ACL for the specified *user*. This denies all access for the specified user. Multiple user names can be specified following the /D switch.

The /G switch specifies an access allowed ACE for the specified *user*. Specify permissions granted to the *user* using *perm*. The following table shows valid characters that can be part of *perm*.

Valid Character	Description
R	Read access.
C	Change (write) access.
F	Full control.
P	Change permissions (special access).
O	Take ownership (special access).
X	Execute (special access).
E	Read (special access).
W	Write (special access).
D	Delete (special access).

The R (read), C (change, that is, write) and F (full control) permissions are normal permissions, which are actually combinations of the other (special access) permissions. These are the only permissions accepted by CACLS; the other permissions are recognized by XCACLS only.

The /P switch is similar to /G, except that the specified permissions replace any that already exist when editing an ACL.

When applied to a directory, the XCACLS command can manipulate the directory permissions and file inheritance permissions separately. Specify directory permissions in *perm* and file inheritance permissions in *sp*.

Notes:

Group names can be substituted for user names anywhere in a CACLS/XCACLS command. These should be quoted if they contain spaces.

When evaluating permissions, Windows NT will stop processing an ACL when access has been explicitly denied or granted. Therefore, always place access denied ACEs before access granted ACEs in an ACL (that is, place all /D switches before /G and /P switches).

CALL

Invokes another script file or script label as a procedure.

Syntax:

```
1. CALL [drive:][path]filename [args]
2. CALL :label [args]
```

The CALL command invokes another script as a procedure. The invoked script is executed and, upon completion, execution of the current script continues at the statement following the CALL statement.

Use CALL(1) to call a script in another file (either .BAT or .CMD). Execution begins at the first line in the file. Use CALL(2) to call a script procedure within the current script file, at the location specified by *label*. Execution begins at the first line following the specified label. You must always precede *label* with a colon.

Execution of the procedure ends when the end of the script file is reached. You can quickly jump to the end of the script file using GOTO :EOF, which therefore acts as a "return" statement for the procedure.

Arguments to the procedure are handled in a similar manner to those passed to a script from a command line, including special parameter substitutions.

The environment is shared between the caller and the callee. Thus the callee can access variables set by the caller, and can use a variable to return a result from the procedure upon completion. A common convention is to use the RET variable for this purpose.

Example:

```
echo Step 1
call :SUB1
echo step 3
goto :EOF


:SUB1
echo Step 2
goto :EOF
```

This sample displays the following when executed:

```
Step 1
Step 2
Step 3
```

See also: GOTO, Labels, Parameter Syntax

CD

See CHDIR.

CHDIR, CD

Changes or displays the current directory.

Syntax

```
1. CHDIR [drive:]
2. CHDIR path
3. CHDIR [/D] drive:path
4. CHDIR ..
5. CD [drive:]
6. CD path
7. CD [/D] drive:path
8. CD ..
```

Switches:

/D   Changes the current drive in addition to changing the current directory.

The CHDIR command displays or alters the current directory for a specified drive. The CD command is a synonym for CHDIR.

Use CHDIR(1) or CD(5) to display the current directory for a drive. If no drive is specified, the current directory for the current drive is displayed.

Use CHDIR(2) or CD(6) to change the current directory on the current drive. The specified path can be absolute (starting at the root of the drive) or relative to the current directory. Use CHDIR(3) and CD(7) to change the current directory on a specified drive. If the /D switch is specified, the current drive changes to drive.

Use CHDIR(4) or CD(8) to move one level up the directory tree (towards the root directory) on the current drive. This command is not valid at the root of a directory tree.

The CHDIR command changes the case of the specified path to match that actually found in the directory tree. If the command shell prompt includes the current path name, this is reflected in the displayed path name.

Unlike most other shell commands, the CHDIR command accepts path names containing spaces without the need to use double quotes, although these can still be used if desired. Also, CHDIR allows wildcards as path names, and changes to the first directory found whose name matches the wildcard specified. This is convenient with long directory names, as it is only necessary to type enough of the path name to uniquely identify the directory, and then add a trailing "*" to the path name.

Command completion editing is particularly useful with the CHDIR command, as only the first few characters of the directory path need to be typed, followed by the command completion key.

Notes:

Current directories are maintained independently for each drive and command shell. New command shells inherit the current drive and directories of the invoking command shell.

See also: MKDIR, RMDIR, Command Line Editing

CHOICE [RK]

Obtains keyboard input for script.

Syntax:

1. CHOICE [/C:choices] [/N] [/S] [/T:c,nn] [prompt]

Switches:

/C	Specifies allowed choices.
/N	Do not display choices and prompt character.
/S	Treat choices as case sensitive.
/T	Default choice after a specified timeout.

The CHOICE command waits for the user to type a keystroke and then returns this keystroke as an exit code. The keystrokes allowed are specified by choices. The default choices are YN. Normally, choices are not case sensitive. Use the /S switch to make choices case sensitive.

Use CHOICE(1) to display the prompt text followed by a list of valid choices in brackets and a question mark. The /N switch suppresses the display of the choice list and question mark, in which case only prompt is displayed.

By default, the CHOICE command waits forever for user input. The /T switch specifies a default choice c and a timeout period of nn seconds. If there is no user input within nn seconds after displaying the choice, CHOICE automatically returns choice c.

The CHOICE command returns the selected choice as an exit code value. The choice is returned as an index into the *choices* choice list, with the first choice corresponding to 1. Thus the default YN choice list returns an exit code of 1 for Y and 2 for N. The exit code value is available via the IF ERRORLEVEL command and %ERRORLEVEL% variable.

Example:

```
cmd /c choice /c:SPX Enter network card type
if errorlevel 3 goto card_X
if errorlevel 2 goto card_P
if errorlevel 1 goto card_S
echo invalid choice
goto exit
```

Notes:

The IF ERRORLEVEL command is true if the exit code is greater than or equal to the specified value. Therefore test choice values in descending order to ensure correct operation.

Some versions of the CHOICE command, including the version shipped with the Windows NT Resource Kit, contain a bug. After the CHOICE command executes, console input is suppressed for future interactive commands within a script. To avoid this problem, execute the CHOICE command within a nested command shell.

CLIP [RK]

Captures command input to the Clipboard.

Syntax:

```
1. CLIP < [drive:][path]filename
2. command | CLIP
```

The CLIP command captures its command input and places it as text in the Windows NT Clipboard. It is then available for pasting into any Windows application.

Use CLIP(1) to place the contents of the specified file into the Clipboard. Use CLIP(2) to capture the command output from *command* and place it in the Clipboard.

Example:

```
dir | clip
```

CLS

Clears the console window.

Syntax:

```
1. CLS
```

The CLS command clears the console window and positions the cursor to the top left location in the window. The window is cleared to the colors specified for this window. These are selected either via the console window menu or via the COLOR command.

If you use large console windows (larger than the default 80 columns by 25 rows), then the CLS command is useful before executing legacy applications that only execute in 80 column by 25 row mode. Using CLS first ensures that the unused portions of the console window are cleared of distracting characters.

See also: COLOR

CMD

Executes the default Windows NT command shell.

Syntax:

```
1. CMD [/X ¦ /Y] [/A ¦ /U] [/Q] [/T:bf]
2. CMD [/X ¦ /Y] [/A ¦ /U] [/Q] [/T:bf] /C command
3. CMD [/X ¦ /Y] [/A ¦ /U] [/Q] [/T:bf] /K command
```

Switches:

/X	Enable command extensions (default).
/Y	Disable command extensions.
/A	All command output to files or pipes will be ANSI (default).
/U	All command output to files or pipes will be Unicode.
/Q	Turn echo off by default when executing scripts (non-functional).
/T	Sets foreground and background window colors.
/C	Execute command specified and then terminate shell.
/K	Execute command specified and then prompt for additional commands.

The CMD command invokes a Windows NT command shell. Use CMD(1) to invoke a normal shell, which then prompts for commands to execute. Use CMD(2) to execute *command*. After execution completes the shell terminates. Use CMD(3) to execute *command*. After execution completes the shell remains in memory and prompts for additional commands.

The /X and /Y switches control command extensions. Windows NT 4.0 introduced numerous extensions to shell syntax and commands, and these extensions are enabled with the /X switch (the default) or disabled with the /Y switch. Generally the new command extensions are backward compatible, but it might be necessary to disable command extensions (using /Y) when executing some legacy scripts.

The default state of command extensions can be toggled using the Registry key:

HKEY_CURRENT_USER\Software\Microsoft\Command
Processor\EnableExtensions

Set this value to a type of DWORD and a value of 0 to disable command extensions by default. In this case, the /X switch is required on each invocation of CMD to enable command extensions.

The /A and /U switches control the format of command output sent to a pipe or file by this command session. If /A is used (the default), output will be 8-bit ANSI characters. If /U is used, output will be 16-bit Unicode characters.

The /T switch changes the foreground and background colors used by the console window. See the COLORS command for the meaning of the bf argument. If /T is not specified, the command shell uses the current console window colors, or the colors specified in the shortcut used to start the console window. If none of these are specified, the colors set in the Control Panel Console settings are used.

Notes:

The /Q switch (not listed in the preceding text) is documented as disabling command script echo. However, it appears to be non-functional in all versions of the command shell tested.

The /E switch is also not functional, although for backward compatibility, CMD.EXE accepts it. Microsoft Knowledge Base article Q158141 states that this switch alters the size of the environment available under Windows NT. This information is incorrect. Windows NT does not set a fixed upper limit on the size of the environment used by 32-bit applications, including CMD.EXE.

Example:

```
cmd /x /c "myscript.bat"
```

This command executes the script MYSCRIPT.BAT with command extensions enabled, and then terminates the shell session.

See also: COMMAND, Command Line Editing, Command Line Syntax, ECHO, COLOR

COLOR

Sets the console window foreground and background colors.

Syntax:

```
1. COLOR
2. COLOR bf
```

The COLOR command changes the foreground and background colors of the current console window. Use COLOR(1) to restore the console window colors to those in effect when the command shell was started.

Use COLOR(2) to set the colors to *bf*. This is a two character parameter, the first character of which specifies the background color, the second the foreground color. The colors are taken from the following table.

0	Black	8	Gray
1	Blue	9	Light Blue
2	Green	A	Light Green
3	Aqua	B	Light Aqua
4	Red	C	Light Red
5	Purple	D	Light Purple
6	Yellow	E	Light Yellow
7	White	F	Bright White

Example:

```
color 17
```

This COLOR command displays white text on a blue background.

Notes:

The console window colors can also be changed using the Properties dialog box for the console window. Click the title bar icon to access this dialog box.

In addition, the /T switch can be used to alter the colors when starting a new command shell via the CMD command. Default colors for a console window can be set using the Properties dialog box for any Command Prompt shortcut. Finally, the default colors for *all* console windows can be set via the Control Panel Console dialog box.

See also: CLS

COMMAND

Executes the MS-DOS command shell.

Syntax:

```
1. COMMAND [/E:nn]
2. COMMAND [/E:nn] /C command
```

Switches:

/E   Specifies the number of bytes to reserve for environment variable storage.

/C   Execute command specified and then terminate.

The COMMAND command invokes an MS-DOS command shell. Windows NT provides a 16-bit MS-DOS compatible command shell, COMMAND.COM. This shell can be used to execute older MS-DOS scripts that do not execute correctly on the default Windows NT shell, CMD.EXE.

Use COMMAND(1) to invoke an MS-DOS shell, which prompts for commands to execute. Use COMMAND(2) to execute *command*. After execution completes, the shell terminates.

The /E switch can be used to specify the size, in bytes, of environment variable storage in the shell.

While an MS-DOS command shell is executing, clicking the close box of the console window will not close the console window. Exit the MS-DOS command shell using the EXIT command first.

The MS-DOS shell does not support the same command line editing as the Windows NT shell (CMD.EXE). However, once a command is submitted for execution (by pressing Enter), the complete command line is passed to a Windows NT shell for execution. Thus the MS-DOS command shell inherits many of the features of the Windows NT shell, including most command line syntax and the ability to execute 16 and 32-bit windows applications.

Notes:

Other switches documented elsewhere for COMMAND.COM are *not* valid under Windows NT and may cause unpredictable behavior.

If you include the current path in your command prompt, the MS-DOS shell displays this using short names, that is, uppercase "8.3" names, not mixed case long file names.

See also: CMD, EXIT, Command Line Syntax.

Command Line Editing

Special keys for command line editing.

When typing a command, several special keys are available allowing command editing and command history recall. These special keys are available in all Windows NT console applications that prompt for lines of input.

Basic editing keys edit a command line while it is being entered. The basic editing keys are shown in the following table.

Keystroke	Description
Left arrow	Move cursor one character left.
Right arrow	Move cursor one character right.
Ctrl+left arrow	Move cursor one word left.
Ctrl+right arrow	Move cursor one word right.
Home	Move cursor to start of command.
End	Move cursor to end of command.
Esc	Clear the command line.
Insert	Toggles insert and overwrite mode.
Delete	Delete the character to the right of the cursor.
Backspace	Delete the character to the left of the cursor.
Enter	Execute the command. The cursor does not need to be at the end of the command.

Template editing keys use the command template. The command template is a hidden copy of the most recent command entered. The template editing keys are shown in the following table.

Key	Description
F1	Copy the template character at the same column position as the cursor into the command.
F2	Search and insert template characters. Press F2 and then a character in the template. Characters are copied from the template up to, but not including, the first character matched in the template.
F3	Copy all remaining template characters starting from the current cursor position.
F4	Delete characters. Press F4 and then a character. Characters in the command line are deleted starting from the cursor up to, but not including, the first character matched in the command.
F5	Copy the entire template into the command.

Command history editing keys access a list of recently typed commands. These can be recalled for editing and re-execution. The history editing keys are shown in the following table.

Keystroke	Description
Up arrow	Recall commands from the newest to the oldest.
Down arrow	Recall commands from the oldest to the newest.
Page Up	Recall the oldest command.
Page Down	Recall the newest command.
F7	Displays the command history list in a popup window. Use the cursor keys to move up and down the list. Press Esc to close the window, or Enter to execute the selected command. Commands in the list are numbered for use by F9. The command history popup does not appear if the history list is empty.
Alt+F7	Clears the command history of all commands.
F8	Recalls commands that match the characters typed at the command line. A command matches if the command starts with the same characters typed at the command line. Repeatedly pressing F8 cycles through all commands in the history buffer that start with the typed characters.
F9	Recalls a command from the history by command number. After recall the command can be edited before execution. Command numbers are displayed by pressing F7.

Command completion editing allows the command shell to automatically complete a partially typed file or directory name. To enable command completion editing, set the following Registry key to the ANSI code for the command completion key (typically the Tab key, 0x9):

HKEY_CURRENT_USER\Software\Microsoft\Command Processor\CompletionChar

Once command completion editing is enabled, type the first few letters of a file or directory name, and then press the command completion key (such as the Tab key). The partial file name will be completed using the first matching file name in the current directory. Press the command completion key again to cycle through all matching files or directories in the current directory.

Notes:

Command history information is maintained independently for each executable program name by the command shell. If the same command is launched several times in succession by the same shell, each copy can access the command history from the earlier copies.

See also: DOSKEY

Command-Line Syntax

Special symbols used in commands.

The Windows NT shell processes certain symbols that are entered as part of a command. These symbols are not visible to the command itself (that is, they are stripped from the command text by the shell before the command is executed).

The command redirection symbols control command input, command output and command error output. The symbols are shown in the following table.

Command	Description
>*file*	Redirects command output to the *file* specified. You can also use a standard device name such as LPT1, CON, PRN or CONOUT$ as the file name. Any preexisting contents of the file are lost.
>>*file*	Redirects command output to the *file* specified. If the file already exists, all command output is appended to the end of the file.
<*file*	Redirects command input from the *file* specified. You can also use a standard device name such as CON or CONIN$.
2>*file*	Redirects command error output to the *file* specified. You can also use a standard device name such as LPT1, CON, PRN or CONOUT$ as the file name. Any preexisting contents of the file are lost.
2>&1	Redirects command error output to the same location as command output. This makes any command output redirection also apply to command error output.
cmd1 ¦ *cmd2*	Pipes the command output of *cmd1* to the command input of *cmd2*. Multiple pipe characters are allowed, creating a chain of commands, each sending output to the next command in the chain.

Command input and output redirection is inherited by commands executed from within a shell. Thus if you start a shell and redirect its output, all commands executed within that shell will also have their output redirected.

Multiple command symbols allow multiple commands to be combined on one command line. The pipe symbol (shown in the preceding table) is both a redirection symbol and a multiple command symbol. The multiple command symbols are shown in the following table.

Command	Description
cmd1 & cmd2	Executes command *cmd1*, then command *cmd2*. Additional commands can be added using additional ampersand symbols.
cmd1 && cmd2	Executes command *cmd1*, then executes command *cmd2* only if *cmd1* completed successfully.
cmd1 ¦¦ cmd2	Executes command *cmd1*, then executes command *cmd2* only if *cmd1* did not complete successfully.
( )	Use parentheses to indicate the nesting of complex multi-command sequences. Also used in IF ... ELSE commands and multi-line commands.

When executing commands using the conditional symbols && and ¦¦, the second command only executes if the previous command either did, or did not, complete successfully. A "successful" command is one that returns an exit code of 0. An unsuccessful command is one that returns an exit code of non-zero. Exit codes can be accessed via the %ERRORLEVEL% variable or the IF ERRORLEVEL command.

To over-ride the meanings of special symbols and treat them as regular characters, precede the symbol by a carat ^character. To enter a literal carat character, use two carat characters in sequence.

Example:

```
dir *.txt >>list.txt
dir *.exe /s ¦ more
(dir c: & dir d:) ¦ more
```

This last example shows the use of parentheses. With the parentheses, the output of both DIR commands is sent through a pipe to the MORE command, one after the other. Without the parentheses, only the output of the second command is sent to the pipe.

Notes:

Variable substitution and parameter substitution occur *before* the shell processes special symbols. Therefore, it is possible to place special symbols within variables or parameters and have them processed by the shell as part of a command.

See also: Variable Syntax, Parameter Syntax, Command Line Editing

COPY

Copies files.

Syntax:

```
(1) COPY [/A ¦ /B] source [/A ¦ /B] [+...] [destination [/A ¦ /B]] [/V] [/N] [/Z]
```

Switches:

/A	Copy files in ASCII mode.
/B	Copy files in binary mode.
/V	Verify file copy operations.
/N	Use short (MS-DOS) file names aduring copy.
/Z	Use restartable copy mode.

The COPY command copies files from one location to another, or to a device (such as LPT1 or CON). COPY copies files either in binary mode or ASCII mode. In binary mode, COPY performs a byte-by-byte exact copy of the file specified. In ASCII mode, COPY performs a byte copy up to, but not including, the first end-of-file character (Ctrl+Z) encountered in the source. If the destination is specified as ASCII, then a single end-of-file character is appended to the end of the file.

The /A switch selects ASCII mode and the /B switch selects binary mode. The default mode is binary, unless the COPY command is combining files. Multiple /A and /B switches can be specified in the COPY command. Place a /A or /B switch before the first source file to set the default COPY mode. Subsequent switches placed *after* a file name change the copy mode for that file and also for additional files specified in the COPY command, until another /A or /B switch is encountered.

The /V switch forces the COPY command to verify all file copy operations. The /N switch uses short (MS-DOS) file names instead of long file names. The /Z switch copies all files in restartable mode. In restartable mode, the COPY command tracks the file copy progress in the destination file so that the copy operation can be restarted. This is used primarily when copying files across WAN network connections.

The *source* can be a single file, a wildcard file name, a path, or a device. The *source* can also be a list of files, separated by +characters. The *destination* can be a single file, a path, or a device. If *destination* is not present, the current drive and directory is assumed as the destination for the copy.

The COPY command can be used to combine files by concatenating several files into one output file. Files are combined if the *source* specifies multiple files separated by +characters, or if a destination file is specified *and* the source is specified using a wildcard. The default mode when combining files is ASCII.

Example:

```
copy c:\bin e:\temp\bin
copy c:\*.txt lpt1:
copy a.cpp+b.cpp+c.cpp sys1.cpp
```

Notes:

Use the XCOPY command to copy complete directory trees.

See also: XCOPY, ROBOCOPY, SCOPY, MOVE, REPLACE

DATE

Displays or sets the system date.

Syntax:

```
1. DATE
2. DATE date
3. DATE /T
```

Switches:

/T   Do not prompt for a new date.

The DATE command displays or sets the system date. Use DATE(1) to display the current date and display a prompt asking for the new date. Press Enter only to leave the date unchanged. Use DATE(2) to set a new date directly from the command line. Use DATE(3) to display the date only.

Dates should be entered in the form **mm-dd-yy**.

See also: TIME

DEL, ERASE

Deletes files.

Syntax:

```
1. DEL [/P] [/F] [/S] [/Q] [/A:attr] [drive:][path]filename
2. ERASE [/P] [/F] [/S] [/Q] [/A:attr] [drive:][path]filename
```

Switches:

/P   Prompt for confirmation before deleting each file.

/F   Force delete of read-only files.

/S   Search specified directory and all sub-directories for files to delete.

/Q   Quiet mode. Skip global wildcard confirmation prompt.

/A:attr   Select files to delete based on attributes.

The DEL command deletes files from directories. It does not delete directories. The ERASE command is a synonym for DEL.

The *filename* specifies the name of the file to delete. Wildcards are allowed. If the *filename* is *.*, the DEL command prompts for confirmation before deleting all files in the directory. This prompt can be defeated by using the /Q switch.

The /P switch prompts for confirmation of each individual file deletion. The /F switch forces DEL to delete read-only files. Normally these files are not deleted.

The /S switch deletes files in the current directory and all subdirectories that match the *filename*. If the *path* is specified, files in the specified directory and all its subdirectories are deleted. (Subdirectories themselves are not deleted, only the files they contain.)

The /A switch selects files by attributes, in addition to name. The *attr* argument can include any of the following items:

Character	Description
R	Select read-only files
S	Select system files.
H	Select hidden files.
A	Select files needing archiving.
-	Prefix an attribute letter to invert the selection.

Example:

```
del /a:-a /s c:\workdir
```

This example deletes all files in the c:\WORKDIR tree which do not require archiving (that is, have already been placed in a backup set).

See also: RMDIR

DIR

Lists files in a directory.

Syntax:

```
1. DIR [drive:][path][filename] [switches]
```

Switches:

/P	Pause after each page of information.
/W	Wide format.
/D	Wide format sorted by column.
/B	Bare format, without summary information.
/N	Long list format (default).
/A[:]attr	Filter files to display by specified attributes.
/O[:]sort	Specify sort order for files.

/T[:]t	Select time field to display.
/S	Display file in directory and all subdirectories.
/L	Use lowercase when displaying file names.
/X	Include MS-DOS compatible names (8.3 names).
/C	Display thousands separator in numbers.
-	Disable switch (such as /-C).

The DIR command lists files found in a specified directory or directories. Specify an optional *drive* and *path*, followed by an optional file name. The file name can contain wildcards. If the file name is not present, *.* is assumed.

The DIR command has numerous switches for controlling output. In addition to reading switches from the command line, the DIR command reads switches from the environment variable DIRCMD. These are included before the switches in the command line. Switches can be disabled (or there effect reversed) by prefixing the switch with a dash. For example, use /-N to disable long format output.

The /P switch paginates DIR output so that long listings do not scroll off the console window. Alternatively, pipe the output of the DIR command into the MORE filter.

The /N switch formats the DIR output using the long file name format, with names in the right-most column. This is the default output format. To output in a format compatible with MS-DOS, use the /-N switch. The /W switch displays DIR output in wide format, with multiple names per line. Directory names are enclosed in brackets. The /D switch is similar to /W, except that names are sorted in columns, rather than in rows. Finally, the /B switch forces "bare" output. This format outputs one name per line and suppresses all additional information output. Bare format is suitable for input into other commands for additional processing.

The /A switch filters files by attributes, as specified by *attr*. The following table shows valid *attr* characters.

Character	Description
D	Filter for directories only.
R	Read-only files and directories only.
H	Hidden files and directories only.
S	System files and directories only.
A	Archivable file and directories only.
-	Invert meaning of filter.

For example, to display files only (no directories), use /A:-D.

The /0 switch sorts files for display. The default is unsorted (although Windows NT NTFS directories are naturally sorted by file name). The following table shows valid *sort* characters.

Character	Description
N	Sort alphabetically by name.
E	Sort alphabetically by file extension.
G	Group directories before files.
S	Sort by file size (smallest first). Directories always have a size of 0.
D	Sort by date and time (oldest first).
-	Invert the sort order.

The /T switch selects the time field for display and/or sorting (if /0:D is also specified). Use /T:C to sort/display by the files creation time. Use /T:A to sort/display by the files last access time. Use /T:W (the default) to sort/display by the files last modification time. File create and access times are only available in NTFS partitions.

The /L switch forces file names to be displayed using all lowercase. The /X switch adds an additional display column to the /N format, showing the MS-DOS compatible (short) file name in addition to the full (long) file name. The /C switch displays thousands separators (commas in North America) in all numeric fields. To disable this, use /-C.

Example:

```
dir c:\winnt\system32\*.exe /O:D /B | FIND /I "ras"
```

This example lists all executable files in the C:\WINNT\SYSTEM32 directory that contain the string "ras", listed in bare format in order of ascending date.

See also: DIRUSE, DISKUSE

DIRUSE [RK]

Displays directory and file space usage statistics.

Syntax

```
1. DIRUSE [/S | /V] [/M | /K | /B] [/C] [/,] [/*] dirs
2. DIRUSE [/S | /V] [/M | /K | /B] [/C] [/,] [/*] /Q:nn [/L] [/A] [/D] [/O]
   dirs
```

Switches:

/S	Include subdirectories in the output.
/V	Display progress while scanning subdirectories.

/M	Display disk use in megabytes.
/K	Display disk use in kilobytes.
/B	Display disk use in bytes (default).
/C	Use compressed file sizes (NTFS only).
/,	Use thousands separator in output.
/*	Use top-level directories in each specified directory.
/Q:nn	Mark directories that exceed *nn* bytes in size (or *nn* kilobytes or megabytes if /K or /M is specified).
/A	Generates an alert if the specified size is exceeded.
/D	Display only directories that exceed the specified size.
/O	Do not check subdirectories for size overflow.
/L	List of directories marked as oversized is sent to log file, diruse.log.

The DIRUSE command computes directory and file size statistics. The totals reported by DIRUSE are computed by adding up the exact file sizes, rather than the space occupied on disk by the files. Therefore, the numbers reported by DIRUSE may be lower than the actual amount of disk space used.

Use DIRUSE(1) to report file sizes only. Use DIRUSE(2) to report file sizes and check for directories that exceed a specified threshold size.

Without any switches, DIRUSE reports the total bytes used by all files in each of the directories specified by *dirs*. Several directories can be specified. For each directory, DIRUSE computes the size of all the files in the directory and all subdirectories. The /S switch displays file size totals for each individual subdirectory in each specified directory. Alternatively, the /V switch shows scan progress during total computations.

The /M, /K and /B switches set the scale value used. The /B switch displays results in bytes. The /K switch displays results in kilobytes (1 kilobyte = 1024 bytes). The /M switch displays results in megabytes (1 megabyte = 1,048,576 bytes). These switches also control the interpretation of the *nn* value specified in the /Q switch as bytes, kilobytes, or megabytes.

If NTFS compression is used, DIRUSE uses the expanded file size when computing totals. The /C switch uses the compressed file size instead.

The /* switch computes totals for each top-level directory within each of the specified *dirs*. This allows a quick break down of a disk drive into usage by directory, by specifying the root of the drive.

The /Q switch sets a threshold level for directory checking. The *nn* value is interpreted according to the /M, /K and /B switches. Any directory whose size exceeds the threshold is marked with a "!" in the output. The /D switch to restricts output only to directories whose size exceeds the threshold. The /A switch generates an administrative alert if the threshold is exceeded. The /O switch prevents subdirectories from being checked for overflow—only the directories specified by *dirs* are checked.

Example:

```
diruse c:\ /* /k /,
```

Displays the disk space used, in kilobytes with comma separators, by each directory off the root of drive C:.

See also: DIR, DISKUSE

DISKUSE [RK]

Displays file usage statistics by user.

Syntax:

```
1. DISKUSE dir [switches]
```

Switches:

/F:*file*	Store command output in the specified *file*.
/E:*file*	Store command error output in the specified *file*.
/U:*user*	Compute usage for the specified *user* only.
/S	Include subdirectories in the scan.
/T	Use table format for output (space or comma delimited).
/W	Unicode output (default is ASCII).
/Q	Quiet mode. No display output.
/R:*file*	Read user restrictions from the specified *file*.
/O	Show only users over the specified limit.
/V	Verbose output. Include information on individual files.
/D:A¦C¦W	Display the access (A), creation (C) or last written (W) date stamp.
/N:*nn*	Display only the largest *nn* files per user.
/X:*nn*	Display only files at least *nn* bytes long.

The DISKUSE command compiles disk usage statistics by file owner. DISKUSE can only be used on NTFS volumes. The specified directory *dir* is scanned and a report compiled of disk space usage by individual user name. The /S switch includes subdirectories in *dir* in the scan.

The compressed sizes of files are always used for the computations. Normally, DISKUSE computes the disk space used for all users. The /U switch computes the disk usage for the specified *user* only. Specify the *user* in normal DOMAIN\Username format.

The /F switch sends DISKUSE output to the specified *file*. The /E switch sends DISKUSE error output to the specified *file*. These switches generate file output in addition to display output. When the /T switch is used, the output generated by the /F switch differs from the display output. The /Q switch suppresses display output and *only* file output is generated.

The /T switch generates output in table format. Output to the display in this mode is space delimited. Output to a file (using the /F switch) is comma delimited. The comma-delimited output can be processed by a FOR command or read into a spreadsheet for further analysis.

The /R switch reads the specified *file* for a list of per-user disk space limits. The file must be a text file containing one user limit per line. The first item on the line must be the user name (in DOMAIN\Username format). The second item, offset from the first by spaces, must be the threshold size, in bytes, for that user. If the /R switch is used, the /O switch limits the report to users who exceed their specified threshold.

The /V switch adds verbose file information to the output, listing all files owned by each user. The /D switch specifies which time stamp to display in this listing. The /N switch displays only the largest *nn* files for each user, while the /X switch displays only files *nn* bytes or larger.

See also: DIRUSE

DOSKEY

Manages command editing, history, and macros.

Syntax:

```
1. DOSKEY /REINSTALL [/LISTSIZE=size]
2. DOSKEY /HISTORY
3. DOSKEY /INSERT ¦ /OVERSTRIKE
4. DOSKEY /MACROS[:ALL ¦ :exename]
5. DOSKEY /MACROFILE=file
6. DOSKEY [/EXENAME=exename] name=[text]
```

Switches:

/REINSTALL	Clears the command history buffer.
/LISTSIZE	Sets the size of the command history buffer.
/INSERT	Select insert mode for command editing.
/OVERSTRIKE	Select overstrike mode for command editing.
/MACROS	Displays currently defined macros.
/EXENAME	Specifies the executable name for the macro.
/MACROFILE	Specifies a macro file for macro loading.

The DOSKEY command manages the command editing features of the command shell, including the command history buffer and command macros. Command history and macro buffers are maintained on a per-shell, per-application name basis. Only programs that use line input can access a command history and use command macros. The command history for a specific application is retained between invocations of the application, provided the application is started from the same command shell.

Use DOSKEY(1) to clear the command history buffer. The /LISTSIZE switch sets the maximum number of commands saved in the buffer. The /REINSTALL switch clears all history buffers for all applications. Use Alt+F7 to clear the history buffer for the current application. Use DOSKEY(2) to display the current history buffer (or press F7).

Use DOSKEY(3) to control the initial insert mode of the cursor. The default is overstrike mode. The mode can also be toggled during editing by pressing the Insert key.

Use DOSKEY(4) to list currently defined macros. By default, macros for the command shell are listed. Use the :ALL option to list macros for all applications, or :exename to list macros for the specified application. When the :ALL option is used, the output is generated in a format suitable for use by the /MACROFILE switch.

Use DOSKEY(5) to load a set of macros from a file. The macros are added to any already defined. Typically this file is generated by using DOSKEY(4) and redirecting command output to a file.

Use DOSKEY(6) to define a macro. By default, the macro is defined for the command shell. Alternatively, the /EXENAME switch defines the macro for use by the application specified by exename. The macro name names the macro command, while text defines the text to be executed by the command. If text is missing, the named macro definition is deleted.

The following table shows special characters recognized within the macro command *text*.

Character	Description
$G or $g	Command output redirection. Equivalent to the > redirection symbol.
GG or gg	Command output redirection with append. Equivalent to the >> redirection symbol.
$L or $l	Command input redirection. Equivalent to the < redirection symbol.
$B or $b	Pipe redirection. Equivalent to the ¦ redirection symbol.
$T or $t	Multiple command separator. Equivalent to the & symbol.
$$	Use to enter a literal $ character.
$1 to $9	Command line arguments to the macro.
$*	Represents all command line arguments.

Example:

```
doskey /macros:all >macfile.mac
doskey /macrofile=macfile.mac
doskey ls=dir/w $*
ls c:\winnt
```

The first two examples show how to create a macro file and then restore it for later use. The last example (line 3) shows how to create a new macro command, ls, to output a Unix-like directory listing.

Notes:

Some Windows NT documentation states that DOSKEY macros are not valid within scripts. This is not true; DOSKEY macros are valid within scripts. However, macros are not advised in scripts, as they may not always be available when the script is executed.

Under MS-DOS, the DOSKEY command loaded a TSR to perform command editing. Under Windows NT, the editing features are built into the operating system, and the DOSKEY command merely provides a means to control these features.

DOSKEY can be used to create simple scripts. First, use DOSKEY /REINSTALL to clear the history buffer. Then enter and execute the script commands. Then save the commands as a prototype script using DOSKEY /MACROS, redirecting the output to a new script file.

See also: Command Editing, Command Syntax

DUMPEL [RK]

Dumps a formatted event log.

Syntax:

> 1. DUMPEL /L *log* [/E *nn*] [/F *filename*] [/M *name* [/R]] [/S *computer*] [/T ¦ /C]
> [/NS] [/FORMAT *fmt*]
> 2. DUMPEL /B /L *logfile* [/E *nn*] [/F *filename*] [/M *name* [/R]] [/T ¦ /C] [/NS]
> [/FORMAT *fmt*]

Switches:

/L	Specifies *log* or *logfile* to dump.
/B	Dump a logfile.
/E *nn*	Filter for event ID *nn*.
/F *filename*	Dump output to *filename*.
/M *name*	Filter for events logged by specified *name*.
/R	Reverses /M name filter.
/S *computer*	Specifies source computer for log.
/T	Delimit dump report using tabs.
/C	Delimit dump report using commas.
/NS	Do not dump strings.
/FORMAT *fmt*	Format the report using *fmt*.

The DUMPEL command dumps the contents of a Windows NT event log or log file. The output can be formatted as required, and is suitable for input to a FOR or FIND command for further processing.

Use DUMPEL(1) to dump an event log. The /L switch specifies the *log* to dump—specify application, system or security. The /S switch specifies the computer containing the log to dump (the default is the local computer). Use DUMPEL(2) to dump an event log file. Event log files are created using Windows NT Event Viewer. The event log dump is displayed in the console window unless the output is redirected to a file, or the /F switch is used.

Normally, the entire log is dumped. The /E switch limits the dump to events having an event ID of *nn*. Up to 10 /E switches can be specified. The /M switch limits the dump to events having a source of *name*, or, if the /R switch is also specified, to events having a source other than *name*.

The log dump output consists of one line per event. Normally the fields in the output are delimited by spaces. The /T switch delimits the fields by tabs, while the /C switch delimits the fields by commas. The fields to dump for each event is controlled by the /FORMAT switch. The *fmt* text specifies the ordering and contents of each field. The following table shows all valid characters in *fmt*.

Valid Character	Description
t	Time of day.
d	Date
T	Event type.
C	Event category.
I	Event ID.
S	Event source.
u	User name.
c	Computer name.
s	Event string.

The default value for *fmt* is dtTCISucs.

Example:

```
dumpel /l application /format dtTC
```

This example dumps the application log of the local computer, and restricts the output to the date, time, event type, and event category.

See also: LOGEVENT

ECHO

Controls command output to console window.

Syntax:

```
1. ECHO
2. ECHO ON ¦ OFF
3. @ECHO %ECHO%
4. ECHO text
```

The ECHO command controls command window script output, or generates script output to the console window.

When executing a script, the command shell, by default, echoes each executed command in the console window. Use ECHO(2) to enable or disable this feature. Use ECHO(1) to display the current state of the echo toggle.

Script commands that begins with an @ character will not be echoed in the console window, regardless of the state of the echo toggle.

It is common practice to disable echo in scripts except during debugging, when echo can be useful to trace commands and monitor variable expansion. To facilitate this, an ECHO variable is often defined, containing the text ON or OFF only. Then, placing ECHO(3) as the first command in a script toggles command echo according to the value in this variable.

Use ECHO(4) to display *text* in the console window. Text is always output, regardless of the state of the echo toggle. Environment variables in *text* are expanded normally before the text is output, allowing ECHO(4) to be used as a general purpose print command. To avoid confusion with ECHO(1) and ECHO(2), *text* cannot be empty, consist only of spaces, or consist only of ON or OFF. To display an empty line, use a single Tab character for *text*.

See also: TITLE, NOW

ENDLOCAL

Ends localized scope for environment variable changes.

Syntax:

```
1. ENDLOCAL
```

The ENDLOCAL command, when used in a script file, ends a local scope for environment variable changes. Any changes made to the environment before an ENDLOCAL command is executed are lost.

Executing an ENDLOCAL command restores the environment to its exact state at the time the most recent SETLOCAL command was executed. Any changed variables are restored to the value they had prior to the SETLOCAL command, and any newly created variables since the SETLOCAL command are deleted.

SETLOCAL/ENDLOCAL commands can be nested up to 32 levels deep, creating additional local scopes within the current scope. If any local scopes exist when the script file ends, an implicit ENDLOCAL is performed to restore the environment at the end of the script.

SETLOCAL/ENDLOCAL is very useful within script procedures, as it allows variables to be made local to the procedure.

Notes:

ENDLOCAL is valid only within a script file. The command is accepted interactively, but no localization occurs.

See also: SETLOCAL, SET

ERASE

See DEL.

EXIT

Exits the current command shell.

Syntax:

```
1. EXIT
```

The EXIT command exits the current command shell, ending the shell session. The program invoking the shell then continues executing. If the command shell exiting is the one that started the console window, the window closes.

Notes:

The exit code from the command shell is the most recent exit code from the last executed program. Thus a nested command shell passes back to its parent shell the exit code from any program it executes.

See also: CMD, COMMAND

FC

Compares files.

Syntax:

```
1. FC /L [switches] [drive1:][path1]filename1 [drive2:][path2]filename2
2. FC /B [drive1:][path1]filename1 [drive2:][path2]filename2
```

Switches:

/A	Display only first and last line for each difference found.
/B	Perform binary comparison.
/C	Perform case insensitive comparison.
/L	Compare files as ASCII.
/LBn	Set maximum consecutive mismatches to n lines.
/N	Display line numbers during comparison.
/T	Do not expand tabs into spaces.
/U	Compare files as Unicode.
/W	Compress whitespace runs for comparison and ignore leading/trailing whitespace.
/nn	Minimum number of lines that must match after mismatch.

The FC command compares files. Files can be compared in two modes: ASCII/Unicode or binary. Use FC(1) to compare files in ASCII or Unicode. Use FC(2) to compare files in binary. If the files being compared have a file extension of .EXE, .COM, .SYS, .OBJ, .LIB, or .BIN then the default comparison mode is binary. Otherwise, the default mode is ASCII/Unicode. Wildcards can be used for *filename1* and *filename2*.

When in ASCII/Unicode mode, FC locates and displays the portions of the files that differ. Normally, FC displays all different lines. The /A switch abbreviates the output so only the first and last lines in a set of lines that are different are displayed.

The /*nn* switch specifies that FC must locate *nn* matching lines from both files before the files are considered re-synchronized after a mismatch. The default is 2 lines.

The /C switch performs a case insensitive comparison. The /W switch forces FC to consider all runs of whitespace (spaces and tabs) to be equivalent to a single space. Also, with this switch, whitespace at the start and end of lines is ignored. FC then treats lines differing only in the amount of whitespace as identical.

Normally, FC expands tabs at every eighth column position. The /T switch treats tabs as tab characters. This can cause FC to consider identically indented lines as different unless the /W switch is used.

When comparing files in binary mode, FC outputs a list of differences as hexadecimal byte values and byte offsets in the file.

Notes:

FC does not return an exit code. The XCPTEST sample script shows how FC output can be filtered by a script to programmatically determine the result of a file comparison.

FIND

Filters text files for matching lines.

Syntax:

```
1. FIND [/V] [/C] [/N] [/I] "string" [drive:][path]filename
2. FIND [/V] [/C] [/N] [/I] "string"
```

Switches:

/V	Invert test. Displays lines *not* matching the string.
/C	Display only the count of matching lines.
/N	Display line numbers of matching lines.
/I	Ignore case when matching line.

The FIND command searches and filters text. Text lines are matched against the specified *string*. Those lines that contain the string are displayed. Those that do not are discarded.

Use FIND(1) to filter text from one or more files. The *filename* can contain wildcards, allowing multiple files to be searched.

Use FIND(2) to filter text from command input. By default, command input is all text typed at the console up to the end of file character, Ctrl+Z. Use the console input redirection symbols to redirect console input from a file or device. Use the pipe command to send the output of any command to the command input of the FIND command for processing.

The /V switch inverts the sense of the string matching. Instead of displaying those lines that contain the *string*, the /V switch displays only those lines that do *not* contain the *string*. The /C switch displays only a count of the matching lines, rather than the lines themselves. The /N switch prefixes each displayed line with the line number in the text file. The /I switch ignores case differences when searching for *string* in the input lines.

Example:

```
dir ¦ find /C "<DIR>"
```

This command counts the number of subdirectories in the current directory.

See also: MORE, SORT, FINDSTR

FINDSTR

Searches for strings in files.

Syntax:

```
1. FINDSTR [switches] [/S] strings [drive:][path]filename
2. FINDSTR [switches] /F:file strings
3. FINDSTR [switches] [/S] /C:string [drive:][path]filename
4. FINDSTR [switches] /F:file /C:string
5. FINDSTR [switches] [/S] /G:file [drive:][path]filename
6. FINDSTR [switches] /F:file /G:file
```

Switches:

/B	Matches strings if they occur at the beginning of the line.
/E	Matches strings if they occur at the end of the line.
/X	Matches strings if they exactly match the line.
/L	Treat search strings as literal text.
/R	Treat search strings as regular expressions (default).
/I	String matches are case insensitive.

/V	Display lines that do *not* match the specified strings.
/N	Display the line number before each line.
/M	Display only the file name for each file containing matches.
/O	Display the file offset before each line.
/C:*string*	Specify a search string.
/G:*file*	Get search strings from the specified *file*.
/F:*file*	Get list of files to search from the specified *file*.
/S	Search all subdirectories of the directory specified.

The FINDSTR command searches one or more text files for lines containing one of the specified match strings. Normally, FINDSTR displays each matching line. Use FINDSTR(1), FINDSTR(3) or FINDSTR(5) to match the files specified by *file-name*. Wildcards can be used. The /S switch searches subdirectories for additional files to process.

Use FINDSTR(2), FINDSTR(4) or FINDSTR(6) to match against a list of files. The *file* specified by the /F switch contains a list of file names to search, one file name per line.

Use FINDSTR(1) or FINDSTR(2) to match file lines against *strings*. Multiple strings can be specified, separated by spaces. Enclose *strings* in double quotes. Thus "one two" matches against the strings "one" or "two". Use FINDSTR(3) or FINDSTR(4) to match file lines against *string*. The *string* specified by the /C switch can contain spaces. Thus /C:"one two" matches against the string "one two" only.

Use FINDSTR(5) or FINDSTR(6) to match file lines against a list of strings contained in a file. The *file* specified by the /G switch contains a list of strings to match, one per line.

Normally, FINDSTR considers a line matched if the line contains an occurrence of at least one of the specified search strings. The /B switch only matches lines in which the search string occurs at the *beginning* of the line, and the /E switch only matches lines in which the search string occurs at the *end* of the line. Using /B and /E together only matches lines that exactly match the search string, and contain no additional characters before or after the string. The /X switch can also be used for this purpose.

By default, FINDSTR displays all matching lines found. The /N switch prefixes each line with its line number, or the /O switch prefixes each line with its byte offset in the file. The /M switch suppresses the display of matching lines, and instead displays only the names of files containing matching lines. Finally, the /V switch inverts the line selection logic; lines (or files if using /M) are displayed that do *not* contain a match against the search strings. The /I switch ignores case during string matching.

The /L switch treats search strings as literal strings. In this case, the text specified by *string* or *strings* is matched character for character against text in the
file being searched. By default (or if the /R switch is used), search strings are
treated as *regular expressions*. Rather than matching literally, FINDSTR uses each
search string as a template that describes the pattern of text to match. This is
similar to the use of wildcard characters in file names, but more powerful. In a
regular expression, most characters are treated as literal characters and match
exactly the character specified (like a literal search string). Some characters are
special, however. These are shown in the following table.

Special Character	Description
. (dot)	Matches any single character.
*	Matches the previous character or class any number of times (including zero).
^	Matches the beginning of the line. Similar in effect to the /B switch.
$	Matches the end of the line. Similar in effect to the /E switch.
[class]	Matches any character listed between brackets.
[^class]	Matches any character *not* listed between brackets.
[x-y]	Matches any character in the range x to y.
\x	Escapes the character x to a literal.
\<	Matches the beginning of a word.
\>	Matches the end of a word.

Example:

```
findstr "a[0-9][0-9]*" *.txt
```

This example finds all lines containing the letter "a" followed by one or more
decimal digits in all .TXT files in the current directory.

```
findstr /i "\\\\[a-z0-9\$][a-z0-9\$]*\\[a-z0-9\$][a-z0-9\$]*" *.doc
```

This example finds all lines containing UNC share names in all .DOC files in
the current directory. The 4 backslashes match the \\ prefix for a UNC name
(two backslashes escaped). The [a-z0-9\$] part of the match string matches
any letter, digit or literal $ character (allowed characters in a UNC name). The
first occurrence matches one letter, digit, or $. The second occurrence is fol-
lowed by an * character, so this matches any number (including zero) of letters,
digits, or $ characters. The following 2 backslashes match a literal backslash.

See also: FIND

FOR

Iterates commands.

Syntax:

```
1. FOR [/D] %var IN (set) DO command
2. FOR /R [drive:][path] %var IN (set) DO command
3. FOR /L %var IN (start,step,end) DO command
4. FOR /F ["opts"] %var IN (set) DO command
5. FOR /F ["opts"] %var IN ("string") DO command
6. FOR /F ["opts"] %var IN ('cmd') DO command
```

Switches:

/D	Match directory names instead of file names.
/R	Recursive directory tree walk.
/L	Iterate a numeric series.
/F	File token parsing.

The FOR command iterates files, directories, text file lines, command output and numeric series. For each step in the iteration, the *command* specified is executed. The iterator variable, *%var*, is substituted in the command in a manner similar to that used for parameter substitution. The iterator variable is named using a single letter after the percent, such as %i or %n. Note that the iterator variable name *is* case sensitive.

When placing a FOR command in a script file, double the % on all references to the iterator variable. Thus, use %%n instead of %n within a script file. Do not do this if entering a FOR command directly at the command prompt.

Use FOR(1) to iterate a set of files or directories. *set* specifies the files to iterate, and must be a file name or a wildcard. You can include a drive letter and path name in *set*, otherwise the current drive and directory is assumed. By default, FOR(1) iterates files. Use the /D switch to iterate directories instead. Parameter qualifiers can be used in *%var* to access portions of the file or path name being iterated (see "Parameter Syntax").

Use FOR(2) to perform a FOR(1) type iteration on an entire directory tree. Specify a drive and/or path name as the root of the directory tree to iterate following the /R switch. If no drive or path is specified, the current directory is assumed. FOR(2) walks the directory tree specified, executing the FOR command for the specified *set* in *each* directory. If *set* is *.*, all files in the entire tree are iterated. If *set* is a single dot, only the directories themselves are iterated.

Use FOR(3) to perform a numeric iteration. The *start*, *step* and *end* values are numeric values specifying the start value, step amount (increment) and end value for the iteration. Start and end values are inclusive. Use an end value less than a start value, along with a negative step value, to perform a descending iteration. The iteration ends when the current iterator value in *var* exceeds the *end* value specified.

Use FOR(4), FOR(5) and FOR(6) to parse text files and strings into tokens. FOR(4) processes each file specified in *set* as a text file, iterating each line in each file. Note that, in this case, *set* is a set of one or more file names separated by spaces. Wildcards are not allowed.

FOR(5) processes the text string specified. In this case, the iterated *command* is called only once, with the results of the parsing in the iterator variable.

FOR(6) processes the output of a command. Enclose *cmd* in single quotes. The command is executed, and each line of output generated by the command is parsed before *command* is executed. This form of the FOR command is very useful, as it allows the output of commands to be captured and parsed for further processing. FOR(6) executes the specified *cmd* to completion before starting the iteration.

To parse a line of text, the FOR command first breaks the line into tokens. A *token* is a portion of an input line delimited by delimiter characters (such as commas or spaces). By default, tokens are delimited by space or tab characters (but see the notes below). The tokens are then assigned to the iterator variable or variables. Finally, the specified *command* is executed. The process then repeats for the next line. Empty lines are skipped (the *command* is not executed). The parsing and tokenizing operation is controlled by the optional *opts*. If present, these must be enclosed in double quotes. Individual options in *opts* are separated by spaces. The following table shows all available options.

Option	Description
eol=c	Specifies an end of line comment delimiter character.
skip=n	Specifies the number of lines to skip at the start of each text file.
delims=xxx	Specifies one or more delimiters to use instead of the default space and tab.
tokens=x,y,m-n	Specifies which tokens on each line are to be placed in variables for iteration.

The *eol* option specifies an optional logical end of line character. Text beyond this character on a line is ignored and not included in any tokens. This is useful to skip comments when delimited by a character such as semi-colon or pound.

The *skip* option can be used to skip a number of lines before tokenizing begins. This is useful when processing command output if the first few lines of output are headers.

The *delims* option specifies an alternate token delimiter set, instead of the default space or tab. Each character specified is recognized as a delimiter when parsing the line. Comma is a common alternative delimiter. The delimiter set breaks each line of text into tokens. Delimiters themselves are not included in the tokens.

The *tokens* option specifies which tokens to include in the iterator variables. Tokens are numbered starting at 1. You can specify a list of tokens, or a range separated by a dash. In addition, if the last character of the *tokens* option is an asterisk, an additional token is generated that contains all remaining text on the line not already assigned to other tokens.

The first token on each line, or the lowest numbered token specified by the *tokens* option, is placed in the iterator variable %*var* when the *command* is executed. If additional tokens are specified by the *tokens* option, then the FOR command automatically creates additional iterator variables to contain the tokens. These are named sequentially up the alphabet, starting at the next letter after %*var*. The ordering of token indices in the *tokens* options is not important: tokens are always assigned from left to right across the command.

Example:

```
for /r %i in (*.bmp) do copy %i c:\bitmaps
for /l %i in (1,1,10) do set ARRAY_%i=0
for /f "delims=, tokens=1-5" %i in ("12,456,777") do echo %i%j%k%l%m
```

The last example shows how the FOR command can strip the commas from numbers. This allows the output of commands that use this format to be processed so that they can be used with (for example) the SET command.

Notes:

In certain versions of Windows NT, the FOR(4) command does not accept tab as a default delimiter. To overcome this, specify a literal tab character using the delims= option.

The FOR(4) command cannot process a file name containing spaces. Instead, use a FOR(6) command in combination with a TYPE command. For example, replace:

```
for /f %I in (name with spaces.txt) do echo %I
```

with

```
For /f %I in ('type "name with spaces.txt"') do echo %I
```

See also: Parameter Syntax

FTYPE

Displays and alters file types.

Syntax:

```
1. FTYPE
2. FTYPE filetype
3. FTYPE filetype=
4. FTYPE filetype=text
```

The FTYPE command displays and alters file type commands in the registry. Once a file type is defined you can use the ASSOC command to associate it with one or more file extensions.

Use FTYPE(1) to display all current file types, and FTYPE(2) to display a specific file type. Use FTYPE(3) to delete an existing file type, and FTYPE(4) to create a new type or change an existing type.

The text can be any valid Windows NT executable program and any additional required parameters (spaces are allowed). Always specify the file name of the executable, including the file extension and (typically) the path name. Within the text, use %0 or %1 to represent the name of the file being opened. %2 onwards represents additional arguments supplied. You can use %* to represent all arguments (from %2 onwards), and %-n to represent all arguments starting at argument n. Generally, %0 or %1 should be enclosed in double quotes to ensure that file names with embedded spaces are correctly processed.

Example

```
ftype Text.File=notepad.exe "%1"
```

Notes:

File type information and file extension associations are stored in the HKEY_CLASSES_ROOT section of the registry. Therefore changes made using the FTYPE command are retained across system shutdowns and affect all users.

See also: ASSOC, ASSOCIATE.

GLOBAL [RK]

Displays the names of members of a global group.

Syntax:

```
1. GLOBAL groupname domain ¦ \\computer
```

The GLOBAL command displays the member list for a specified global group. The global group is specified using groupname. GLOBAL locates the group either in the specified domain or on the specified computer.

Example:

```
global Administrators \\styx
```

See also: LOCAL, IFMEMBER, NET GROUP

GOTO

Transfers control to a script label.

Syntax:

```
1. GOTO [:]label
2. GOTO :EOF
```

The GOTO command transfers control to a different location within the script. GOTO executes a *jump* to the specified location—no automatic return to the caller location is possible.

Use GOTO(1) to jump to another location in the current script specified by *label*. The colon before the label in the GOTO statement is optional. Use GOTO(2) to jump to the end of the current script file. This either terminates the current script, or (if the script was invoked via a CALL statement) returns to the calling script.

Example:

```
goto :exit
 .
 .
 .
:exit
```

See also: CALL, Label

IF

Executes commands conditionally.

Syntax:

```
1. IF [NOT] ERRORLEVEL level command
2. IF [NOT] [/I] str1==str2 command
3. IF [NOT] EXIST file command
4. IF [/I] val1 op val2 command
5. IF CMDEXTVERSION version command
6. IF [NOT] DEFINED varname command
7. IF test (command) ELSE (command)
```

Switches:

/I   Specifies string comparisons are to be case insensitive.

The IF command provides conditional command execution. A test condition is evaluated and, if true, the specified *command* is executed. Frequently, the *command* is a CALL or GOTO command. However, any valid command can be used, including another IF command. Use the NOT clause with IF(1), IF(2), IF(3) or IF(6) to invert the sense of the conditional test performed.

Use IF(1) to test the exit code from a previous command. Commands generally return 0 if successful, and a non-zero error code if not successful. IF(1) evaluates true if the previous command set ERRORLEVEL equal to, or greater than, *level*. A command's exit code is also available via the %ERRORLEVEL% variable.

Use IF(2) to compare two strings for equality. The /I switch performs a case-insensitive comparison. The strings must be enclosed in double quotes if they contain spaces, or if one or both of the strings is a variable name. When comparing parameter values, which may already contain double quotes, enclose both strings in alternate delimiters, such as braces.

Use IF(3) to check if the specified *file* exists. IF(3) evaluates true if the specified file exists. Full path names and wildcards can be used for *file*. If a wildcard is used, the test evaluates true if at least one file matches the pattern specified. You can also test for the existence of a directory by specifying a directory name for *file*. To test that *file* is a directory and not a file, test for the existence of a file named "." within the directory—all directories contain at least this file.

Use IF(4) to compare strings or numbers. The two values, *val1* and *val2* are compared using the operator *op*. If the comparison evaluates to true, the *command* is executed. The following table shows valid comparison operators.

Comparison Operator	Value
EQU	True if the two values are equal.
NEQ	True if the two values are not equal.
LSS	True if *val1* is less than *val2*.
LEQ	True if *val1* is less than or equal to *val2*.
GTR	True if *val1* is greater than *val2*.
GEQ	True if *val1* is greater than or equal to *val2*.

In some versions of Windows NT, the comparison operators must be specified as uppercase. Using lowercase operators results in a syntax error.

If both *val1* and *val2* are comprised entirely of decimal digits, the comparison if performed numerically. Otherwise, the comparison is performed as a text comparison. In this case the /I switch can be used to indicate that the comparison should be case insensitive.

Use IF(5) to test for the command script extensions revision. This test evaluates to true if the current script extension revision is greater than or equal to *version*. Currently, the command extension revision is 1. If future versions of Windows NT alter the script language by adding new features, this value will be incremented. This allows scripts to verify which syntax and commands are available and adapt accordingly.

Use IF(6) to see if a variable is defined. The test evaluates to true if *varname* is a defined environment variable. Do *not* enclose *varname* in percent symbols.

Use IF(7) as a variation on any other IF command type to add an ELSE clause. Replace *test* with any of the tests described previously. If the test evaluates to true, the first command in parentheses is executed. If the test evaluates to false, the second command in parentheses, after the ELSE clause, is executed. Note that IF(7) and the ELSE clause are presently undocumented by Microsoft, and should therefore be used with caution.

Example:

```
if "%OS%"=="Windows_NT" echo Running on Windows NT..
if exist c:\winnt if exist c:\winnt\. echo Valid Windows NT directory found!
if %ERRORLEVEL% LEQ 1 echo Command completed ok!
```

The last example shows the use of %ERRORLEVEL% and a comparison operator as an alternative to the IF ERRORLEVEL command.

See also: SET, Variable Syntax, Standard Variables

IFMEMBER [RK]

Tests group membership.

Syntax:

```
1. IFMEMBER groupname [...]
```

The IFMEMBER command checks Windows NT group membership for the current logged-on user. Specify a list of one or more group names for checking, separated by spaces. For each group, IFMEMBER checks to see if the current logged-on user is a member of that group. IFMEMBER then returns a count of the number of matches as its exit code.

The exit code can be accessed using the IF ERRORLEVEL command and %ERROR-LEVEL% variable.

Example:

```
ifmember Administrators
if not errorlevel 1 exit
```

This example exits the script if the current user is not an administrator.

See also: GLOBAL, LOCAL, NET GROUP

INSTSRV [RK]

Installs or removes a Windows NT service executable.

Syntax:

```
1. INSTSRV servicename drive:path\filename [-A acct] [-P pwd]
2. INSTSRV servicename REMOVE
```

Switches:

-A *acct* Execute the service using the specified account name.

-P *pwd* Logon to the specified account name using the specified password.

The INSTSRV command installs a Windows NT service executable file. Services are special .EXE files designed specifically to execute as Windows NT services. They are managed by the service control manager (SCM), and execute independently of interactive logons.

Use INSTSRV(1) to install a new service. The service is assigned the specified *servicename*, which then appears in lists of services, such as that presented by Control Panel. The executable for the service must also be specified. Always include the full drive and path name to the executable file.

The -A switch specifies an account in which to execute the service. If this is not specified the SYSTEM (also known as the LocalSystem) account is used. The -P switch supplies a password when logging on using the specified account.

Use INSTSRV(2) to remove a previously installed service. The .EXE file is not deleted by this operation.

Example:

```
instsrv SysMonitor c:\bin\sysmon.exe -a MonitorAccount -p pwd42
```

See also: SC, SCLIST

KILL [RK]

Kills a process.

Syntax:

```
1. KILL [-F] pid
2. KILL [-F] name
```

Switches:

-F Force the process kill.

The KILL command kills a Windows NT process. The -F switch forces the process to be killed.

> **Troubleshooting Tip**
>
> *Using the* -F *flag can result in the loss of unsaved data.*

Use KILL(1) to kill a process by process ID (*pid*). Use Task Manager or PULIST to obtain process IDs for all processes.

Use KILL(2) to kill a process by task name or window name. The *name* can be either a task name (typically the executable name) or a window name (typically the applications main window title). In either case, wildcards can be used to match the name to the process.

See also: PULIST

Labels

Marks a target for control flow transfers.

Syntax:

    1. :label

A *label* is a line in a script file comprised of a colon followed by a label name. Valid label names follow the same syntax conventions as file names, except that spaces are not allowed. Labels must appear at the start of a line, and cannot be part of a compound or multi-line command. Spaces are permitted before and after the colon character.

The label :EOF is special. If this label is not defined in the script file, it is assumed to exist at the very end of the file. In this way, the statement GOTO :EOF means jump to the end of the script and can be interpreted as an "exit" or "return" statement.

See also: CALL, GOTO

LOCAL [RK]

Displays the names of members of a local group.

Syntax:

    1. LOCAL groupname domain ¦ \\computer

The LOCAL command displays the member list for a specified local group. The local group is specified using *groupname*. LOCAL locates the group either in the specified *domain* or on the specified *computer*.

Example:

```
local Administrators \\styx
```

See also: GLOBAL, IFMEMBER, NET GROUP

LOGEVENT [RK]

Logs an event in the application event log.

Syntax:

```
1. LOGEVENT
2. LOGEVENT [-M \\computer] [-S severity] [-C category] text
```

Switches:

-M	Logs event on specified *computer*.
-S	Log with the specified *severity*.
-C	Log event with the specified *category*.

The LOGEVENT command adds events to the Windows NT application event log. This allows scripts to record information messages and success/failure results. This is particularly useful when the script is scheduled via the AT command, as these scripts typically do not interact with the desktop.

Use LOGEVENT(1) to install the event log program. This step is necessary on any computer that is to view the event log information generated by LOGEVENT. LOGEVENT(2) also performs the installation step if it detects that LOGEVENT has not been execute previously.

Use LOGEVENT(2) to add an event to the event log. The event should be described using *text*. The -M switch specifies which computer receives the event log entry. The default is the local computer. The -S switch sets the severity of the event being logged. Severity values are shown in the following table.

Value	Description
S	Success audit.
F	Failure audit.
I	Information event.
W	Warning event.
E	Error event.

Each severity is displayed using a different icon in the event log viewer.

The -C switch includes an optional event category. The *category* is a numerical value stored as part of the event. Its meaning is specific to the event being logged.

Example:

```
logevent -s i -c 400 "File write error: log.txt"
```

See also: DUMPEL

LOGOFF [RK]

Logs off the current Windows NT session.

Syntax:

```
1. LOGOFF [/F] [/N]
```

Switches:

/F	Force applications to close without saving un-saved data.
/N	Do not confirm before logoff.

The LOGOFF command terminates the current Windows NT session. Normally, LOGOFF confirms that a logoff is desired and then prompt the user to save unsaved data before proceeding. The /F switch forces applications to close without saving data. The /N switch skips the logoff confirmation request.

MD

See MKDIR.

MKDIR, MD

Creates directories.

Syntax:

```
1. MKDIR [drive:]path
2. MD [drive:]path
```

The MKDIR command creates a new directory or directories. The MD command is a synonym for MKDIR.

The MKDIR command can create a complete tree of directories in a single command, by creating all intermediate directories specified in *path*. For example, the command MKDIR C:\A\B\C\D creates directory C:\A, then C:\A\B, then C:\A\B\C etc as necessary.

See also: RMDIR, CHDIR

MORE

Filters text files into pages.

Syntax:

```
1. MORE
2. MORE /E [/C] [/P] [/S] [/Tn] [+n]
3. MORE /E [/C] [/P] [/S] [/Tn] [+n] file [...]
```

Switches:

/E	Enable extended features.
/C	Clear screen before displaying page of output.
/P	Expand form-feed characters.
/S	Collapse multiple blank lines into one.
/Tn	Expand tabs to column *n*.
+n	Start output at line *n*.

The MORE command splits text files up into pages. This allows command output to be viewed that would otherwise scroll off the console window.

Use MORE(1) or MORE(2) to filter command input. By default, command input is all text typed at the console up to the end of file character, Ctrl+Z. Use the console input redirection symbols to redirect console input from a file or device. Use the pipe command to send the output of any command to the command input of the MORE command for processing.

Use MORE(3) to filter one or more text files. File names are separated by spaces.

The /C switch clears the console window before each page is displayed. The /P switch expands form-feed characters in the input. The /S switch collapses multiple blank lines into a single blank line, compacting the output. The /T switch expands tabs, setting tab stops at the specified columns. Finally, the +n switch starts displaying output at line *n*, skipping earlier lines. For MORE(3), only lines in the first file are skipped.

At the end of each page of output, MORE displays the prompt —More - and waits for user input. Press any key to continue to the next page. If the /E switch is used, the following commands can be entered at the prompt.

Command	Description
Pn	Display next *n* lines.
Sn	Skip next *n* lines.
F	Display next file. Only applicable to MORE(3).
Q	Quit.
=	Show line number.
?	Show help.
Spacebar	Display next page.
Enter	Display next line.

Notes:

In some versions of Windows NT, the /T switch does not correctly expand tabs to spaces.

See also: FIND, SORT

MOVE

Moves files from one directory to another.

Syntax:

```
1. MOVE [drive:][path]filename [drive:]dstpath
2. MOVE [drive:]srcpath [drive:]dstpath
```

The MOVE command moves files and directories from one location to another.

Use MOVE(1) to move individual files to the specified *dstpath* directory. Wildcards can be used with *filename* to move multiple files.

Use MOVE(2) to move a complete directory to the specified *dstpath* directory. The entire directory, including all files and subdirectories, is moved.

Notes:

MOVE operates rapidly when the source and destination drives are the same.

Under MS-DOS, the MOVE command was used to rename directories. Windows NT uses the REN command to rename directories.

See also: COPY, XCOPY, ROBOCOPY, RENAME

NET ACCOUNTS

Manages user account database policies.

Syntax:

```
1. NET ACCOUNTS [/DOMAIN]
2. NET ACCOUNTS /SYNC [/DOMAIN]
3. NET ACCOUNTS [switches]
```

Switches:

/SYNC	Synchronize all account databases.
/DOMAIN	Perform the specified operation on the domain controller.
/FORCELOGOFF:*nn* ¦ NO	Set number of minutes before forced logoff occurs.
/MINPWLEN:*nn*	Specifies the minimum password length.

`/MAXPWAGE:nn ¦ UNLIMITED`	Specifies the maximum password age, in days.
`/MINPWAGE:nn`	Specifies the minimum password age, in days.
`/UNIQUEPW:nn`	Sets unique password count to *nn*.

The NET ACCOUNTS command manages user account database policies. All commands operate on the local computer account database, unless the /DOMAIN switch is specified, in which case the commands operate on the domain account database. On Windows NT domain controllers, the local and domain account databases are synonymous.

Use NET ACCOUNTS(1) to display current account database policy information. Use NET ACCOUNTS(2) to synchronize all account databases within the domain. This command is not valid on computers that are not members of a domain.

Use NET ACCOUNTS(3) to change account database policies. Individual switches change specific policy options. The /DOMAIN switch changes policies in the current domain. If this switch is not present, policies on the local computer are changed.

The /FORCELOGOFF switch sets the number of minutes before a user is forced to log off. Forced logoffs occur either when the user account expires, or when valid logon hours expire (if the account has restricted logon hours). The /FORCELOGOFF:NO switch disables forced logoffs.

The /MINPWLEN switch sets the minimum length of a password allowed. Valid minimum lengths range from 0 to 14 characters. The default is six characters. The /UNIQUEPW switch sets the size of the old password buffer. Valid sizes range from 0 to 24. The unique password buffer is used to check password uniqueness for each account. If (for example) a buffer size of 4 is set, then Windows NT will reject attempts to change an account password to any of the four most recently used passwords for that account.

The /MINPWAGE switch sets the minimum password age, in days, before the password can be altered for a user account. The range is 0 to 49710 days. The default is 0, which allows passwords to be changed at any time. The /MAXPWAGE switch sets the maximum password age, in days, before a password expires and a new password must be supplied. The range is 0 to 49710 days, and the default is 90 days. The /MAXPWAGE:UNLIMITED switch disables password expiration.

Example:

```
net accounts /minpwage:5 /maxpwage:30 /domain
```

This example sets the password aging policy such that password cannot be changed more frequently than once every five days, and expire every 30 days. The policy is changed in the domain.

See also: NET USERS

NET COMPUTER

Adds or deletes computers from a Windows NT domain.

Syntax:

```
1. NET COMPUTER \\computer /ADD
2. NET COMPUTER \\computer /DEL
```

Switches:

/ADD	Adds specified *computer* to the domain.
/DEL	Deletes specified *computer* from the domain.

The NET COMPUTER command manages computer accounts within a domain. The command is only valid when executed on a Windows NT domain controller.

Use NET COMPUTER(1) to add a computer to the domain. Use NET COMPUTER(2) to delete a computer from the domain. Windows NT workstation and server computers must become members of a domain to pass logon requests to the domain controllers in that domain.

NET CONFIG SERVER

Configures the server service.

Syntax:

```
1. NET CONFIG SERVER
2. NET CONFIG SERVER [/AUTODISCONNECT:nn] [/SRVCOMMENT:"text"] [/HIDDEN:[YES ¦ NO]]
```

Switches:

/AUTODISCONNECT:*nn*	Sets the auto-disconnect time to *nn* minutes.
/SRVCOMMENT:"*text*"	Sets the server announce comment to *text*.
/HIDDEN:[YES ¦ NO]	Hides or un-hides the server.

The NET CONFIG SERVER command configures the server service. All Windows NT computers (servers and workstations) provide a server service. Use NET CONFIG SERVER(1) to display the current configuration, and NET CONFIG SERVER(2) to change the configuration.

The /AUTODISCONNECT switch specifies the numbers of minutes before a remote session is automatically disconnected. The range is 1 to 65535 minutes, and the default is 15 minutes. Specify -1 minutes to disable auto-disconnection.

The /SRVCOMMENT switch specifies a comment that is displayed on other computers when browsing this computer. Comments are displayed in the Windows NT Explorer and with the NET VIEW command.

The /HIDDEN switch hides the computer from other computers when browsing. Hiding a computer does *not* provide any additional security, it merely excludes the computer from the list of computers displayed by Windows NT Explorer or the NET VIEW command.

Example:

```
net config server /hidden:yes
```

This example hides the computer from other computers browsing the network.

See also: NET VIEW

NET CONFIG WORKSTATION

Configures the workstation service.

Syntax:

```
1. NET CONFIG WORKSTATION
2. NET CONFIG WORKSTATION [/CHARCOUNT:nn] [/CHARTIME:nn] [/CHARWAIT:nn]
```

Switches:

/CHARCOUNT:nn	Sets the number of bytes buffered before data transmission occurs.
/CHARTIME:nn	Sets the timeout, in milliseconds, before data transmission occurs.
/CHARWAIT:nn	Sets the amount of time Windows NT waits for a device to become available, in seconds.

The NET CONFIG WORKSTATION command configures the workstation service. All Windows NT computers (servers and workstations) provide a workstation service. Use NET CONFIG WORKSTATION(1) to display the current configuration, and NET CONFIG WORKSTATION(2) to change the configuration.

The /CHARCOUNT switch sets the maximum number of bytes buffered by Windows NT before data is sent to a communications port. The range is 0 to 65,535 bytes, and the default is 16 bytes.

The /CHARTIME switch sets the idle timeout period, in milliseconds, before Windows NT sends data to the communications port. The range is 0 to 65,535,000 ms, and the default is 250 ms.

The /CHARWAIT switch sets the number of seconds Windows NT will wait for a communications port to become available. The range is 0 to 65535 seconds, and the default is 3,600 seconds.

Example:

```
net config workstation /charwait:60
```

This example sets the communications port timeout to 60 seconds.

NET CONTINUE, NET PAUSE, NET START, NET STOP

Starts, stops, continues, or pauses services.

Syntax:

```
1. NET START
2. NET START service
3. NET STOP service
4. NET PAUSE service
5. NET CONTINUE service
```

These commands control services running on the local Windows NT computer. Services can also be controlled using the Windows NT Control Panel or the SC[RK] command.

Use NET START(1) to display a list of running services. Use NET START(2) to start a service, and NET STOP(3) to stop a service. Use NET PAUSE(4) to pause a service, and NET CONTINUE(5) to restart the service after a pause.

Use the Control Panel dialog box's Services icon to obtain a list of available services. This list also provides the names that should be used when specifying the service to process.

Example:

```
net stop remote access service
```

This example stops the Windows NT remote access service.

Notes:

The SC[RK] command can also control services running on remote computers.

See also: SC, INSTSRV

NET FILE

Manages open files on a server.

Syntax:

```
1. NET FILE
2. NET FILE id /CLOSE
```

Switches:

> /CLOSE   Closes the specified file.

The NET FILE command manages remotely opened files on a server. Use NET FILE(1) to display a list of all remotely opened files, including each file's unique *id* number. Use NET FILE(2) to force a file to close. Specify the *id* number for the file to close.

> ### Troubleshooting Tip
>
> *Closing open files with* NET FILE *can result in a loss of file data.*

See also: NET FILE

NET GROUP, NET LOCALGROUP
Manages local and global groups.

Syntax:

```
01. NET GROUP [/DOMAIN]
02. NET LOCALGROUP [/DOMAIN]
03. NET GROUP group [/DOMAIN]
04. NET LOCALGROUP group [/DOMAIN]
05. NET GROUP group /ADD [/COMMENT:"text"] [/DOMAIN]
06. NET LOCALGROUP group /ADD [/COMMENT:"text"] [/DOMAIN]
07. NET GROUP group /DELETE [/DOMAIN]
08. NET LOCALGROUP group /DELETE [/DOMAIN]
09. NET GROUP group username [...] [/ADD ¦ /DELETE] [/DOMAIN]
10. NET LOCALGROUP group name [...] [/ADD ¦ /DELETE] [/DOMAIN]
```

Switches:

> /DOMAIN   Perform the specified operation on the domain controller.
>
> /ADD   Adds the group to the account database *or* adds the specified names to the group.
>
> /DELETE   Deletes the group from the account database *or* deletes the specified names from the group.
>
> /COMMENT   Adds a comment describing the group.

The NET GROUP and NET LOCALGROUP commands manage local and global groups. Only Windows NT servers can maintain global groups—Windows NT workstations only maintain local groups. All commands operate on the local computer account database, unless the /DOMAIN switch is specified, in which case the commands operate on the domain account database. On Windows NT domain controllers, the local and domain account databases are synonymous.

Use NET GROUP(1) or NET LOCALGROUP(2) to display a list of all global or local groups. Use NET GROUP(3) or NET LOCALGROUP(4) to display a list of all members of the specified *group*. Global groups can only have user accounts as members. Local groups can have user accounts and global groups as members.

Use NET GROUP(5) or NET LOCALGROUP(6) to add a new group to the account database. The /COMMENT switch adds the specified *text* as a descriptive comment to the group.

Use NET GROUP(7) or NET LOCALGROUP(8) to delete an existing group. Members of the group themselves are not deleted, but their membership in the group *is* deleted.

Use NET GROUP(9) or NET LOCALGROUP(10) to add or delete group members. Follow the group name with a list of one or more names to add to the group. Enclose names containing spaces in double quotes. The /ADD switch adds names to the group, while the /DELETE switch deletes names from the group. Only user accounts can by added to global groups, while user accounts or global groups can be added to local groups.

Example:

```
net group "Power Users" BobM PollyC KurtB /add
```

This example adds three users to the global Power Users group.

See also: ADDUSERS, NET USERS, GLOBAL, LOCAL, IFMEMBER

NET LOCALGROUP

See NET GROUP.

NET NAME

Manages messenger service names.

Syntax:

```
1. NET NAME
2. NET NAME name [/ADD]
3. NET NAME name /DELETE
```

Switches:

/ADD	Adds the specified *name* to the name list.
/DELETE	Deletes the specified *name* from the name list.

The NET NAME command manages the list of alias names used by the Windows NT messenger service. These names can be used as target names with the NET SEND command. In addition to names added using the NET NAME command,

Windows NT automatically adds the computer name and the interactive user logon name to the list of available names.

Use NET NAME(1) to display the list of names currently maintained by this computer. Use NET NAME(2) to add the specified *name* to the alias list. The /ADD switch is optional. Use NET NAME(3) to delete the specified *name* from the alias list. Computer names cannot be deleted from the list.

If any computer sends a message via the messenger service, and that message is sent to a name that appears in the alias name list, the message will appear in a dialog box on the computer.

Notes:

The Windows NT messenger service must be running on a computer for messages to be received on that computer.

See also: NET SEND

NET PAUSE

See NET CONTINUE.

NET SEND

Sends a messenger service message.

Syntax:

> 1. NET SEND [*name* ¦ * ¦ /DOMAIN[:*name*] ¦ /USERS] "*message*"

Switches:

/DOMAIN	Sends the message to the specified domain.
/USERS	Sends the message to all connected users.

The NET SEND command sends a message to the computers specified. Enclose the *message* in double quotes.

The destination can be one of the following:

name	Sends the message to the specified computer or user name, or alias name created via the NET NAME command.
*	Sends the message to all computers in the workgroup.
/DOMAIN	Sends the message to all the names in the domain.
/DOMAIN:*name*	Sends the message to all the names in the specified domain.
/USERS	Sends the message to all users remotely connected to this computer.

Example:

```
net send * "Server STYX will be shut down in 10 minutes."
```

This example sends the message shown to all computers in the workgroup.

Notes:

The Windows NT messenger service must be running on a computer for messages to be received on that computer.

See also: NET NAME

NET SESSION

Manages server computer connections.

Syntax:

```
1. NET SESSION
2. NET SESSION \\computer
3. NET SESSION \\computer /DELETE
```

Switches:

/DELETE   Deletes the connection to the specified computer and closes all open files.

The NET SESSION command manages remote computer connections. It can only be used on Windows NT servers.

Use NET SESSION(1) to display a list of all open connections, and NET SESSION(2) to display details of open connections from the specified *computer*. Use NET SESSION(3) to break the connection from the specified computer and close all open files.

> ### *Troubleshooting Tip*
>
> *Using* NET SESSION(3) *can cause the loss of file data.*

See also: NET FILE

NET SHARE

Manages printer and directory shares.

Syntax:

```
1. NET SHARE
2. NET SHARE share
3. NET SHARE share=drive:path [/USERS:nn ¦ /UNLIMITED] [/REMARK:"text"]
4. NET SHARE share [/USERS:nn ¦ /UNLIMITED] [/REMARK:"text"]
5. NET SHARE [share ¦ device ¦ drive:path] /DELETE
```

Switches:

/USERS	Limits maximum number of simultaneous users to *nn*.
/UNLIMITED	Allows unlimited users.
/REMARK	Sets share comment to *text*.
/DELETE	Deletes existing share.

The NET SHARE command manages shared printers and directories (folders) on the local computer.

Use NET SHARE(1) to display information about all shares defined on the local computer. Use NET SHARE(2) to display detailed information about the specified *share*.

Use NET SHARE(3) to create a new shared directory named *share*, which maps to the specified *drive:path*. The /USERS switch limits the number of simultaneous connections to the share to *nn*, while the /UNLIMITED switch (the default) allows an unlimited number of simultaneous connections. The /REMARK switch assigns a descriptive comment to the share, which is available when the share is browsed by a remote computer.

Use NET SHARE(4) to modify the properties of an existing share. Use NET SHARE(5) to delete a share. Specify the share to delete using either the share name, the device name (if the share is a printer share), or the drive and path name.

Example:

```
net share cdrom=g:\ /remark:"Local CD-ROM drive"
```

This example creates a new share named CDROM that maps to the local path G:\.

Notes:

Shares names that end in a $ character are not displayed when browsing the local computer from a remote computer.

See also: NET USE, RMTSHARE

NET START

See NET CONTINUE.

NET STATISTICS

Display server and workstation service statistics.

Syntax:

```
1. NET STATISTICS SERVER
2. NET STATISTICS WORKSTATION
```

The NET STATISTICS command displays statistics about the server or workstation services on a Windows NT computer. Both services normally run on both Windows NT servers and Windows NT workstations.

Use NET STATISTICS(1) to display statistics for the server service, and NET STATISTICS(2) to display statistics for the workstation service.

NET STOP

See NET CONTINUE.

NET TIME

Displays and synchronizes to remote computer time.

Syntax:

```
1. NET TIME [/SET]
2. NET TIME \\computer [/SET]
3. NET TIME /DOMAIN:name [/SET]
```

Switches:

/SET   Sets the local computer time to that obtained from the remote computer.

/DOMAIN   Specifies the domain with which to synchronize the time.

The NET TIME command displays the time on a remote computer and optionally synchronizes the local computer time to that computer.

Use NET TIME(1) to obtain the time from the computer designated as the time server for the domain. Use NET TIME(2) to obtain the time from the specified *computer*. Use NET TIME(3) to obtain the time from the designated time server in the specified domain.

The /SET switch sets the local computer time to match the time obtained from the remote computer.

Only Windows NT servers can be designated as time servers. To designate a server as a time server, add a new Registry value to this key on that server:

HKEY_LOCAL_MACHINE\SYSTEM\CurrentControlSet\Services\LanMa nServer\Parameters

The value to add should be named TimeSource, should have a type of REG_DWORD, and should have a value of 1.

Example:

```
net time \\server-1 /set
```

This example sets the local computer time to that obtained from the server
SERVER-1.

NET USE

Manages remote connections.

Syntax:

```
1. NET USE
2. NET USE device
3. NET USE [device ¦ *] \\computer\share [password ¦ *] [/USER:username]
[/PERSISTENT:[YES ¦ NO]]
4. NET USE [device ¦ *] [password ¦ *] /HOME
5. NET USE [device ¦ *] /DELETE
6. NET USE /PERSISTENT:[YES ¦ NO]
```

Switches:

/USER	Specifies the user account to use when connecting to the share.
/PERSISTENT	Specifies if the connection should persist across logoff/logon operations.
/DELETE	Deletes the connection.

The NET USE command manages remote connections on the local computer to shares on remote computers. NET USE maps remote resources, such as shared directories, to local resources, such as drive letters.

Use NET USE(1) to display a list of all current connections to remote computers, and NET USE(2) to display detailed connection information for the specified device.

Use NET USE(3) to map a local device to a remote share. The local device may be a drive letter, D: through Z:, (used when the remote share is a directory) or a printer, LPT1: through LPT3: (used when the remote share is a printer). Specify an * instead of a device name to automatically use the next available device name. The remote share to map is specified by the UNC name, \\computer\share. Use the NET VIEW command to view available network shares.

If the remote share is password protected, specify the password following the UNC name. Specify an * to make NET USE prompt for a password interactively. This avoids the need to embed passwords in scripts, where their secrecy may be compromised. Use the /USER switch to specify a different user account to use when connecting to the share. The username may include a domain name in the form DOMAIN\username.

The /PERSISTENT switch controls the persistence of the connection. Specify /PERSISTENT:NO to create a connection which will exist only for the current interactive session. Specify /PERSISTENT:YES to specify a connection which will be automatically restored at the next logon. The default value of the /PERSISTENT switch is set using NET USE(6).

Use NET USE(4) to map the designated home directory to the specified *device*, which must be a drive letter or *. The home directory is specified as part of a user's account profile.

Use NET USE(5) to delete an existing connection, including persistent connections.

Example:

```
net use g: \\server-1\cdrom-a /persistent:no
```

This example makes a temporary connection to the share \\SERVER-1\CDROM-A and maps it to local drive G:.

See also: NET SHARE, NET VIEW.

NET USER

Manages user accounts.

Syntax:

```
1. NET USER [/DOMAIN]
2. NET USER user [/DOMAIN]
3. NET USER user [password ¦ *] /ADD [switches] [/DOMAIN]
4. NET USER user [password ¦ *] [switches] [/DOMAIN]
5. NET USER user /DELETE [/DOMAIN]
```

Switches:

/DOMAIN	Processes accounts in the domain.
/DELETE	Deletes the specified user account.
/ACTIVE:[YES ¦ NO]	Activates or deactivates the account.
/COMMENT:"*text*"	Adds a descriptive comment to the account.
/COUNTRYCODE:*nnn*	Specifies the country code for localized messages.
/EXPIRES:[*date* ¦ NEVER]	Specifies an account expiration date; NEVER indicates that the account never expires.
/FULLNAME:"*name*"	Specifies the full name of the account.
/HOMEDIR:*path*	Specifies the home directory for the account.
/PASSWORDCHG:[YES ¦ NO]	Allows or disallows password changes by the user.

/PASSWORDREQ:[YES ¦ NO]	Specifies if this account must have a password.
/PROFILEPATH:*path*	Specifies the profile *path* for this account.
/SCRIPTPATH:*path*	Specifies the script *path* for this account.
/TIMES:[*times* ¦ ALL]	Specifies allowed logon hours, or ALL to allow unlimited logon hours.
/USERCOMMENT:"*text*"	Specifies a user comment for the account.
/WORKSTATIONS:[*list* ¦ *]	Specifies a list of computers from which the account may logon, or * for no restrictions.

The NET USER command manages user accounts. All commands operate on the local computer account database, unless the /DOMAIN switch is specified, in which case the commands operate on the domain account database. On Windows NT domain controllers, the local and domain account databases are synonymous.

Use NET USER(1) to display a list of all user accounts in the account database. Use NET USER(2) to display details for the specified *user*. Use NET USER(3) to add a new account. Follow the new user account name with a *password* or an * to obtain the password interactively. Use NET USER(4) to modify the properties of an existing account, and NET USER(5) to delete an account.

The /ACTIVE switch activates or deactivates the account. An inactive account cannot be used for logon operations, but still exists in the account database. The /COMMENT switch specifies a descriptive comment, while the /USERCOMMENT switch adds a user comment to the account. The /EXPIRES switch specifies an expiration date for the account. Format the date according to the conventions specified by the Control Panel's Regional Settings icon.

The /FULLNAME switch specifies the full name for the account. This is displayed in some security dialog boxes. The /HOMEDIR switch specifies the home directory for the account. The /PASSWORDCHG switch prevents or allows the user to change the account password. The /PASSWORDREQ switch specifies that a password *must* be specified for this account. The /PROFILEPATH switch specifies the profile path for this account, while the /SCRIPTPATH switch specifies the logon script path for this account.

The /TIMES switch specifies the allowed logon hours for this account. Use /TIMES:ALL to specify unlimited logon hours. Restrict logon hours by specifying a set of allowed logon *times*. *times* is specified as a list of allowed time slots, separated by semi-colons. Each time slot can specify a day or the week, or a range of days, and a range of hours (in one-hour increments). For example: mon-wed,8am-5pm;thu-fri,8am-4pm.

The /WORKSTATIONS switch specifies a list of workstations from which the account is permitted to logon. Specify /WORKSTATIONS:* to allow unrestricted logon, or specify a comma separated list of workstations to restrict logon to only those computers.

Example:

```
net user PerryM Secret /add /fullname:"Perry Mason"
/scriptpath:d:\winnt\system32\repl\import\scripts\logon.bat
```

This example creates a new account called PerryM with a password of Secret, and sets the script path to D:\WINNT\SYSTEM32\REPL\IMPORT\SCRIPTS\LOGON.BAT.

See also: NET ACCOUNTS, ADDUSERS

NET VIEW

Displays available network resources.

Syntax:

```
1. NET VIEW [/DOMAIN[:name]]
2. NET VIEW \\computer
```

Switches:

> /DOMAIN   Specifies the domain name for display.

The NET VIEW command views available network resources (directory and printer shares).

Use NET VIEW(1) to display a list of server computers in the local workgroup or domain. The /DOMAIN switch displays a list of computers in the domain named *name*. If *name* is omitted, the /DOMAIN switch displays a list of available domains.

Use NET VIEW(2) to display a list of all resources on the specified *computer*.

Notes:

Only servers which are not hidden are displayed by the NET VIEW(1) command. Individual resources with share names ending in a $ character are not displayed by the NET VIEW(2) command.

See also: NET USE

NOW [RK]

Displays text with a time stamp.

Syntax:

```
1. NOW text
```

The NOW command displays the *text* entered on the command line prefixed by the current time and date. NOW(1) is similar to the ECHO command except for the date and time prefix.

Example:

```
now Script execution begun...
```

See also: ECHO, TITLE

NTBACKUP

Automatic volume backup.

Syntax:

```
1. NTBACKUP EJECT /TAPE:n
3. NTBACKUP BACKUP paths [switches]
```

Switches:

/A	Appends backup sets to the end of the tape.
/V	Verifies the backup operation.
/R	Restricts access to the tape owner or administrators.
/D"text"	Specifies a descriptive comment for the backup set.
/B	Includes the local registry in the backup operation.
/HC:[ON | OFF]	Enables or disables hardware compression on the tape drive.
/T type	Specifies the type of backup to perform.
/L"filename"	Specifies a file name for the backup log.
/E	Restricts the backup log to exceptions only.
/TAPE:n	Specifies the destination tape drive for the operation.

The NTBACKUP command provides tape archival facilities for complete volumes or directory trees. NTBACKUP is a Windows NT GUI application, but it can be controlled completely from command line switches and is frequently used in scripts to automate regular backup schedules.

Use NTBACKUP(1) to eject the tape from the specified drive. Use NTBACKUP(2) to initiate a complete backup operation, with optional verify. Specify one or more *paths* to backup. Separate individual paths from each other with spaces. Each path must refer to a local drive or a mapped network drive—UNC names are *not* accepted by NTBACKUP. Each path creates a new, distinct, backup set on the tape.

The /A switch appends the new backup sets to the end of the tape, preserving any existing backup sets. If /A is not specified, all existing sets on the tape will be over-written by the new backup sets. The /V switch performs a verify pass after the backup operation is complete. All files on the tape are verified against the original files on disk. Verify results are recorded in the log file and in the system event log.

The /R switch restricts subsequent access to the backup sets to the tape owner or an administrator. The /D switch specifies a descriptive comment for all backup sets. Do not place a space between the switch and the opening double quote.

The /B switch backs up the local registry. This switch is only applicable to paths that specify the drive containing the Windows NT directory. The /HC switch controls hardware compression on the tape drive (if this feature is supported).

The /T switch specifies the type of tape backup operation to perform. Follow the switch with a space and then one of the types specified in the following table.

Type	Description
normal	Back up all files, then clear the archive flag on all files.
copy	Back up all files, but do not clear the archive flags.
incremental	Back up only changed files, then clear the archive flag on these files.
differential	Back up only changed files, but do not clear the archive flags.
daily	Back up only those files changed today, but do not clear the archive flags.

The /L switch specifies the name of a log file which can be used to record backup operation results. The /E switch restricts this log file information to exceptions and errors only.

The /TAPE switch specifies which tape device to use for the backup operation.

Example:

```
ntbackup backup c:\Library d:\Library /v /d"Library Backup" /t normal
```

This example performs a normal backup of the paths C:\Library and D:\Library.

Notes:

NTBACKUP operations that are run by the Schedule Service must take special precautions to ensure correct operation. First, ensure that the Windows NT

Schedule Service is running in an account with sufficient rights to access the drives, directories, and network shares to be backed up. Second, ensure that all network shares are mapped to the appropriate local drive before starting the backup operation. The UNCBACK sample script can provide this mapping automatically.

Parameter Syntax

Command shell parameter substitution.

Arguments to a script are accessible within the script via script parameters. Arguments are specified either on the command line or in a CALL statement, and are separated by spaces, tabs, commas, equal signs, or semi-colons. To pass any of these characters as part of an argument, enclose the argument in double quotes. The double quotes enclosing the argument *are* passed as part of the argument—the command shell does not strip them.

Parameters are named %n, where n is the parameter index, 0 to 9. The first argument is passed in parameter %1, the second in %2 and so on. %0 always contains the name of the script file itself (exactly as typed). Arguments beyond the ninth are accessed using the SHIFT command. The special parameter %* refers to all script arguments, exactly as typed, excluding %0.

Parameter names can also be qualified so that only part of the argument is returned. Qualifiers are placed between the percent sign and the parameter index, and are prefixed by a tilde. For example, %~fd1 applies the "f" and "d" qualifiers to parameter 1. Qualifiers treat the parameter text as a file or path name, and extract portions of the name. The following table shows all parameter qualifiers.

Qualifier	Description
f	Expand parameter to a fully qualified path name.
d	Expand parameter to a drive letter only.
p	Expand parameter as a path only.
n	Expand parameter as a file name only.
x	Expand parameter as a file extension only.
s	Modify n and x qualifiers to refer to the short (MS-DOS) name.
$var:	Treat var as a directory list, and search all directories for the file specified by the parameter. Then expands to the full path name of the first match found.

For example, assume that Windows NT is installed in C:\WINNT, that the current directory is D:\HOME, and that parameter %1 contains XCOPY.EXE. The following table shows some examples of qualified parameter substitution and the resulting text.

Parameter	Result
%~f1	D:\HOME\XCOPY.EXE
%~d1	D:
%~p1	\HOME\
%~n1	XCOPY
%~x1	.EXE
%~nx1	XCOPY.EXE
%~$PATH:1	C:\WINNT\SYSTEM32\XCOPY.EXE
%~dp$PATH:1	C:\WINNT\SYSTEM32\

Notes:

Qualifiers can also be used with the iterator variables used in FOR commands.

See also: FOR, CALL, CMD, SHIFT

PATH

Sets the command search path.

Syntax:

```
1. PATH
2. PATH path
3. PATH ;
4. SET PATH=path
5. SET PATH
```

The PATH command alters the Windows NT command search path. The command search path is used when the command shell attempts to locate a command for execution. See the START command for more information concerning the use of the search path.

The command search path is a list of directory names, separated by semi-colons. To locate a command to execute, Windows NT first searches the current directory, and then searches each directory listed in the search path, in order, until the executable is located. The current search path is stored in the PATH environment variable.

Use PATH(1) or PATH(5) to display the current search path. Use PATH(3) to clear the current search path. This restricts command execution to the current directory only.

Use PATH(2) or PATH(4) to set a new search path. You can include %PATH% in the path specification to add the new path information to the existing path.

Example:

```
path c:\bin;%PATH%
```

See also: START

PAUSE

Pauses script execution.

Syntax:

> 1. PAUSE

The PAUSE command stops execution of the script command and displays the prompt Press and key to continue.. Script execution continues when any key is pressed, except Ctrl+C, which terminates script execution.

See also: SLEEP, CHOICE, TIMEOUT

PERMCOPY [RK]

Copies share permissions.

Syntax:

> 1. PERMCOPY \\srccomputer srcshare \\dstcomputer dstshare

The PERMCOPY command copies access rights (ACLs) from one share to another, either on the same or a different server. PERMCOPY cannot copy to or from system maintained shares (such as C$).

To copy permissions, specify a source computer and share name, and a destination computer and share name.

Example:

> permcopy \\styx files1 \\arbiter files2

POPD

Restores previously saved drive and directory.

Syntax:

> 1. POPD

The POPD command reverses the operation of a PUSHD command by recovering the most recently saved drive and directory from the save stack.

If the previous PUSHD mapped a UNC name, which resulted in the allocation of a temporary drive letter, POPD deletes the drive mapping and release the drive letter.

See also: PUSHD, CHDIR

PROMPT

Sets the command shell prompt.

Syntax:

```
1. PROMPT
2. PROMPT prompt
3. SET PROMPT=prompt
4. SET PROMPT
```

The PROMPT command alters the Windows NT command shell prompt. This prompt is displayed when the command shell is ready to accept input, either from the keyboard or from a script (if echo is on). The current command prompt is stored in the PROMPT environment variable. Use PROMPT(4) to display the current prompt (unless it is set to the default value).

Use PROMPT(1) to reset the prompt to the system default. This also clears the PROMPT variable. The default prompt displays the current path and a greater then symbol, and is equivalent to the prompt string pg.

Use PROMPT(2) or PROMPT(3) to set a specific prompt. The prompt is set to prompt, and this value is also set in the PROMPT variable. The prompt argument is used literally as the prompt. Within this argument you can specify the codes shown in the following table.

Code	Description
$A	Ampersand character.
$B	Pipe (I) character.
$C	Left parenthesis.
$D	Current date.
$E	Escape code (ASCII 27).
$F	Right parenthesis.
$G	Greater than character.
$H	Backspace character.
$L	Less than character.
$N	Current drive letter.
$P	Current drive letter and directory path.
$Q	Equal sign.
$S	Space.
$T	Current time.
$V	Windows NT version number.
$_	New line.
$$	Dollar sign.
$+	Displays a series of "+" signs, corresponding to the number of pushed directories on the PUSHD stack. See PUSHD.
$M	Displays the remote name (UNC name) for the current drive.

Notes:

Changing the prompt always changes the PROMPT variable, and vice versa.

PULIST [RK]

Displays process and user accounts.

Syntax:

```
1. PULIST [\\computer] [\\computer...]
```

The PULIST command displays a list of executing processes on each of the computers specified. Processes executing on the local computer are displayed if no computer names are specified. The list specifies the process executable, the process ID assigned by the system, and (for the local computer only) the user name associated with the process.

The process ID can be used as an argument to the KILL command.

See also: KILL

PUSHD

Saves current directory and change to new drive/directory.

Syntax:

```
1. PUSHD
2. PUSHD [drive:]path
3. PUSHD ..
4. PUSHD uncname
```

The PUSHD command saves the current drive and directory on a stack and optionally switches to a new drive and directory. The saved drive and directory can subsequently be restored from the stack using the POPD command. PUSHD/POPD command pairs can be nested, allowing multiple saved directories to be stacked up. If $+ is part of the current PROMPT string, the nesting depth of pushed directories is indicated by a string of + signs in the command prompt.

Use PUSHD(1) to save the current drive and directory. This is useful before calling another script that can alter the drive and/or directory. After calling the script, use POPD to restore the drive and directory.

Use PUSHD(2) to save the current drive and directory and then change the drive and directory to that specified by path. The specified path can be absolute (starting at the root of the drive) or relative to the current directory. Use PUSHD(3) to save the current drive and directory and then move one level "up" the directory tree on the current drive towards the root. This command is not valid at the root of a directory tree.

Use PUSHD(4) to save the current drive and directory and then change to the
UNC path specified by *uncname*. A UNC path takes the form
\\servername\sharename\path. To switch to this directory, PUSHD creates a
temporary drive mapping to map the UNC share onto a drive letter. Temporary
drive letters are allocated starting at Z: and working down the alphabet, skipping letters already in use. When a POPD command is executed the drive letter is
un-mapped from the share.

Example:

```
pushd e:\workdir
pushd \\master-serv\data1\archive\temp
```

See also: POPD, CHDIR, PROMPT

RD

See RMDIR.

REG [RK]

Manipulates the Windows NT Registry.

Syntax:

```
01. REG QUERY [rootkey\]keypath[\valuename] [\\computer] [/S]
02. REG ADD [rootkey\]keypath\valuename=value [type] [\\computer]
03. REG UPDATE [rootkey\]keypath\valuename=value [\\computer]
04. REG DELETE [rootkey\]keypath[\valuename] [\\computer] [/F]
05. REG COPY [rootkey\]keypath1[\valuename] [\\computer1]
[rootkey\]keypath2[\valuename] [\\computer2]
06. REG SAVE [rootkey\]keypath filename [\\computer]
07. REG BACKUP [rootkey\]keypath filename [\\computer]
08. REG RESTORE filename [rootkey\]keypath [\\computer]
09. REG LOAD filename [rootkey\]keypath [\\computer]
10. REG UNLOAD [rootkey\]keypath [\\computer]
```

Switches:

/S	Display keys and values for all subkeys.
/F	Skip delete confirmation.

The REG command manipulates the Windows NT Registry on the specified
computer or (by default) the local computer.

Troubleshooting Tip

*The Windows NT Registry contains information critical to the operation
of the system. Inappropriate changes to the contents of the Registry can
compromise Windows NT stability.*

Registry entries are specified using a hierarchy of *keys,* which are similar to directories, and *values,* which are similar to files. Elements in a registry path are separated by backslashes. The root of the hierarchy is one of the *root keys,* which are predefined. Valid root key values are shown in the following table.

Root Key	Value
HKLM	HKEY_LOCAL_MACHINE, the local machine hive.
HKCU	HKEY_CURRENT_USER, the current users hive.
HKCR	HKEY_CLASSES_ROOT, the root of the class information.
HKU	HKEY_USERS.
HKCC	HKEY_CURRENT_CONFIG, the current machine configuration.

When accessing remote computers, only HKLM and HKU root keys are valid. If the root key is not specified, HKLM is assumed.

Use REG(1) to query the registry and display key and value information for the specified *keypath.* If a *valuename* is specified, this item is displayed. Otherwise, all keys and values in the specified *keypath* are displayed. The /S switch displays values in all subkeys under the key specified. Key names are shown in brackets in the query output.

Use REG(2) to add a new value to the Registry. The value *type* can be one of the following types:

REG_SZ	A text string (the default type).
REG_DWORD	A 32-bit binary value, entered as a decimal number.
REG_EXPAND_SZ	A text string that can contain environment variables in percent signs. These are expanded when the string is used.

Use REG(3) to update an existing value with new data, and use REG(4) to delete a value or a key. Specifying a key only (no value) deletes the entire key, including all values and subkeys it contains. The /F switch skips the confirmation prompt.

Both REG(2) and REG(3) use the backslash character in the *value* as an escape. Therefore, to store a literal backslash character, specify a double backslash (\\) instead.

Use REG(5) to copy a complete key or individual value from one location or computer to another. Entire trees of keys can be copied using this command.

Use REG(6) or REG(7) to save a registry key to the specified file. Do not specify a file extension with *filename.* Use REG(8) to restore a registry key previously saved using REG(6) or REG(7).

Use REG(9) to load a registry hive at the specified key. This key is created and the hive is then linked to the registry at this location. The hive is then accessible at the specified location in the registry until it is unloaded. Use REG(10) to unload a previously loaded hive.

Example:

```
reg add HKLM\Software\AcmeCorp\WonderApp\V1.0\LoadDir=c:\apps REG_SZ
reg delete HKLM\Software\AcmeCorp\WonderApp /f
```

REM

Comments.

Syntax:

```
1. REM text
```

The REM command provides comments in a script file. The command performs no actions. The command shell ignores any text entered as part of the REM command.

REN, RENAME

Renames files and directories.

Syntax:

```
1. REN [drive:][path]filename1 filename2
2. REN [drive:]path1 path2
3. RENAME [drive:][path]filename1 filename2
4. RENAME [drive:]path1 path2
```

The REN command renames a file or directory. The RENAME command is a synonym for the REN command.

Use REN(1) or RENAME(3) to rename a file. The new file name is specified using *filename2*. You cannot specify a new drive or directory for the new file name—the REN command cannot move files. Wildcards are allowed for both *filename1* and *filename2*, allowing multiple renames. The wildcards in the source and destination should correspond, so that valid file names are formed when renaming the file.

Use REN(2) or RENAME(4) to rename a directory. The new directory name is specified using *path2*. You cannot specify a new drive for the new directory—the REN command cannot move directories. Wildcards are allowed for both *path1* and *path2*, allowing multiple renames. The wildcards in the source and destination should correspond, such that valid directory names are formed when renaming the file.

To ensure source and destination wildcard names correspond, make sure that the wildcard characters occur at the same location in the source and destination names.

See also: MOVE

RENAME

See REN.

REPLACE

Replaces files with updated versions.

Syntax:

```
1. REPLACE [drive1:][path1]filename [drive2:][path2] [/A ¦ /U] [/P] [/R] [/W]
2. REPLACE [drive1:][path1]filename [drive2:][path2] /S [/P] [/R] [/W] [/U]
```

Switches:

/A	Add new files to destination directory.
/P	Prompt for confirmation before all operations.
/R	Allow replacement if destination file is read only.
/W	Prompt for a key press before copying files.
/S	Replace all files in all subdirectories of the destination.
/U	Only replace files that are older than the source.

The REPLACE command searches for and updates files in the destination (path2) with files in the source (path1). The source filename can use wildcards. If no destination is specified, the current directory is assumed. The destination must be a directory, not a file name.

Use REPLACE(1) to replace files in the specified destination. Each source file that also exists in the destination is copied to the destination, over-writing the file replaced. The /A switch adds source files that do not exist in the destination. The /U switch updates files in the destination that are older than the corresponding source file.

Use REPLACE(2) to replace files in an entire directory tree. For each source file, REPLACE searches the destination directory tree for any matching file names. For each file found, REPLACE copies the source file into the appropriate directory, over-writing the file. The /U switch updates files in the destination that are older than the corresponding source file.

The /P switch prompts before each file replacement. The /R switch allows replacing read only files. The /W switch prompts for a key press before starting the replace operation.

Example

```
replace c:\src e:\distribution /s /u
```

See also: COPY, XCOPY

RMDIR, RD

Deletes directories and their contents.

Syntax:

```
1. RMDIR [/S] [/Q] [drive:]path
2. RD [/S] [/Q] [drive:]path
```

Switches:

/S   Delete all files and directories in the specified directory.

/Q   Quiet mode. Skip confirmation prompt if /S is used.

The RMDIR command deletes directories or directory trees. The RD command is a synonym for RMDIR.

Specify the directory to delete with *path*, optionally including a drive letter. By default, RMDIR will not delete a directory that is not empty.

The /S switch deletes a directory that is not empty. In this case, RMDIR deletes all files in the directory before deleting the directory itself. If the directory contains subdirectories, they are also deleted, and so on down the directory tree.

Use the /S switch with care, as it allows RMDIR to delete entire directory trees in a single command. RMDIR prompts before proceeding, unless the /Q switch is used.

Notes:

The RMDIR includes the functionality of the MS-DOS DELTREE command. DELTREE is not a Windows NT command, although the DELTREE command may work if a earlier version of MS-DOS or Windows 95 is present in the current path.

See also: DEL

RMTSHARE [RK]

Manages shares on a remote computer.

Syntax:

```
1. RMTSHARE \\computer
2. RMTSHARE \\computer\share
3. RMTSHARE \\computer\share=[drive:]path [switches]
4. RMTSHARE \\computer\share [switches]
5. RMTSHARE \\computer\share /DELETE
```

Switches:

/G	Removes access control from share.
/G *user*:*perm*	Sets specified permissions for specified user.
/REMOVE *user*	Removes specified user from access control list for share.
/USERS:*nn*	Sets maximum number of simultaneous users to *nn*.
/UNLIMITED	Sets an unlimited number of users on the share.
/REMARK:*text*	Sets the share comment to *text*.
/DELETE	Deletes the share.

The RMTSHARE command manages shares available on a remote server computer. Use RMTSHARE(1) to display a list of available shares on the specified *computer*. Use RMTSHARE(2) to display details about a specific share.

Use RMTSHARE(3) to create a new share, named *share*, on the specified remote *computer*. This new share refers to the *drive* and *path* specified on this computer (so C:\ refers to the root of drive C: on the remote computer, not the computer where the RMTSHARE command is executed). Use RMTSHARE(4) to modify the properties of an existing share. Use RMTSHARE(5) to delete an existing share.

The /G (or /GRANT) switch sets access control for the share. Use /G by itself to remove all access control, and grant everyone full access to the share. Use /G with a *user* and *perm* to set specific access permissions for the specified user or group. Use R (read), C (change), F (full) or N (none) for *perm*. Use the /REMOVE switch to remove *user* from the permissions list.

The /USERS switch sets the maximum number of simultaneous users for the share and the /UNLIMITED switch removes this limitation.

The /REMARK switch adds a comment to the share. Enclose the comment *text* in double quotes.

Example:

```
rmtshare \\MOTHRA\C_Root=C:\
```

ROBOCOPY [RK]

Replicates file and directory trees.

Syntax:

```
1. ROBOCOPY srcpath dstpath [file [...]] [switches]
```

Switches:

/S	Copies subdirectories, excluding empty ones.
/E	Copies subdirectories, including empty ones.

/T	Timestamps all copied and skipped files.
/R:*n*	Sets retry count to *n* (default 1,000,000).
/W:*n*	Waits *n* seconds between retries (default 30).
/REG	Saves /R and /W as new default settings.
/X	Reports all extra files.
/V	Verbose report output.
/L	Lists actions only, but don't actually perform them.
/A+:R ¦ S ¦ H ¦ A	Sets the specified attributes.
/A-: R ¦ S ¦ H ¦ A	Resets the specified attributes.
/XA: R ¦ S ¦ H ¦ A	Excludes files with the specified attribute set.
/A	Copies only files with the archive attribute set.
/M	Copies only files with the archive source attribute set, then resets it. Destination attribute is always set.
/XF *file*	Excludes files matching *name*.
/XD *dir*	Excludes directories matching *dir*.
/XC	Excludes changed files.
/XN	Excludes newer files.
/XO	Excludes older files.
/XX	Excludes extra files.
/XL	Excludes lonely files.
/IS	Includes same files.
/ETA	Shows estimated time remaining during each copy.
/MOVE	Moves files, rather than copy them.
/PURGE	Deletes files in destination that do not exist in source.

The ROBOCOPY command replicates files and directories from one location to another. Unlike other copy commands, ROBOCOPY only copies the minimum number of files to synchronize the source and destination directories. This is useful on WAN links where bandwidth can be limited.

To ensure robustness on WAN links, ROBOCOPY performs retries when errors occur. The number of retries to perform is set by the /R switch, and the wait period between retries is set by the /W switch. Use the /REG switch in conjunction with these switches to set new default values.

The file source for ROBOCOPY is *srcpath*. This can be either a local drive/directory, or a UNC path. Similarly, the destination for ROBOCOPY is *dstpath*. This can also be either a local drive/directory, or a UNC path. Both *srcpath* and *dstpath* must specify directory names, not file names.

By default, ROBOCOPY only processes files in the specified *srcpath*. The /S switch processes files in subdirectories of *srcpath*. This allows ROBOCOPY to replicate an entire directory tree. Use the /E switch instead of /S if ROBOCOPY should also replicate empty directories.

In addition to copying files, ROBOCOPY generates a report of which files are copied. The /V switch generates a verbose report, and the /X switch includes "extra" files in the report. The /ETA switch displays display estimated copy times while copying files. The /L switch only generates a report—no actual copying is performed.

Normally, ROBOCOPY copies file contents exactly, including time stamp information and attributes, except for the archive attribute, which is always set in the copied file. The /A+ switch sets the specified attributes in the destination files, and the /A- switch resets the specified attributes in the destination files. The /XA switch excludes source files that have the specified attributes set. Finally, The /A switch copies only files that have the archive attribute set, or the /M switch copies only these files and then resets this attribute in the source files. The /M switch is the only switch that changes source files in any way.

All command arguments after the *srcpath* and *dstpath* that are not switches are assumed to be file names that are used to specify which files and directories in the *srcpath* are to be considered for copying. By default, *.* is assumed, causing ROBOCOPY to copy all files in the source path to the destination (and all files in all subdirectories, if /S or /E is specified). Multiple file names can be specified, each of which can be a wildcard.

If the command includes a /XF switch, then all subsequent file names on the command line are *excluded* from the file copy operation. For example, the command:

```
ROBOCOPY c:\ e:\ *.* /XF *.EXE *.COM
```

copies all files from C:\ to E:\ *except* .EXE and .COM files. Similarly, if the command includes a /XD switch, then all subsequent names are assumed to be directory names to exclude from the copy. Directory names cannot contain wildcards. /XF and /XD switches can be mixed on the command to switch between excluding directory names and file names.

Before copying a file, ROBOCOPY assigns it a category, depending upon the state of the file and any corresponding file of the same name in the destination. These categories are shown in the following table.

Category	Description
Lonely	A file that exists only in the source.
Same	A file that exists in the source and destination. Both files have identical size and time stamps.
Changed	A file that exists in the source and destination, but the destination file has a different size than the source.
Newer	A file that exists in the source and destination, but the source file is newer than the destination.
Older	A file that exists in the source and destination, but the source file is older than the destination.
Extra	A file that exists only in the destination.
Mismatched	A file exists in the source, but the destination contains a directory, not a file, of the same name.

By default, after a file has been categorized, ROBOCOPY copies all files that are lonely, changed, newer or older. The default copying of older files means that ROBOCOPY can overwrite newer versions of files with older versions, so care must be used when using the default behavior.

The /XL switch excludes lonely files from the copy. Only files which exist in the destination will be copied from the source.

The /IS switch includes same files in the copy. Normally this is not needed, but can be used to force a refresh of the destination from the source.

The /XC switch excludes changed files from the copy. The /XN switch excludes newer files from the copy, and the /XO switch excludes older files from the copy. The /XX switch excludes extra files from all processing.

The /XO switch is normally used to prevent older versions of files in the source from overwriting newer versions in the destination. It can also be used to implement a bi-directional replication. By executing two ROBOCOPY commands with the /XO switch, and swapping the srcpath and dstpath in the second command, a given directory tree can be kept fully replicated in both directions. The /XO switch must be used carefully, however. During the file copy process, the destination file temporarily has a time stamp that is newer than the source file. If the copy operation is interrupted, then a later use of the /XO switch can cause ROBOCOPY to accidentally over-write the original source file, mistakenly thinking that the partially copied file is *newer* than the original.

The /MOVE switch moves files rather than copies them. The /PURGE switch processes extra and mismatched files. If the /PURGE switch is included (and the /XX switch is not present), then ROBOCOPY deletes all extra files found in the destination. In addition, all mismatched directories in the destination are deleted, including their contents. This ensures that the destination is an *exact* duplicate of the source tree. However, using /PURGE with a mis-entered *dstpath* can have disastrous results, as ROBOCOPY rapidly purges all directories and files in the destination. Therefore, use /PURGE with great caution.

Example:

```
robocopy c:\ e:\archive\drive_c /e /xo /xn *.bak pagefile.sys
```

See also: COPY, XCOPY

SC [RK]

Manages Windows NT services.

Syntax:

```
01. SC [\\computer] QUERY [servicename ¦ switches]
02. SC [\\computer] QC servicename [switches]
03. SC [\\computer] GETDISPLAYNAME servicename
04. SC [\\computer] GETKEYNAME servicedisplayname
05. SC [\\computer] ENUMDEPEND servicename
06. SC [\\computer] CREATE servicename [switches]
07. SC [\\computer] DELETE servicename
08. SC [\\computer] CONFIG servicename [switches]
09. SC [\\computer] START servicename [args]
10. SC [\\computer] STOP servicename
11. SC [\\computer] PAUSE servicename
12. SC [\\computer] CONTINUE servicename
13. SC [\\computer] INTERROGATE servicename
14. SC [\\computer] CONTROL servicename value
```

Switches:

TYPE= *type*	Type of service. Can be Own, Share, Interact, Kernel, or Filesys (default is Share).
START= *start*	Startup control for the service. Can be Boot, System, Auto, Demand or Disabled (default is Demand).
ERROR= *error*	Error severity if service fails. Can be Normal, Severe, Critical or Ignore (default is Normal).
BINPATH= *path*	Path name (including drive) to the service executable or driver file.
GROUP= *group*	Name of service group for this service.
DEPEND= *groups*	List of groups upon which this service depends.
OBJ= *account*	Name of user account for service, or driver object name for drivers (default is LocalSystem).
DISPLAYNAME= *name*	The friendly display name for the service.

PASSWORD= *pwd*	The password used to logon to the user account specified by OBJ.
STATE= *state*	Service states to enumerate. Can be Inactive or All (default is Active).
BUFSIZE= *nn*	Sets service enumeration buffer size to *nn* bytes.
RI= *rindex*	Sets the resume index for long enumerations.

The sc command controls Windows NT services and drivers. Note that some sc commands, if used incorrectly, can leave Windows NT in an un-bootable state.

The sc(1) to sc(5) commands query the service control manager for information regarding services. No changes are made to services or drivers by these commands. The sc(6), sc(7) and sc(8) commands create, delete or configure services. The sc(9) to sc(14) commands control the execution of installed services. Each command works with the service control manager (SCM) on the specified *computer*, or (by default) on the local computer.

Each service is referred to by its *servicename*, which is a short name used internally by the service control manager. Typically, this name is not used for display purposes. Instead, each service also has a service *display* name, which is more descriptive and can be localized. The sc(1) command can be used to obtain a list of service names.

Some sc commands accept one or more switches to set command options. Switches require a space between the equal sign and the switch value, as shown in the following table.

Switch	Description
TYPE=	Specifies the type of service being installed.
START=	Indicates when the service should be started by the service control manager.
ERROR=	Indicates the severity of the error that should be reported if the service fails to start as specified.
BINPATH=	Specifies the full path to the service executable or driver binary.
GROUP=	Specifies to which dependency group the service belongs.
DEPEND=	Specifies which dependency groups the service depends upon before it can start.
OBJ=	Specifies the account name under which the service is run.
DISPLAYNAME=	Specifies the "friendly" display name for the service.
PASSWORD=	Specifies the password to use when logging on to the account specified with the OBJ= switch.

STATE=	Specifies which services to enumerate when querying service information.
BUFSIZE=	Specifies the size of internal buffers used by SC (use larger buffers if SC requests this).
RI=	Restarts a long enumeration at the specified index.

Use the SC(1) command to display service information for installed services. Without a *servicename* or *switches*, SC(1) displays details of all active services. Specify a *servicename* to display details for a specific service. Specify the TYPE=, STATE= and GROUP= switches to display details for services of the specified type, group, and state.

Use the SC(2) command to display service configuration information for the specified *servicename*. Use the SC(3) command to display the full display name for the specified *servicename*, and use the SC(4) command to display the service name for the specified service display name. Use double quotes with the *servicedisplayname*. Use SC(5) to list all services upon which the specified *servicename* depends.

Use the SC(6) command to create a new service called *servicename* and the SC(7) command to delete a service called *servicename*. Deleting a service removes it from the registry, and is *not* the same as stopping the service. Use switches with the SC(6) command to specify (at the minimum) the path to the service executable. Use the SC(8) command to reconfigure a previously created service.

Use the SC(9) command to start an installed service. The optional *args* are passed to the service as startup arguments. Use the SC(10) command to stop a service, and the SC(11) command to pause a service. Use the SC(12) command to resume execution of a paused service. The actual effect of pausing a service is service dependent. Use the SC(13) command to interrogate the current state of a service. Use the SC(14) command to send a control code (a decimal *value*) to the service. The meaning of control codes is service dependent.

Example:

```
sc start PlugPlay
sc create NewService binpath= c:\bin\service\autotest.exe start= auto
    displayname= "New Service"
sc pause NewService
sc \\mothra query NewService
```

Notes:

Most SC commands that alter service status require administrator privilege.

See also: SCLIST, INSTSRV, NET CONTINUE

SCLIST [RK]

Displays services on specified computer.

Syntax:

1. SCLIST [/R ¦ /S] [/M computer]

Switches:

/R	Displays only running services.
/S	Displays only stopped services.
/M computer	Displays services for computer.

The SCLIST command lists services present on the specified computer, or (by default) on the local computer. The /R switch restricts the list to running services, and the /S switch restricts the list to stopped services.

The list is displayed with one service per line. The first column shows the status of the service, the second shows the service short name, and the third column the full display name.

See also: SC

SCOPY [RK]

Copies files and security information.

Syntax:

1. SCOPY [drive1:][path1][filename1] [drive2:][path][filename2] [/O] [/A] [/S]

Switches:

/O	Copy owner security information.
/A	Copy auditing information.
/S	Copy all files in subdirectories.

The SCOPY command copies files from one location to another on NTFS volumes. The NTFS security information (if present) for each file is copied with the file. Security information includes access control lists (ACLs), ownership information, and auditing information.

Use SCOPY(1) to copy files. Wildcards can be used for filename1. If filename1 is not present, *.* is assumed. The /S switch copies files in subdirectories as well as files in the specified directory.

By default, SCOPY copies the access control list of each file as well as file data. The /O switch copies file ownership information as well. Use of the /O switch requires administrator privilege. The /A switch copies auditing information. Use of the /A switch requires Manage Auditing rights.

Example

```
scopy c:\users e:\backup\users /s /a /o
```

See also: COPY, XCOPY, ROBOCOPY

SET

Sets environment variables and performs arithmetic computations.

Syntax:

```
1. SET
2. SET var
3. SET var=
4. SET var=value
5. SET /A expression
```

Switches:

/A   Evaluates a numeric expression.

The SET command sets the values of environment variables, or performs arithmetic computations.

Use SET(1) to display the entire list of variables defined in the current environment. Use SET(2) to display the list of all variables that begin with the var text.

Use SET(3) to delete an existing variable named var from the environment. Use SET(4) to define or redefine a variable named var with the value specified. Expansion of environment variables within value occurs before the value is stored in var. The value can contain equal sign characters, but not it cannot begin with an equal sign.

Use SET(5) to evaluate a numeric expression. If the command is entered interactively, the numeric result is displayed in the console window. If the command is part of a script, the result is not displayed. Note that the expression can contain assignment operators, allowing numeric results to be assigned to environment variables.

The *expression* is comprised of operators, variables, and literal numbers. Literals are can be either decimal (the default), hexadecimal (by prefixing the literal with 0x), binary (by prefixing with 0b) or octal (by prefixing with 0). Take care not to prefix a decimal literal with a leading zero—doing so causes the literal to be treated as an octal number. The following table shows some examples of literals.

Literal	Description
123	Decimal literal.
-14	Negative decimal literal.
0x100	Hexadecimal literal, equal to 256 decimal.
0b1001	Binary literal, equal to 9 decimal.
014	Octal literal, equal to 12 decimal.

Variables can also be used in expressions. Percent characters are *not* required in the expression; the SET command evaluates the values of variables directly. Undefined variables are assumed to have a value of zero. Variable values are evaluated using the same syntax as literals—decimal, hexadecimal, binary and octal numbers are all valid.

The operators allowed in an expression are shown in the following table. All operators except the expression separator and unary minus are binary operators—they take two values as arguments. The operators are listed in decreasing order of precedence.

Operator	Description
( )	Use parentheses to group sub-expressions.
* / %	Multiplication, division and modulus.
+ -	Addition and subtraction.
<< >>	Left and right logical bitwise shift.
&	Bitwise logical AND.
^	Bitwise logical exclusive OR.
¦	Bitwise logical OR.
=	Basic assignment
*= /= %= += -= &= ^= ¦= <<= >>=	Assignment operators.
,	Expression separator.

The operators are shown in order of precedence. Operators at the top of the list are evaluated before those lower in the list. This means that 1+2*3 is evaluated as 1+(2*3), yielding 7. Parentheses can be used to override this evaluation order.

The % operator is the modulus operator. The expression A % B computes the integer remainder when A is divided by B.

The << and >> operators perform logical bitwise shift operations. The expression x << N logically shifts all the bits in x left by N bits by adding N zero bits onto the right of x. For example, 12 << 1 yields 24. The expression x >> N logically shifts all the bits in x right by N bits by deleting N bits from the right of x. For example, 13 >> 1 yields 6. The << and >> operators must be escaped to avoid conflict with the redirection commands. Use `^>^>` or `^<^<` to enter these operators. This is also true for the `<<=` and `>>=` assignment operators.

The bitwise logical operators `&` (AND), `¦` (OR) and `^` (exclusive OR) combine the bits in their two arguments according to the boolean AND, OR and exclusive OR functions. Since the characters `&`, `¦` and `^` are all command syntax characters, these operators must be escaped using a `^` character when entered in shell scripts. Therefore use `^&`, `^¦` and `^^` to enter these operators. This is also true for the `&=`, `¦=` and `^=` assignment operators.

The `=` operator is the basic assignment operator. The left of the `=` operator must be a variable name. The result of the expression on the right is stored, as a decimal result, in the specified variable.

The extended assignment operators, such as `+=`, `*=` etc, are a shorthand way of writing an expression such as `X=X+4`. This expression can be re-written using the `+=` assignment operator as `X+=4`.

The expression separator operator, "`,`", allows multiple expressions to be evaluated using a single SET command. Separate each expression by a comma. Typically, the expressions are assignment expressions. When the SET command is typed at the console, the last (right-most) expression result is displayed.

Example:

```
set VARARGS=14,15,16
set DIRCMD=/w
set /a X=(I*14) + (B << 1) + (C ^& 0b1100)
set /a X=4,Y=5,Z=10
```

Notes:

An expression that is comprised only of a single variable name, with no other operators or literals, is not always evaluated correctly. Instead of SET /A X, use SET /A X+0 as a workaround. This appears to be a shell bug.

> **Troubleshooting Tip**
>
> *In some versions of Windows NT, using parentheses results in a syntax error. This appears to be a shell bug.*

See also: SETLOCAL, ENDLOCAL, Standard Variables, SETX

SETLOCAL

Begins localized scope for environment variable changes.

Syntax:

```
1. SETLOCAL
2. SETLOCAL ENABLEEXTENSIONS ¦ DISABLEEXTENSIONS
```

The SETLOCAL command, when used in a script file, begins a local scope for environment variable changes. Any changes made to the environment after a SETLOCAL command is executed are local to the script.

Executing an ENDLOCAL command restores the environment to its exact state at the time the most recent SETLOCAL command was executed. Any changed variables are restored to the value they had prior to the SETLOCAL command, and any newly created variables since the SETLOCAL command are deleted.

SETLOCAL/ENDLOCAL commands can be nested up to 32 levels deep, creating additional local scopes within the current scope. If any local scopes exist when the script file ends, an implicit ENDLOCAL is performed to restore the environment at the end of the script.

SETLOCAL/ENDLOCAL is very useful within script procedures, as it allows variables to be made local to the procedure.

Use SETLOCAL(1) to begin a new localized variable scope. Use SETLOCAL(2) to begin a new scope and also explicitly enable or disable shell command extensions. As with the environment, the current state of the shell extensions toggle is saved and restored when an ENDLOCAL command is executed.

Notes:

SETLOCAL is valid only within a script file. The command is accepted interactively, but no localization occurs.

See also: ENDLOCAL, SET

SHIFT

Accesses additional command arguments.

Syntax:

```
1. SHIFT
2. SHIFT /n
```

Switches:

/n   Parameter index from which to start shifting (such as /2).

The SHIFT command accesses command arguments beyond the first nine entered. The standard parameter syntax (%1, %2, and so on) provides direct access to only nine command arguments. The shift command provides access to additional arguments by shifting the arguments down the parameter list. The first argument is discarded.

Use SHIFT(1) to shift all arguments one place in the parameter list. The argument in parameter %0 is discarded and replaced by the argument from %1. The argument in parameter %1 is replaced by the argument from %2. This continues up to parameter %9, which receives a new argument from the command line. Thus each SHIFT(1) command discards the argument in %0, moves arguments in %1 through %9 down one parameter index, and moves a new argument from the command line into %9.

Use SHIFT(2) to start the shift operation at parameter index *n*. The command SHIFT /3 starts the shift at parameter %3. This leaves parameters %0, %1 and %2 unaltered by the shift process.

See also: Parameter Syntax

SHUTDOWN [RK]

Initiates Windows NT shutdown on the specified computer.

Syntax:

```
1. SHUTDOWN \\computer [/R] [/T:nn] [/Y] [/C] message
2. SHUTDOWN /L [/R] [/T:nn] [/Y] [/C] message
3. SHUTDOWN \\computer /A
4. SHUTDOWN /L /A
```

Switches:

/L	Shuts down local computer.
/A	Aborts shutdown.
/R	Restarts computer after shutdown.
/T:*nn*	Sets timeout to *nn* seconds.
/Y	Forces confirmation for all questions.
/C	Forces applications to close (can result in data loss).

The SHUTDOWN command initiates the shutdown of a Windows NT computer. After the specified timeout interval, the Windows NT computer will shutdown normally.

Use SHUTDOWN(1) to shutdown the specified computer remotely. Use SHUTDOWN(2) to shutdown the local computer. Use SHUTDOWN(3) or SHUTDOWN(4) to abort the shutdown. Shutdowns can only be aborted during the specified timeout period.

The /R switch forces a restart after the shutdown is complete. The /T switch sets the timeout period before the shutdown starts to *nn* seconds. The /Y switch assumes a yes response to all questions asked by SHUTDOWN.

The /C switch forces a shutdown at a computer regardless of the state of running applications. Use this switch with caution, as it forces applications to close *without* saving data first. This can result in data loss.

Example:

```
shutdown \\MOTHRA /T:45
```

SLEEP [RK]

Pauses execution for a specified period of time.

Syntax:

```
1. SLEEP nn
```

The SLEEP command pauses command execution for *nn* seconds and then continues. This is useful when waiting for asynchronous operations to complete.

Example:

```
sleep 4
```

See also: PAUSE, TIMEOUT

SOON [RK]

Executes a scheduled command in the near future.

Syntax:

```
1. SOON [\\computer] [delay] [/INTERACTIVE] "command"
2. SOON /D
3. SOON /D [/L:nn] [/R:nn] [/I:ON ¦ /I:OFF]
```

Switches:

/INTERACTIVE	Allows the scheduled command to interactive with the desktop.
/D	Modify or display default settings.
/L	Set default local machine delay.
/R	Set default remote machine delay.
/I	Set default interactive switch.

The SOON command schedules a command to execute via the Windows NT scheduler in the near future. Executing a SOON command is equivalent to executing an AT command with the time set to *delay* seconds in the future.

Use SOON(1) to schedule a command for execution. The command is executed on the local computer unless *computer* is specified. The command is scheduled to execute *delay* seconds in the future. If no *delay* is specified, SOON uses default values set with the /D switch. The /INTERACTIVE switch allows the command to interact with the Windows NT desktop.

Use soon(2) to display the current default values for the local and remote delays, and the interactive switch. Use soon(3) to alter these values. The /L switch sets the default delay for commands executed locally, and the /R switch sets the default delay for commands executed remotely. The /I switch sets the default state of the /INTERACTIVE switch.

Example

```
soon \\polycrates 300 "copy c:\logfiles e:\archives"
```

Notes:

You can create a script that executes periodically by placing a soon command in the script itself. Each time the script executes it schedules another run of the same script after the specified delay.

See also: AT

SORT

Sorts text lines.

Syntax:

```
1. SORT [/R] [/+n]
```

Switches:

/R	Reverses the sort order.
/+n	Sorts based on the characters in column *n*.

The SORT command sorts text lines into alphanumeric order using the ASCII character set as the collating sequence. SORT reads command input for lines to sort. By default, command input is all text typed at the console up to the end of file character, Ctrl+Z. Use the console input redirection symbols to get console input from a file, device, or another command.

The /R switch reverses the sort order. The /+n switch sorts the lines according to data starting in column *n* of each line. The first column is numbered 1.

See also: FIND, MORE

SRVINFO [RK]

Displays general computer and server information.

Syntax:

```
1. SRVINFO [switches]
2. SRVINFO [switches] \\computer
```

Switches:

/NS	Do not display service information.
/D	Display service drivers and services.
/V	Display Exchange and SQL information.
/S	Display share information.

The SRVINFO command displays general computer, server, and service information. Use SRVINFO(1) to display information for the current computer, and SRVINFO(2) to display information for the specified *computer*.

The basic information displayed includes the computer name, Windows NT type and version information, the current domain (if any) and Primary Domain Controller (PDC), and the current IP address. Following this is a list of installed CPUs, disk drives, and services. If the /D switch is specified the service list also includes device drivers. Finally, a list of network adapter cards is displayed followed by the system up time.

Example:

```
srvinfo ¦ find "PDC"
```

This example displays the name of the PDC for the domain.

Standard Variables

Standard environment variables defined by Windows NT.

Windows NT defines a number of standard environment variables. These generally provide information on the NT system environment and status of the machine and current user. Standard environment variables are collected from a number of sources to form the default environment available to a command shell when it starts execution.

The sources for standard variables are:

- Special values built-in to the system (such as OS).

- The system environment as defined in Control Panel System (stored in the Registry).

- The user environment as defined in Control Panel System (stored in the Registry).

- Any SET commands in C:\AUTOEXEC.BAT (if parsing is enabled).

- Any SET commands in a Windows NT logon script.

The following table lists the standard Windows NT environment variables.

Variable	Description
CMDCMDLINE	Command line passed to CMD.EXE, provided no variable exists of this name.
COMPUTERNAME	Network name of the computer, as defined in Control Panel Network.
COMSPEC	Path to Windows NT command shell executable.
ERRORLEVEL	Numeric value of last program exit code, provided no variable exists of this name.
HOMEDRIVE	Drive letter corresponding to path of home directory.
HOMEPATH	Path to home directory, excluding drive letter.
HOMESHARE	UNC name of share if home directory is on a network share.
LOGONSERVER	Name of server that performed the logon.
NUMBER_OF_PROCESSORS	Number of CPUs detected (1 for single CPU systems).
OS	Specifies the name of the running OS. Always "Windows_NT" on Windows NT systems.
PATH	A semi-colon separated list of directory names to search when trying to locate an application to execute (see PATH command).
PATHEXT	A semi-colon separated list of file extensions to test when attempting to locate a command executable (see START command),
PROCESSOR_ARCHITECTURE	Name of CPU architecture (such as "x86").
PROMPT	Defines the format of the shell command prompt (see PROMPT command).
SystemDrive	Drive letter of drive containing Windows NT.
SystemRoot	Path (including drive) to Windows NT directory.
USERDOMAIN	Name of domain or local machine used to log user on.
USERNAME	Name of user logged on.
USERPROFILE	Path to user profile of current user.

The command shell specially handles the ERRORLEVEL and CMDCMDLINE variables. If these variables are defined by a SET command, they behave normally. If, however, these variables are *not* defined and they are then expanded in a command, the shell replaces %ERRORLEVEL% with the exit code of the most recently executed application, and %CMDCMDLINE% with the exact text of the command line used to invoke the shell. %CMDCMDLINE% can be used to access the switches used to invoke the current command shell.

Notes:

Some standard variables are not available when executing a scheduled script via the AT command. Specifically, those which contain information regarding the current logon session (such as USERNAME) are not available.

See also: SET, START, CMD

START

Executes a command in a new window or console window.

Syntax:

```
1. START ["title"] [switches] command [args]
2. START [drive:]path
```

Switches:

/Dpath	Sets the current drive and directory for the command to *path*.
/I	Initializes the environment from the initial environment used by this command shell.
/MIN or /MAX	Starts the new command window minimized or maximized.
/SEPARATE or /SHARED	Starts a 16-bit Windows application in a shared (default) or separate memory space. Ignored for other application types.
/LOW, /NORMAL, /HIGH or /REALTIME	Specifies the priority class for the command. The default is /NORMAL.
/WAIT	Waits for the application to terminate before continuing.
/B	Executes command without creating a new window.

The START command starts a new application or executes a command in a new console window. Any valid application or command can be executed using the START command, including built-in shell commands, scripts, 16-bit Windows applications, 32-bit Windows applications, console applications, POSIX and OS/2 applications.

Use START(1) to execute a command. If the command is a script command or script file, then a new command shell is started to execute that command. This shell is started with the /K switch. This means that the new console window remains active when the command has finished executing, allowing command output to be viewed. To over-ride this behavior, use START to explicitly execute

CMD, the command shell, and then submit the *command* to this shell using the /C switch.

title specifies the title of the new command window. This is also displayed in the Windows NT task bar. The *title* is ignored for Windows applications, which provide their own title text. The /D switch specifies a starting drive and directory for the application.

Normally, the new application or command inherits the environment of the command shell executing the START command. The /I switch makes the command inherit the environment exactly as it was when the command shell began operation. Changes to the environment made within the command session are not passed to the new application.

The /MIN and /MAX switches control the position of the new window created for the application. Without these switches, Windows NT creates a new, normal, window for the application. The /MIN switch starts the application with a minimized window (just a new entry on the task bar). The /MAX switch starts the application with a maximized window.

If the application specified by *command* is a 16-bit Windows 3.x application, the /SHARED switch specifies that the application is started in the shared memory space used by 16-bit applications. (This is the default.) The /SEPARATE switch starts the application in a new address space. Using /SEPARATE increases robustness if the application crashes, but can use additional resources while the application executes.

The /LOW, /NORMAL, /HIGH and /REALTIME switches control the priority class for the application. The default priority class is normal, which should be used for the majority of applications. Use low priority if you want the application to execute as a background task when Windows NT is not busy. Use high priority to execute the application as an urgent task, ahead of other regular applications. Use the real-time priority only for special real-time applications. Incorrect use of the real-time priority can cripple a Windows NT system. Use the priority switches (except /LOW) with restraint, as they interfere with Windows NT ability to correctly balance system loads.

Without the /WAIT switch, the START command begins execution of the specified application or command and then immediately completes—the START command does *not* wait for the application to complete. With the /WAIT switch the START command waits until the application terminates before completing.

The /B switch applies only to script and console commands, not Windows applications. The /B switch executes the specified command within the current console window, rather than in a new console window. The command is executed under the control of a new command shell, and this shell is started with the /K switch. Therefore, when the command completes, the new shell is still running. Use the EXIT command to exit this shell and return to the original shell.

If the first token of *command* is the exact text CMD, then this is replaced by the contents of the COMSPEC variable. This ensures that the correct command shell is executed, and allows the token CMD to act as a placeholder for whichever command shell is specified with the COMSPEC variable.

If the first token in *command* does *not* specify an explicit file extension, then the START command uses the PATHEXT variable as a list of file extensions to test when searching for an executable file. PATHEXT must contain a list of file extensions, separated by semi-colons. START tests each file extension in turn when trying to locate a command to execute. The default value for PATHEXT is .COM;.EXE;.BAT;.CMD. When searching for the file to execute, START searches the current directory, and then each directory specified by the PATH variable. File extensions in the PATHEXT are applied first. That is, START first checks the current directory for all possible file extensions, then searches the first entry in the PATH for all possible PATHEXT file extensions, then the second entry in PATH and so on.

Use START(2) to start a copy of Windows NT Explorer in the drive and directory specified.

Example:

```
start /de:\database /i /low /min cmd /c cleanup.bat
```

This example executes the script CLEANUP.BAT in a minimized window as a low priority task, using the initial shell environment and starting in the E:\DATABASE directory.

See also: CMD, Command Syntax

SUBST

Creates virtual drive mappings.

Syntax:

```
1. SUBST
2. SUBST drive1: [drive2:]path
3. SUBST drive1: /D
```

Switches:

/D   Deletes virtual drive mapping.

The SUBST command creates virtual drives by mapping a drive letter to an arbitrary location in a directory tree on a local drive. Once mapped, the virtual drive letter can be used as a shortcut to access the specified drive and path.

Use SUBST(1) to display a list of all currently mapped virtual drive letters. Use SUBST(2) to create a new virtual drive. Specify the virtual drive to create in *drive1*, which must be an unassigned drive letter. Use *drive2* and *path* to specify the actual path for the virtual drive.

Use SUBST(3) to delete a virtual drive mapping.

Example:

```
subst v: c:\winnt\system32\logfiles
```

Notes:

The SUBST command implementation was flawed under MS-DOS and Windows 95. It is fully operational in Windows NT.

Drives created using the SUBST command are present only in the current Windows NT session. They are not persistent.

TIME

Displays or sets the system time.

Syntax:

```
1. TIME
2. TIME time
3. TIME /T
```

Switches:

/T   Do not prompt for a new time.

The TIME command displays or sets the system time. Use TIME(1) to display the current time and display a prompt asking for the new time. Press Enter only to leave the time unchanged. Use TIME(2) to set a new time directly from the command line. Use TIME(3) to display the time only.

See also: DATE

TIMEOUT [RK]

Pauses execution for a specified period of time or until a key is pressed.

Syntax:

```
1. TIMEOUT nn
```

The TIMEOUT command pauses for *nn* seconds and then continues. The command also continues if a key is pressed during the timeout period. This is useful when waiting for asynchronous operations to complete.

During the timeout period a count-down timer is displayed showing the remaining time before execution continues.

See also: PAUSE, SLEEP

TITLE

Sets the title text of the console window.

Syntax:

    1. TITLE *text*

The TITLE command alters the title displayed in the title bar of the console window. This is also displayed in the Windows NT task bar. Use TITLE(1) to set the title to *text*.

TITLE is useful to show the progress of long scripts without having to fill the console window with distracting output.

See also: ECHO, NOW

TRANSLATE [RK]

Translates a Windows NT error code to text.

Syntax:

    1. TRANSLATE *code*

The TRANSLATE command converts a Windows NT error code (a Win32 error code) into text form. This is useful when a command returns an exit code with a numeric Windows NT error. In this case, use TRANSLATE %ERRORLEVEL% to obtain the error message text.

Example:

    translate 5

This example returns the text Access is denied.

TYPE

Displays a text file in the console window.

Syntax:

    1. TYPE [*drive:*][*path*]*filename*

The TYPE command displays a text file in the console window. The file contents are dumped directly to command output for display. Command output redirection can be used to redirect output to a file or device.

Example:

```
type readme.txt
```

USRSTAT [RK]

Displays user statistics for a domain.

Syntax:

```
1. USRSTAT domain
```

The USRSTAT command displays a report listing the user name, full name, and last logon date/time for each user in the specified *domain*.

Example:

```
usrstat nevada
```

Variable Syntax

Environment variable substitution.

Variable substitution is the first operation that occurs after a command is entered. The shell searches the command text for variable names bracketed by % signs. For each such name found, the shell deletes the variable name and replaces it with the current value of the variable. If a pair of % characters surround a variable name that is not defined, the name and the percent characters are not altered in interactive mode. In script mode, the name and the percent characters are deleted.

The shell also defines two substitute-only variables: %ERRORLEVEL% and %CMDCMD-LINE%. If there is no user variable named ERRORLEVEL in the environment, then the shell replaces %ERRORLEVEL% with the exit code returned by the most recently executed command. If there is a user variable of this name, then normal substitution occurs. Similarly, if there is no user variable named CMDCMDLINE, then the shell replaces %CMDCMDLINE% with the full text of the command line used to invoke this copy of the shell.

There are several additional ways to modify the variable substitution process. These are shown in the following table.

Variable	Description
%var%	Substitutes the value of *var* for the variable name in the command. If *var* is not defined, does not alter the command text.
%var:str1=str2%	Substitutes the value of *var* for the variable name in the command. Before substitution, each occurrence of *str1* in the *var* is replaced with *str2*.

`%var:str1=%`	Substitutes the value of *var* for the variable name in the command. Before substitution, each occurrence of *str1* in the *var* is deleted.
`%var:~n%`	Substitutes the value of *var* for the variable name in the command. Substitution of the value of *var* begins at the *nth* character of the value. The first character is numbered 0.
`%var:~n,len%`	Substitutes the value of *var* for the variable name in the command. Substitution of the value of *var* begins at the *nth* character of the value and continues for *len* characters, or until the end of the value. The first character is numbered 0.
`%var:~0,len%`	Substitutes the value of *var* for the variable name in the command. Substitution of the value continues for *len* characters, or until the end of the value.

Example:

```
set VAR1=d:\winnt40\system32
set VAR2=cmd.exe
echo %VAR1:\=/% %VAR2:~0,3%
```

The output of the ECHO command is d:/winnt40/system32 cmd. Note the replacement of backward slashes by forward ones, and the extraction of the first three characters from variable VAR2.

See also: Parameter Syntax, Command Syntax, SET

VER

Displays Windows NT version information.

Syntax:

```
1. VER
```

The VER command displays the Windows NT command shell version information.

Example:

```
for /f "skip=1 tokens=4" %i in ('ver') do set OSVER=%i
```

This example uses the parse features of FOR to extract the version number of Windows NT from the VER command output.

WHOAMI [RK]

Displays the current user name and domain name.

Syntax:

```
1. WHOAMI
```

The WHOAMI command displays the domain name and user name of the currently logged in user. The names are displayed in the standard DOMAIN\UserName format.

Example:

```
for /f "delims=\ tokens=2" %i in ('whoami') do set USER=%1
```

The user name is available via the USERNAME variable. However, the user can alter this with a SET command. The example above shows how to obtain the true user name from the output of WHOAMI.

WINAT

See AT.

XCACLS

See CACLS.

XCOPY

Copies files and directories.

Syntax:

```
1. XCOPY source [destination] [switches]
```

Switches:

/A	Copies files that have the archive attribute set (modified).
/M	Copies files that have the archive attribute set, and reset the attribute.
/D	Copies only files with a source time newer than the destination time.
/D:mm-dd-yy	Copies files changed on or after the specified date.
/P	Prompts before creating each destination file.
/S	Copies directories and subdirectories, except empty ones.
/E	Copies directories and subdirectories, including empty ones.
/V	Verifies all copy operations.
/W	Prompts for a key press before copying files.
/C	Continues even if errors occur.
/I	Assumes destination is a directory if it does not exist.

/Q	Quiet. Do not display names while copying.
/F	Shows full source and destination names.
/L	Displays names that would be copied, but do not do actual copy.
/H	Copies hidden and system files as well as normal files.
/R	Copies even if destination file is read only.
/T	Creates directory tree, but do not copy files.
/U	Only copies files that already exist in the destination.
/K	Copies attributes.
/N	Use short (MS-DOS) file names during copy.
/Z	Use restartable copy mode.

The XCOPY command copies files and directories from one location to another. XCOPY has numerous switches to control the copy process.

The *source* can be a single file, a wildcard file name, or a directory name. If *source* is a directory name, all files in the directory are copied. The *destination* can be a file name or a directory name. If no destination is specified, the current directory is assumed. If *destination* does not exist, XCOPY prompts to choose between creating a file or directory with the specified name. The /I switch assumes that the destination is to be a directory. The /P switch prompts before creating each destination file. The /W switch prompts before starting the copy. This is useful if the destination specifies removable media, such as a floppy disk.

By default, XCOPY copies only the files in the source directory. The /S switch copies files in all subdirectories as well. The /E switch copies empty subdirectories as well as those containing files. The /T switch only copies directories, not files. Use the /E switch with /T to copy empty directories as well.

The /A switch only copies files that have the archive attribute set (that is, have been modified since the last backup). The /M switch copies these files are then reset this attribute on each source file. The /D switch only copies files when the source file time and data is newer than the destination file time and date. Alternatively, specify an explicit time and data with the /D switch to copy only those files newer than that date. The /H switch copies hidden and system files, in addition to normal files. Finally, the /U switch only copies files that already exist in the destination.

The /Q switch prevents the display of file name while copying. The /F switch displays the full source and destination file names during the copy. The /L switch *only* displays the file names—no actual file copy operations occur.

The /K switch copies attributes as well as file data. Normally, XCOPY resets the attributes on the destination file. The /R switch copies to a destination file marked read only. The /N switch copies files using short (MS-DOS) file names only.

The /V switch verifies all file copy operations. The /Z switch copies all files in restartable mode. In restartable mode, XCOPY tracks the file copy progress in the destination file so that the copy operation can be restarted. This is used primarily when copying files across WAN network connections.

See also: COPY, ROBOCOPY, SCOPY, MOVE, REPLACE

Part **IV**

Appendixes

Appendix **A**

The RCMD Resource Kit Utility

One tool in the Windows NT Resource Kit that is particularly useful is the RCMD utility. This utility provides a remote command execution facility for Windows NT servers and workstations. The utility only ships with the Windows NT Server version of the Resource Kit, although it can be used with Windows NT workstations or servers in both the client and target roles.

RCMD executes command-line programs (including scripts) on a remote computer (the *target*) and displays the results of these commands on the local computer (the *client*). The command results are displayed in the same console window on the client used to initiate the RCMD session. Because the command executes on the remote computer, it can access all the local resources on that computer.

Commands that can be executed remotely are restricted to 32-bit Windows NT console applications that use the command input, command output and command error output streams only (see Chapter 2). MS-DOS applications, 16-bit and 32-bit Windows applications, and Windows NT console applications that use cursor positioning *cannot* be used.

RCMD Client and Target Computer Installation

The RCMD client is installed as part of the Windows NT Server Resource Kit. The only file needed for the client is the executable RCMD.EXE. In addition to client installation, each target computer (i.e. each computer which will execute commands on behalf of an RCMD client) must have the Remote Command Server service installed.

To install the Remote Command Server service on a target computer, proceed as follows:

1. Copy the files RCMDSVC.EXE and OEMNSVRC.INF from the Resource Kit installation directory to the %SYSTEMROOT%\System32 directory on the target computer.

2. On the target computer, open the Control Panel and select the Network icon. In the Network dialog box, select the Services tab and click the Add button.

3. In the Select Network Service dialog box that opens, select Remote Command Server and Click OK.

4. Click OK to close the Network dialog box.

Repeat the steps above on each target computer.

After the Remote Command Server service is installed on a target computer it can be started and stopped manually, or set to auto-start when NT boots. The service can be started and stopped locally using the Control Panel Services icon, remotely using the Windows NT Server Manager utility, or by using the SC command line utility (described in the Command Reference).

Command Execution

To execute a command on a target computer from a client computer, use the following syntax:

```
1. RCMD \\computer command
2. RCMD \\computer
```

Use RCMD(1) to execute a single command on the specified target computer. For example:

```
rcmd \\pythagoras dir c:\
```

This command will display a directory of all files in the root of drive C: on the computer PYTHAGORAS.

Use RCMD(2) to establish an interactive session on the specified target computer. This starts a command shell on the target computer and displays the shell prompt locally (on the client). Normal shell commands (including scripts) can then be entered and executed on the target computer. To terminate the session, either exit the remote shell using the EXIT command, or press Ctrl+Break to terminate the RCMD session.

Because commands are executed remotely in a remote command shell on the target computer, command shell state information local to the client is not used or altered by remote commands. For example:

```
01. C:\>set VAR=Test
02. C:\>echo %VAR%
03. Test
04. C:\>rcmd \\pythagoras
05. Connected to \\pythagoras
06.
07. Microsoft(R) Windows NT(TM)
08. (C) Copyright 1985-1996 Microsoft Corp.
09.
10. D:\USERS\DEFAULT>echo %VAR%
11. %VAR%
12. D:\USERS\DEFAULT>exit
13. Remote server \\pythagoras disconnected
14. C:\>
```

In this example, the variable VAR is defined in the local command shell (as shown by the first ECHO command). However, this variable is not available to the command shell executing on the target computer—the second ECHO command does not expand %VAR%.

RCMD Security Features

RCMD provides several security features that prevent unauthorized access to target computers.

- The Remote Command Server service must be running on a target computer before it will accept commands for remote execution. Therefore this service can be stopped to prevent unauthorized remote command access. Starting and stopping the service is a privileged operation protected by Windows NT security mechanisms.

- A user who submits a remote command via RCMD must have the interactive logon user right on the target computer. By default, only administrators have this user right on Windows NT Server computers.

- The Remote Command Server impersonates the remote user when executing all remote commands. Thus the command executes with the same rights and privileges as the remote user, and no others.

Appendix **B**

Other Useful Command Line Tools

The Command Reference in Part III of this book covers all of the Windows NT and Windows NT Resource Kit utilities that are typically used in scripts. However, there are a number of additional command line utilities and tools that may be useful in some circumstances. These are listed in this appendix. For a full description of the operation of these commands, consult the Windows NT and the Windows NT Resource Kit on-line documentation.

AUTOEXNT[RK]   A service that executes a script when Windows NT boots. Equivalent to the MS-DOS AUTOEXEC.BAT facility.

COMPREG[RK]   Compares two registry keys, looking for differences. Useful to determine differences in system configurations.

COMPACT   Provides command-line control of the built-in compression available on NTFS volumes.

COMPRESS[RK]   Provides manual file compression. Use the EXPAND command to restore the original file or files.

DELSRV[RK]   Deletes an installed Windows NT service.

DHCPCMD[RK]   Provides command-line control of the Windows NT DHCP server.

DHCPLOC[RK]   Locates DHCP servers on the local subnet.

DISKMAP[RK]   Displays information on hard disk partitions, fault-tolerance setup data and other disk information.

DNSCMD[RK]   Provides command-line control of the Windows NT DNS server.

DRIVERS[RK]   Displays a complete list of all installed Windows NT device drivers. Useful to determine which devices are installed.

EXETYPE[RK]   Determines the type of executable represented by a file (script, 16-bit Windows application etc.).

FILEVER[RK]	Displays the internal version stamp information present in many EXE and DLL files.
FREEDISK[RK]	Checks the amount of free disk space against a specified minimum.
GETMAC[RK]	Gets the MAC (physical) network address or addresses. Provides a useful way to get a unique value on each computer.
INSTSRV[RK]	Installs a Windows NT service executable and assigns the service a name.
IPCONFIG	Displays IP configuration information.
NETDOM[RK]	Provides command-line domain management.
PASSPROP[RK]	Controls password policy on a server.
PATHMAN[RK]	Edits the PATH variable values stored in the registry.
RASLIST[RK]	Displays RAS server announcements.
RASUSERS[RK]	Displays a list of all accounts that have dial-in rights.
REGDMP[RK]	Dump the registry in a format compatible with the REGINI[RK] command.
REGFIND[RK]	Searches the registry for values or key names.
REGINI[RK]	Edits the registry by reading a special editing script.
SECADD[RK]	Adds security control to registry entries.
SETX[RK]	Sets environment variables in the user or computer portions of the registry. Changes made are persistent, unlike those made with the SET command.
SHOWDISK[RK]	Displays disk partition information.
SRVCHECK[RK]	Displays information about all non-hidden shares on a computer.
TIMETHIS[RK]	Times how long a command takes to execute.
WINSCHK[RK]	Verifies WINS database and replication integrity.
WINSCL[RK]	Provides command-line control of the Windows NT WINS server.
WINSDMP[RK]	Dumps a WINS database.

Index

Q-R

W

X-Z